MOTHER R.

MOTHER R.

Eleanor Roosevelt's Untold Story

Elliott Roosevelt and James Brough

G.P. PUTNAM'S SONS

NEW YORK

SBN: 399-11998-1

Library of Congress Cataloging in Publication Data

Roosevelt, Elliott, 1910-
  Mother R. : Eleanor Roosevelt's untold story.

  Includes index.
  1.   Roosevelt, Eleanor Roosevelt, 1884-1962.
  2.   Presidents—United States—Wives—Biography.
  3.   Roosevelt family.   4.   Roosevelt, Elliott, 1910-
  I.   Brough, James, 1918-   joint author.   II. Title.
  E807.1.R48R66 1977   973.917'092'4 [B]   77-7281

PRINTED IN THE UNITED STATES OF AMERICA

*To F.D.R., a man of conviction,
and A.E.R., a woman of faith*

Acknowledgments

In addition to the personal files and records that provided the essence of this book, five other works proved to be valuable and much appreciated reference sources in establishing chronology and stirring recollections: *Eleanor: The Years Alone*, by Joseph P. Lash (New York, W. W. Norton & Company, Inc., 1972); *Eleanor Roosevelt: Her Day*, by A. David Gurewitsch, M.D. (New York, Quadrangle/The New York Times Book Company, in cooperation with the Interchange Foundation, 1974); *I Love A Roosevelt*, by Patricia Peabody Roosevelt (Garden City, Doubleday & Company, Inc., 1969); and David Jacob's essay "Harry S. Truman" and Charles L. Miller, Jr.'s, "Dwight David Eisenhower," both in *The American Heritage History of the Presidents* (New York, American Heritage Publishing Company, Inc., 1968).

Contents

Preface

You who have read *An Untold Story* and *A Rendezvous With Destiny*, the first two books in the trilogy which this volume completes, will be aware of its concept of my father, Franklin Delano Roosevelt, as a man of towering strength, intellectual capacity, patience and vision. No attempt has been made to conceal the fact that he had weaknesses, as all mortals do, but he performed herculean tasks in times of peril for the United States and the world whose impact will continue to be felt by mankind for generations to come.

It has never ceased to astonish me that throughout his career he could have been married to an equally fascinating personality, my mother, Anna Eleanor Roosevelt. Hers was a character that grew and developed in their years together, but the true greatness in her did not mature until after her husband's death. Her achievements and contributions to human betterment will live on with equal brilliance.

Of course, she had failings. Nobody but God is without fault. But in spite of the difficulties the two of them experienced in the simple act of living as man and wife for more than forty years, they came to understand each other's mind and heart and so project the hopes and ambitions they shared for the well-being of all people.

Never in any history book have I read of such attainments of a husband and wife; I have enormous pride in them. All five of us children who lived to maturity came to realize, I believe, how fortunate we were to have been born of their union and to have known intimately two unforgettable parents.

I have often heard comments about how sad it is that none of us offspring has achieved anything approaching the records of Franklin and Eleanor. Without attempting apology or explanation for this failure, I offer a few observations.

We were brought up in a country where great change was under way, altering the moral tenets of society while one crisis after another added obstacles to normal development. While Father and Mother tried hard to give their children a happy upbringing, their preoccupation with personal and public commitments precluded for the most part a successful, closely knit family life.

The eldest child, Anna, who died in 1976, did experience during her lifetime some great sorrows, followed in the latter years by a real degree of happiness, enjoying moments of true closeness and, with the help of her husband, Dr. James Halsted, managing to establish with her own children deep family rapport.

James, the eldest son, who now lives in California, had many advantages to serve Father, but personal difficulties intervened to remove Jimmy from his prestigious position in Washington. During World War II, he more than redeemed the faith of those who loved him. He continues to work hard in politics and business, but he has known only limited joy or sense of worthwhile accomplishment.

Franklin junior, the third son, according to one's viewpoint either enjoyed or suffered being Father's namesake. He still has political hopes, though the years are advancing, and in his personal life he has had a number of sad encounters to augment political disappointments. In business, he has been more fortunate; his success there has proven a great solace.

The youngest child, John, had much less opportunity to experience closeness with our parents during his formative years; they were both immersed in public life. He seems to have no political ambitions as he spends a quiet existence in New York City and Tuxedo Park.

I was the second son and always a rebel. I confounded my parents with divorce, previously unheard of in our family. In the war, I had some satisfaction in doing a creditable job, enjoying occasional comradeship with Father, then after he died there were the many years when I had the glorious chance of living and working with Mother. I loved them both dearly and appreciated more than words can say the many beautiful things they did for me. I revere their memories.

There is only one source of sadness: With their passing, our family as a unit disappeared. In spite of our parents' absorption by the world, they always provided us, albeit fleetingly, with a sense of being a part of their grand crusade that convinced them of the urgency of serving to help people everywhere to a better life on earth. The pity of it is that we did not follow their example.

E.R.

Book I
The Seeking

"MEN AND WOMEN WHO LIVE TOGETHER THROUGH
LONG YEARS GET TO KNOW ONE ANOTHER'S FEELINGS,
BUT THEY ALSO COME TO KNOW WHAT IS WORTHY OF
RESPECT AND ADMIRATION IN THOSE THEY LIVE WITH
AND IN THEMSELVES."

—ELEANOR ROOSEVELT

1

Aunt Polly was the obvious candidate to make the tricky first call. She had deceived Cousin Eleanor often enough before, and no twinges of conscience were likely to trouble Polly over what she was about to try. The terror which everyone else in the little clapboard cottage shared would not be detectable in her perennially crisp voice. If the scheme worked, the bleak grief of this April day would be leavened for her by a certain, sardonic satisfaction that she had succeeded in tinkering with history.

After the turmoil of the past hour, the still disordered living room was oddly quiet when she stretched out a thin arm to pick up the telephone in her fingers heavy with rings. On the easel set up by a window stood the unfinished portrait, abandoned when the artist and the woman for whom it had been commissioned fled the scene together. The canvas depicted a bland likeness of the thirty-second President of the United States, Franklin Delano Roosevelt, aged sixty-three years and sixty-two days, sporting his Harvard-crimson tie, his shoulders covered by his old Navy cape, which was easier to handle than an overcoat for a man whose wasted legs would not allow him to stand unaided. A vase that Polly had filled with flowers while lunch was being prepared in the kitchen sat in the center of the dining table at a far end of the room, where five places were set for a meal that was never eaten.

Joe Espencilla, the Filipino houseman, had helped Arthur Prettyman, the valet, and George Fox, the physical therapist, carry my father's inert body into his bedroom after the massive cerebral hemorrhage struck like a bolt of lightning. The time was then some minutes after one o'clock. Polly had gone running for the nearest Secret Serviceman. A call to the swimming pool two miles away had brought Father's cardiologist speeding back by car within a quarter of an hour. Lieutenant Commander Howard G. Bruenn, a reserve officer in the Naval Medical Corps, had been attending him for the past thirteen months.

The young doctor employed his skills at the bedside in the hopeless effort to maintain life in the pale, cold, profusely sweating body covered in blankets and warmed with hot-water bottles. He tried an injection of papaverine and then amylnitrate with the aim of relieving contraction of the arteries to keep the blood coursing. Father was totally unconscious, legs numbed, muscles twitching, and soiled by loss of continence, yet for the present the heartbeat was steady. Each labored breath could be heard outside the flimsy bedroom door where his black scottie, Fala, waited.

As soon as time could be spared from attending to his patient, Bruenn would call Washington on the private line to report the news to Admiral Ross McIntire, the Navy nose and throat specialist who served as the President's personal physician. The word Bruenn used to describe the situation was "catastrophe." "It was just like . . . getting hit by a train," he said later. The prognosis was not in doubt.

There had been four guests in the place that newspapers grandiosely labelled the Little White House when Father complained of a headache, raised a hand to his neck, then slumped, head lolling, in his worn leather armchair. Now, besides Polly, only Margaret (Daisy) Suckley remained, another of his multitude of cousins, a goodhearted, homespun woman fond of dogs and crocheting, who would do anything for her adored Franklin, including connive in the subterfuge that Polly had in mind.

Its purpose was to conceal from my mother and the world at large the fact that Mrs. Winthrop Rutherfurd II, whom Father had set above all other women, had been with him on this occasion as she had been on uncounted other days during the past two years. It was for Lucy Mercer Rutherfurd, a widow now, that Father had agreed that Elizabeth Shoumatoff should paint this portrait, a gift due to be passed along to Lucy's daughter Barbara. Lucy herself had commissioned a watercolor of him from the same artist in 1943.

Perhaps she sensed at the moment of Father's collapse that he would not live to speak to her again, making it both futile and hazardous to stay at the cottage any longer. A stroke of those proportions inflicts such physical damage that even untrained eyes could foresee the inevitable outcome. Lucy, for whose gentle, smiling love Father had been ready to leave Mother after thirteen years of marriage in 1918, hurried away with Madame Shoumatoff almost immediately.

Rehearsing what she would say, Aunt Polly asked the White House operator to put her through to Mother. A spinster with a fancy for romance (albeit once with a close relative), Laura Delano—which was her true name—had always delighted in taunting Cousin Eleanor. In her opinion, Mother was a poor choice as a bride for Father in the first place. Polly, a sprite no more than four feet nine inches tall with parchment skin and purple hair, invited us children up to her two-hundred-acre place at Rhinebeck, New York, and, as we grew, plied us with the liquor that Mother abhorred.

"Don't be so stuffy, Eleanor," she would tease, sharp eyes glittering, when Mother objected. More than anyone else, Polly acted as the go-between, responsible for restoring Lucy to Father's life when the age of passion had passed for both of them.

Mother's calendar of appointments for the day had been more or less routine. At her morning press conference, she spoke up for the United Nations, whose birth was scheduled for thirteen days ahead in San Francisco, emphasizing how important it was for the United States to work in harmony with its fellow members. Tomorrow's frenzied newspapers would spare scarcely an inch of space for the story. She had a spokeswoman for Russian War Relief in for lunch and persuaded Anna to join them. The afternoon promised nothing more momentous than a four o'clock benefit tea at the Sulgrave Club for one of her long list of good causes, the Thrift Shop, which she would attend together with a President's widow, Mrs. Woodrow Wilson.

There was no set time for one caller she had promised to see on this Thursday, April 12, 1945. Leo Szilard, nuclear physicist, was one of the progenitors of the atomic bomb. Along with the Italian, Enrico Fermi, he had prompted Albert Einstein to write to Father, warning him that the most powerful weapon of destruction science had yet conceived might well become a reality. The outcome was the Manhattan Project, for which FDR appropriated $2 billion of completely unauthorized federal funds to make the bomb before Germany did.

Szilard, who was employed on the supersecret undertaking, had an uncanny prevision of the future before America's bomb had even been tested. He foresaw the necessity of avoiding another desperate contest—between the United States and the Soviet Union to achieve postwar nuclear supremacy. His memorandum must be read only by the President, but Father had not replied to Szilard's last letter, so Szilard had sought a meeting with Mother, to use her as a conduit. Though she knew from Father that a fantastic new means of dealing death was indeed being developed, she had no idea of the progress that had been made. She was willing to see Szilard and pass along the sealed document—but the appointment was lost in the chaos of the day.

Polly had to play for time. The cover-up meant that all trace of Lucy's presence must be erased. If Mother were told the truth about Father's collapse, she would be aboard a plane for Warm Springs in a matter of minutes. Not a second was frittered away whenever she felt one of the family or a dear friend was in need or in distress.

Since his return from Yalta in the Crimea at the end of February, Mother had recognized that Father was growing prematurely old, worn out by the pressures of conducting the war. The evidence was there in his drawn, tense face, the voice that had lost its resonance, the hands that sometimes shook uncontrollably. With my sister Anna, she watched from the gallery of the House of Representatives when he told the Congress and the nation what had been consummated at the latest round of meetings with Winston Churchill and Josef Stalin.

"I hope that you will pardon me for an unusual posture of sitting down during the presentation of what I want to say," he began, "but I know that you will realize that it makes it a lot easier for me in not having to carry about ten pounds of steel around on the bottom of my legs."

He had been wheeled into the well of the chamber to sit at a small table in a red plush chair. Sitting while he spoke in public was highly unusual. Never before had he mentioned the braces without which his legs could not support him. She concluded that he had reconciled himself to infirmity and the repellent truth that, no matter what effort he made, he would not realize the dream of walking again, which he had cherished from the time that polio crippled him in 1921.

He brooded over the death of Pa Watson, Presidential naval aide and one of the last survivors in the innermost circle around Father, who had been felled by a cerebral hemorrhage aboard the battleship *Quincy* two days out of Algiers on the voyage home from the Black Sea. Louis Howe, the gnome of a man who had steered Father on his political career; Missy LeHand, the secretary who had served him with body and soul; Gus Gennerich, who was simultaneously bodyguard and intimate friend—they were all dead. The condition of Harry

Hopkins, the New Deal's heir apparent until illness intervened, was so critical at Yalta that he had been compelled to
fly back to the United States.

So Father's solitude increased. There was scarcely anyone
left for him to chat and joke with in his study as he had done
by the hour in the past. He saw less and less of people and cut
their visits short. In contrast with Winston, who took to his
bed every afternoon, Father's habit had been to work on unless he was exceptionally weary. Now he, too, needed a nap
in the middle of the day.

Anna was eager to keep him sheltered from every form of
intrusion. She gloried in supervising Father's days in her chosen role as chatelaine and Presidential protector. With her
three children, she had moved in to fill the gap after a stroke
left Missy partially paralyzed and compelled to retire. Anna's
first marriage, to Curtis Dall of Wall Street, had broken up.
Her new husband, John Boettiger, who used to work as a reporter for the *Chicago Tribune*, was a colonel serving in Europe with the army's military government branch. For the
past year, my sister had been living in the redecorated Lincoln
Suite of the White House, where Harry Hopkins had once
made his home. She made the care of Father a full-time occupation and relished every moment of it.

He had needed no urging to get away to Warm Springs.
Mother found him "anxious" to spend a couple of weeks re-
cuperating in the sun. He was itching to be off all through
March, tantalized by the certainty that Lucy would arrange to
be there too. So far as Mother knew, Mrs. Rutherfurd belonged to the buried past and to memories too agonizing to be
dwelt on. She was the golden-haired, slim-waisted girl who
had worked for her as a part-time social secretary after Father
became an assistant secretary of the Navy in 1912 and the
family made its first move to Washington, D.C. It was twenty-
five years ago that she was married to Wintie Rutherfurd,
whose own first love had been Consuelo Vanderbilt, and that
was the end of the chapter in Mother's estimation.

Father managed to leave just before the month was over.

Mother felt relieved that he could find the rest he so obviously needed to rebuild his health and strength. The original plan had been for Anna to go with him as she had to Yalta, but her youngest child, Johnny, lay gravely ill in the Washington Naval Hospital, and she asked to stay close to him.

Father drove himself off in the little blue Ford with the specially fitted hand controls after the Presidential train had delivered him to Warm Springs. Dogwood, wild violets and azaleas already bloomed along the road up the mountain on Good Friday, March 30. According to the timetable, he would be back at Forest Glen railroad station in Silver Spring, Maryland, at eight-thirty precisely on the morning of April 16. On April 9, Lucy arrived at the Little White House from the Rutherfurd estate, Ridgeley Hall, in Aiken, South Carolina, where Father had visited on occasion.

Mother was in her second-floor sitting room in the White House when Polly's call came into the switchboard. She was with a visitor, Charles Taussig, a veteran New Dealer, president of the American Molasses Company, and lately an adviser to the United States delegation assembled for San Francisco. He was asking for further details on Father's thinking about the trusteeships that he proposed for governing Axis colonies once the war was won. She promised to telephone Father on Taussig's behalf, but there was this interruption. Mrs. Malvina Thompson, the plump, genial secretary whom we all called Tommy, signaled her to pick up the telephone.

The hands on the old-fashioned watch, a gift from Father that she forever wore pinned to her dress, pointed to some minutes before three-thirty. In the bedroom at Warm Springs, the pupils of my father's eyes were dilated pitch black, his breath faltered, and the purple of cyanosis replaced the tan which in recent days had returned to his cheeks. Summoned by telephone by Admiral McIntire, Dr. James A. Paullin, an Atlanta heart specialist, was heading toward the cottage as fast as his car would carry him.

Polly's tone would betray no more than her careful sentences. "Eleanor? There is no cause for you to upset yourself, but I think you should know that Franklin has had a fainting spell down here.''

For as long as she could remember, Mother had kept a tight rein on her responses. The standards of conduct she set for herself were as rigid as those of a Victorian finishing school. A visitor should not be disturbed by any unseemly display of emotion. It was unthinkable for Mr. Taussig to be allowed a hint of a confidential family matter. She asked only a guarded question or two of Polly.

"Where did this happen?"

"He was having this portrait painted and he just keeled over.''

"Who is looking after things?''

"He was put right to bed. Dr. Bruenn is with him.''

With customary politeness, Mother brought the conversation with Taussig to an early close so that she might speak privately with Ross McIntire, who for the better part of an hour had known the truth concerning Father's condition. He assured her that there was no cause for alarm. Inevitably by now the cover-up extended far beyond Aunt Polly. In times of stress, those who serve a President apparently feel obliged to accept as an article of faith as binding upon them as anything written in the Constitution that he must be preserved from scandal at whatever cost.

Mother's instincts were not completely satisfied. She must go to Warm Springs. McIntire convinced her that she should wait until evening, playing on her abiding desire to do whatever was *proper.* "He thought I had better go on with my afternoon engagements,'' she recalled, "since it would cause great comment if I canceled them at the last moment.''

No breath of life or beat of heart remained in Father at three-thirty-one when Dr. Paullin hurried into the cottage to join Dr. Bruenn. Artificial respiration was attempted. It worked no better than the adrenalin injected straight into the heart muscle. At three-thirty-five, Bruenn pronounced the end.

On Pine Mountain, the charcoal had been lit for the barbecue which Father had been looking forward to attending later in the afternoon. A trio of shirt-sleeved reporters swapped gossip in the sunlight, and in his uniform of chief petty officer in the United States Navy, black Graham Johnson stood by with his accordion to entertain the President. An abrupt summons from the Little White House brought the newsmen filing into the tidied-up living room, where Bill Hassett, Presidential press secretary, stood, his perpetually mournful face lined with deeper sorrow. "Gentlemen," he whispered, "it is my sad duty to inform you. . . ."

The ladies at the Sulgrave Club, after some introductory words from Mother, had settled down to enjoy themselves when she was called to the telephone. Steve Early, the suave Virginian who had begun masterminding Father's press relations a quarter-century ago, could say no more than, "Come back at once, please," before his voice broke.

It was not necessary to ask him why. "In my heart I knew what had happened," she remembered, "but one does not actually formulate these terrible thoughts until they are spoken." Politeness demanded her return to the tea party. Something had come up at home that required her attention, she explained. "I am so sorry to have to leave so soon."

The clenching of her strong hands was the only outward sign of distress as she waited in her second-floor sitting room for Steve Early and Ross McIntire. Otherwise, she retained total control. She sat in silence for a minute after they put into words what her sensibilities had already told her: that the husband she had served rather than loved during most of the forty years of their marriage lay dead in Warm Springs.

She said nothing of personal grief, and her eyes were dry. As a patriot, she realized what should be done next. She asked for Harry Truman. At the Vice-President's podium in the Senate, he was about to wind up business for the day when he received the call. My mother, inches taller than he, walked across to him as he entered her room and put an arm around his shoulders. Anna and Steve Early were beside her.

"Harry," she said calmly, "the President is dead."

For a while, he could not find his voice. "Is there anything I can do for you?" he said at last.

"Is there anything *we* can do for *you?*" she answered, "for you are the one in trouble now." At this point, the cover-up held firm. Steve Early's discretion could be counted on. She still spoke of sorrow only in terms of others, of the country that had lost its leader before the war was won, but with never a word about her own feelings.

To each of her sons, Jimmy, Franklin, Johnny and me, she sent the same radiogram: FATHER SLEPT AWAY. HE WOULD EXPECT YOU TO CARRY ON AND FINISH YOUR JOBS. I would reflect later that of all the family, she was the only one to do precisely that. As it was, I learned the numbing news in England, where I was serving in the United States Army Air Force, before her message reached me. I was aboard a flight to Washington some hours after Mother had seen the thirty-third President take the oath of office at seven-nine p.m. precisely. Finding a Bible had delayed the ceremony. At seven-fifteen she left for Warm Springs with Early and McIntire. The United States had spent half a day without a functioning President while the war remained to be won.

It was close to midnight when she entered the cottage, giving a quick embrace to Polly and Margaret Suckley and a kiss to Grace Tully, who had been Missy's right-hand assistant. "I am so very sorry for all of you," she told them. She listened briefly to what they had to tell her about Father's last hours before she walked alone into his bedroom, closing the door behind her. When she came out, her face was grave. There and then, she ordered the coffin to be sealed. That, she said, was in accordance with a decision that she and Father had reached in the past.

There was another, unspoken consideration. The violence of the damage to his brain had so disfigured Father that he bore little resemblance to the living man whose mouth was always ready to smile. She would have no one share the shock with her but those who had already been into the room. Only once did she ask for the lid to be raised; in the East Room of the White House, she alone stood beside the coffin for a moment or two to place a handful of flowers inside.

In Moscow, a diplomatic outcry was to arise for an autopsy to be conducted. Stalin himself suspected that, as part of a dark capitalistic plot, poison had done away with Father, on whom he relied to maintain the Big Three partnership through victory into a lasting peace. When more than one or two Allied commanders were hoping to entice the Red Army into mutually destructive conflict with the Japanese, xenophobia among the Soviets was not entirely unjustified. But Mother would not dream of allowing pathologists to perform their acts of mutilation. The coffin stayed sealed. She wanted him to be remembered as he had been when alive.

In the predawn hours of April 13, as she tried to compose herself for sleep, she could detect some inexplicable omissions in the account so far given of the events of the previous day. Father had trained her in observing, listening and asking questions when he sent her off as his roving reporter in his first term, touring the country to bring back to him first-hand accounts of how America was surviving the Depression. She had developed an insatiable curiosity and determination to get to the roots of any situation. The information she was able to pry out when the household awoke made for a day which she described as "long and heartbreaking." She unearthed the story of Lucy's presence, and she pieced together what had occurred minute by minute as he died.

As Mother could be relentless in her questioning, too many people were involved for the secret to be kept. Besides Polly and Margaret, there were Grace Tully to quiz; Arthur Prettyman; Joe Espencilla; George Fox; Daisy Donner, the cook at the cottage; Bill Hassett; Lizzie McDuffie, the maid sent down from the White House; perhaps Lieutenant Commander Bruenn. Just when was the President taken ill and what was he doing at the time? Exactly who was in the room with him? For what purpose was the portrait intended? Why the delay in telephoning her? She found everyone, she said afterwards, "as self-controlled and calm as possible," but piecing their answers together, she could confront Polly with the crucial question: How did Mrs. Rutherfurd come to be there?

The cover had failed. It was useless to try to brazen things out or continue the dissembling. From Polly she learned how Lucy and Father had been reunited in companionship. Mother would not allow herself to show any sign of distress, and it would be impossible for Polly to resist a final question of her own: "And was anything wrong with that?"

When her own account of the turmoil came to be written, Mother did not mention the name of Lucy, yet in her characteristically oblique way she was compelled to leave those who knew her best in no doubt about her feelings. "Though this was a terrible blow," she said, "somehow one had no chance to think of it as personal sorrow. It was the sorrow of all those to whom this man who now lay dead, and who happened to be my husband, had been a symbol of strength and fortitude."

She made it a point of honor not to nurse grudges, but she could never completely forgive Laura Delano. On the surface, nothing changed between them. Polly received the usual invitations to visit Mother, and she kept up her gibes at Cousin Eleanor, but Mother seldom set foot in Polly's house again.

At ten o'clock on the morning of April 13, to the drumbeats of an army band from Fort Benning, the procession wound between ranks of paratroopers past the unassuming white cottages of the Warm Springs Foundation. Polio victims in wheelchairs waved farewell, and out from the portico of Georgia Hall came Graham Johnson, seizing his final chance to play for the man the world could still think of only as *the* President. "Going Home" was the song he chose, with tears descending his cheeks.

A guard of honor surrounded the flag-covered coffin in the end car of the Presidential train in which Father had spent days at a time, campaigning for reelection or seeking to instruct Americans in his striving to achieve peacetime prosperity and victory in the war. Mother sat in the lounge car as the twenty-three-hour journey northward began, staring in a state of abstraction at the tense figures in the crowds gathered at the stations, the crossroads and along the track, some of them on their knees in prayer. When night came and the train was darkened except for the dimly lit last coach, she lay in her berth with the shade up, maintaining her vigil while her mind raced.

Snatches of lyrics kept intruding on her thoughts. *A lonesome train on a lonesome track,/Seven coaches painted black. . . .* But there was no way in which she might suppress memories of Lucy Mercer. As always in hours of stress, she felt inadequate and insecure.

She remembered her first contact with Lucy when young Miss Mercer arrived to work most mornings at our little red-brick row house at Number 1733 N Street, a picture of innocence turned out in a white blouse and long skirt, with a black velvet ribbon encircling her neck. She would compose herself on the living room rug, spreading out the letters and invitations which overwhelmed Mother on her introduction to social life in Washington. Father called her "the lovely Lucy," but that seemed to be in character with his bantering with everyone.

Mother's suspicions did not begin to stir until after the birth of her last child, my brother Johnny, in March, 1916, which marked the conclusion of all physical relations between husband and wife. When Lucy enlisted as a Navy yeoman the following summer and joined his staff at the Navy Department, he openly met her after working hours. Mother was too miserable and too timid to do more than upbraid him for his increasing lack of attention to her. She had no proof of infidelity.

A slow train, a quiet train,/Carrying Lincoln home

*From the musical drama *The Lonesome Train*, text by Millard Lampell, music by Earl Robinson. Copyright © MCMXLIII, Earl Robinson. Copyright © MCMXLV, Sun Music Co., Inc. U.S. Copyright Renewed. Copyrights assigned to Shawnee Press, Inc., Delaware Water Gap, Pa. 18327. Used with permission.

again. . . . * The proof fell into her hands by chance. For the
first time, Lucy and Father exchanged letters when he took
off for Europe in the summer of 1918 to see London, Paris and
the battle lines at Verdun. He sailed home suffering from double pneumonia and was carried in a stretcher to bed. Unpack-
ing his bags, Mother found Lucy's letters, the evidence she
had been waiting for.

Her impulse was to seek divorce on grounds of adultery,
which was all that the courts of New York recognized. Sara
Delano Roosevelt, our patrician grandmother, averted that by
bringing pressure on Father. If the marriage were shattered,
she would cut off the flow of cash that he needed to supple-
ment his income. If that would not be sufficient punishment, a
divorce would mean political suicide, she noted. So Father
was persuaded to agree to give up Lucy, and Mother on reflection reconciled herself to that solution. Yet he had broken
that promise, if he had ever intended to keep it, and he had
contrived to withhold the truth from her. She had been
tricked, and she could not tell yet how many people had lied
to her in the course of keeping Father's secret.

Six white horses pulled the black-draped caisson from Union Station to the front steps of the White House, with a seventh pacing along as outrider. The roar of bombers flying in
homage overhead occasionally blanketed the music of the
bands to which battalions of uniformed men and women
marched between the tens of thousands who lined the route.
The coffin was borne up the steps and wheeled down to the
East Room, where Lincoln had lain on this same date eighty
years before.

It seemed to Mother that "everyone in the world" was
there for the funeral service—the President, the Cabinet, jus-
tices of the Supreme Court, Senators, Congressmen, the elite
of the diplomatic corps, union bosses and bureaucrats, with a

---

*From the musical drama *The Lonesome Train*, text by Millard Lampell, music by
Earl Robinson. Copyright © MCMXLIII, Earl Robinson. Copyright © MCMXLV,
Sun Music Co., Inc. U.S. Copyright Renewed. Copyrights assigned to Shawnee
Press, Inc., Delaware Water Gap, Pa. 18327. Used with permission.

spill-over congregation gathered in the Blue Room next door. There was a curious twist of courtesy: everyone stood when Mother entered, but they remained sitting on the little gilt chairs when Harry Truman came in. She waited until the hymns had been sung and the prayer was over, then she was the first to leave. She had business to attend to with Anna.

Her face was bleak when she went into my sister's room. "Why was *I* not told about Mrs. Rutherfurd? *You* certainly must have known about her. Why did you say nothing to me?"

Anna dissembled like a child—she was then thirty-eight years old. "I didn't know she would be at Warm Springs."

"Has she ever been in the White House?"

My sister confessed that she had. Father had invited Lucy to dinner when Mother was away and Anna was hostess. Did she know who Mrs. Rutherfurd was? Yes; there was no pretending otherwise. Anna, the eldest of us, was twelve at the time it appeared inevitable that our parents would part.

The realization that her only daughter had been an accomplice added immeasurably to Mother's anguish. The confrontation left both of them disturbed, but Anna made a rapid recovery. Blonde, lean, and almost as tall as Mother, she was the first to greet me when I reached the White House. Her account of the showdown was lighthearted.

"Boy, am I in the doghouse!" she said. "But she'll get over it in a day or so."

Elsewhere, she put a less frivolous gloss on her feelings: "I was upset enough to wonder whether it would make my relationship with Mother difficult. It did, for two or three days. That was all. We never spoke about it again." That was not at all what happened. For years, there was little warmth in Mother's approach to Anna. Forgiveness had to wait until my sister suffered an illness that made her an invalid for months.

The long journey home to Hyde Park and Granny's house in which Father was born was resumed before midnight. Another procession brought the cortege back to Union Station to rejoin the Presidential train. Crowds packed the sidewalks along the way. I sat with Mother in one of the seventeen cars, together with such friends as Harry Hopkins and Henry Morgenthau, Secretary of the Treasury from 1934 on, a close friend and fellow resident on the banks of the Hudson River. My brother Jimmy should have been here by now from Manila, where he was stationed as a lieutenant colonel in the Marines, but he had missed some travel connections and would be with us later. Franklin junior and Johnny were serving with the Pacific Fleet, which had begun the invasion of Okinawa on April 1, so there was no chance of their arrival. The new President and his men were gathered in the car ahead.

At the moment, Mother was incapable of assessing the surgings of affection, disappointment, indignity and anger. She would be sixty-one in October, and she could see no future for herself except as a widow in retirement, endeavoring to instill in five fractious children her own upright standards of behavior. Yet even then, her fascination with politics asserted itself. A parade of Father's followers kept passing between our coach and Truman's, bringing back tidbits of information about what was going on up ahead.

Jimmy Byrnes, a wheeler-dealer whom Father had never trusted, was tipped as the next Secretary of State, replacing Ed Stettinius. "This is the worst mistake in the world," Mother murmured. The names of Bob Hannegan, chairman of the Democratic National Committee, and Ed Pauley, whose influence in the party was tainted by his deals in oil, were bandied about. It appeared that they would carry weight with Truman, and neither of them fitted her concept of a good, liberal Democrat.

One more wish of Father's had to be fulfilled. He wanted to be buried in his own backyard, in the rose garden close by the Hyde Park house. Mother discovered belatedly that this posed problems. It was private, unconsecrated ground, and emergency arrangements had to be completed to rectify that in advance of tomorrow's ceremony. As for the tombstone, Father had written the specifications years before: "A plain white monument—no carving or decoration—to be placed over my grave, east and west, as follows: Length, 8 feet; width, 4 feet; height, 3 feet. Whole to be set on marble base extending 2 feet out from monument all around—but said base to be no more than 6 inches from the ground.'' There was to be ''no device or inscription except the following on the south side: FRANKLIN DELANO ROOSEVELT 1882-19—''

We spent a second night without sleep, watching through the windows of the train, stirred by the sight of the throngs who congregated in the darkness to pay tribute to FDR. Mother had already reached one decision about her future: she would not return to live in the Hyde Park house. It had been Granny's before she died and left it to Father. The presence of our commanding grandmother was almost tangible within its walls. It never felt like home to Mother.

As a young wife, she had consistently bowed to Granny's whims for fear of disapproval. The seed of independence began to germinate, I believe, when Mother learned of Father's original involvement with Lucy. As soon as young Johnny was old enough to follow in the path of Father and us older boys and be sent off as a school boarder at Groton, she started with great deliberation to create a separate existence for herself, ''to use my own mind and abilities for my own aims,'' as she put it.

As First Lady, she was not content to be only the President's helpmate. The objectives he chose were his, not hers. So was the pattern established to meet the physical limitations of a man almost literally tied to his chair. To be independent, she must have an environment of her own. She found it in the apartment that she rented at Number 11 East Eleventh Street in New York City, found for her by her brother Hall, who at one time lived in the same building before his death from cirrhosis reinforced her loathing of the evils of alcohol. And she constructed independence in another way by maintaining a whirlwind round of appointments, speaking engagements and out-of-town travels that filled most of her time.

This provided her with the separateness from Father that

she found essential. If he wanted her at his side on any occasion, she could choose to be there with him or not, depending on her inclination. When the prospect appealed to her, she was quick to cancel a conflicting commitment on her calendar. If she had no desire to be involved, she would say, "Oh, dear, I *should* like to be with you, but I'm afraid that it's *quite* impossible," citing an obligation she had sought for herself. The excuse was valid and ready-made, politeness had been preserved, and the fabric of a disjointed marriage left intact.

We saw the first glint of light brighten the Sunday sky, and soon the train was winding alongside the Hudson on the curving route that Father had ridden so many times before. The day was clear, and a spring breeze was flecking the water white. Garrison, Beacon, Poughkeepsie, then the cars were switched into the siding at the little Hyde Park station.

A fresh half-dozen horses, brown this time, were hitched to a waiting caisson. At its rear stood a seventh, with stirrups reversed, a sword and black riding boots suspended upside down at the saddle. A twenty-one gun salute was fired as the bearers lifted the coffin from the rear coach. I rode with Mother in the automobile that crept along as the cortege moved off to the beat of muffled drums.

It seemed as if every man and woman of Hyde Park village had turned out to stand at the little station and all the way up the climbing, graveled road to the highway, then along the highway itself to the turn-in past the fieldstone gatehouse between the avenue of elms leading toward the house. I recognized some inveterate opponents of Father, akin to those sworn enemies of his who in Washington had clamored for a place aboard the train. But I saw only tears on every face that we passed.

Widow's black made Mother's face seem gaunt and sallow. The veil reached only to her forehead, leaving her majestic, dark-blue eyes uncovered. The look in them was unfathomable. She would not weep then or later. She sat still as stone except, once again, for the constant flexing of her fingers. She had withdrawn completely into herself as I had seen her do before in times of interior conflict between overwhelming emotions. She spoke not a word.

With Anna on one side and I on the other, she walked, head bowed, through the entrance in the towering hemlock hedge into the myrtle-bordered rose garden to which Granny, in straw hat and gardening gloves, had given personal, daily care. Ahead of us, eight servicemen of matched height carried the coffin on the final few yards of its journey. A detachment of West Point cadets, rigid in gray, formed a backdrop for the President, his Cabinet, the Chiefs of Staff, foreign diplomats and the rest of the congregation of men great and small. Lines of soldiers, sailors and marines whose ribbons testified to battles won across the world formed the other three sides of the square.

Harry Hopkins, with signs of his own imminent end on his starch-white cheeks, had argued his doctors at St. Mary's Hospital in Rochester, Minnesota, into letting him be here. Jim Farley, Postmaster General until he broke with Father in 1940, was sobbing as if heartbroken; before very long, he would be complaining to friends that Mother treated him as her social inferior.

The gray-haired rector of St. James Episcopal Church raised his right hand in benediction as the pallbearers inched the coffin down into Father's native earth. *Now the laborer's task is o'er*, the Reverend Gordon Kidd recited, *Now the battle day is past,/Now upon the farther shore,/Lands the voyager at last*. Three volleys cracked out and echoed in the stillness. The bugle notes of taps rose in a lament to the blue sky. Mother turned into Granny's house to express her gratitude to these friends and officials of an era that was over for taking the trouble to attend today, particularly those for whom it had meant leaving home so very *early*.

Not one of them sensed what she had endured. They would praise her courage, but they had no inkling of the degree of discipline she had required of herself. One cover-up had fallen apart—Mother's own magnificent effort had succeeded completely. She accepted President and Mrs. Truman's invitation to go back to Washington on the train with them. She could not be finished with the White House soon enough for her personal satisfaction.

She turned over in her thoughts the events of the past three days, struggling to place them in perspective before trying to evaluate their significance. What had driven Father to act as he did? Where did the responsibility lie? Could there have been a happier outcome to her marriage?

Before many more days had elapsed, we sat together in her latest New York City retreat, apartment 15A at 29 Washington Square West, which she had rented for the past year. Everything there held meaning for her. Pride of place on the dining room walls was given to the Hunting portrait of her father, for whom I was named, picturing him when he was the daredevil master of hounds of a Virginia hunt in the prime of his brief life.

Much of the furniture was authentic handwrought copies of early American pieces made by local carpenters working in the cottage industry set up by Mother in an earlier bid for independence with the help of two women friends at Val-Kill, a few miles up the hill from Hyde Park; that was in the year before Father became Governor of New York. On the living room walls hung the Turner watercolors he gave her—scenes of Venice, where they spent part of their honeymoon sharing the delights of gondolas, St. Mark's Square and tea at the Lido, until her conscience stung her and she reminded herself, "Nothing could be quite so lovely as long as you wished to be idle."

Today, she had reached some conclusions about the circumstances surrounding Father's death, and she wished to share them. "Do you recall the talk we had when you were home last November, Elliott?"

"Every word of it."

"You mentioned that Father had been telling you how he hoped he and I might spend more time together?"

"That is correct." I teased her a little. "He also said, if you remember, 'I only wish she wasn't so darned busy!'"

There was an answering smile. "I also hoped that the day would come when we could make a fresh start. He grew so *alone* after Missy died."

"You wanted to go to Yalta with him, didn't you?"

"He thought there might be *difficulties* with Mr. Churchill and Marshal Stalin and I would be in the way. I think Anna must have been a comfort to him, though."

"I guess she was."

"I should have tried much *harder* to help him all through this awful war. I used to pray every night that he would be spared to carry on, but he did not know that. He did *so* want to see a good peace."

"I don't think the end is too far off in Germany. I'm not so sure about the Pacific."

She was too absorbed in her thoughts to be turned to a different theme. "Oh, I was pigheaded! Unbending during all those years since the first war. Always so insistent on doing what *I* wanted to do."

"Father could have tried harder, too, you know. He kept too many things from you. Maybe the habit was hard to break."

"You mean what happened at Warm Springs? I have thought very hard about that. I can only blame my own pigheadedness, not Father. Neither can I blame Polly nor any of them. It was really my responsibility."

"And Lucy Rutherfurd?"

"She deserves forgiveness as much as anyone."

I fancied that I could make it easier for her by introducing a touch of gossip. "Did I ever tell you I used to know her son, Winthrop III? I met him when he was a single sculler with the Penn Athletic Club. It was he who got me to take up single sculling on the Schuylkill River. He trained me for months— that would be 1930. *His* coach had been Jack Kelly. Wintie and I discovered that Father and Mrs. Rutherfurd had known each other once, but that was all there was to it."

She was not really interested in what I was saying. "If only I had found the *courage* to talk to Franklin as I wanted to do. I could have said, 'Let us bury this whole matter and begin over again together.' I ought to have done that when I said I would. But I left it too late. I contributed to his loneliness. I should have shared his burdens——''

The person she blamed for Father's dying was herself. She found it impossible to form any other judgment. The guilt remained for the rest of her life. She felt certain that had she supported and comforted him, they might have shared some autumn years content with each other's company. Atonement for what she accepted as a sin of omission was to drive her on the course that made her perhaps the best loved woman in the world.

She was mistaken in believing that the reconciliation for which she yearned was frustrated because of her own shortcomings. The fault lay elsewhere.

2

Aboard the train returning south toward Washington on the Sunday evening after Father's burial, President Truman did all he could to lighten the burden for Mother. "Now don't you be in any hurry to leave the White House," he urged. "Take all the time you need in the world." Bess Truman echoed her husband. They would be perfectly happy to stay on in Blair House on the opposite side of Pennsylvania Avenue for a month or more if that would help.

Mother had no desire to waste a minute in leaving. Somehow in the past seventy-two hours she had made time to start one of the prodigious lists with which she imposed order on her days, this latest containing instructions for tagging, crating and shipping out the household possessions accumulated by our family of seven plus grandchildren over the past twelve years.

She was possessed with the idea of putting life as First Lady behind her. "I lived those years very impersonally," she reflected. "It was almost as though I had erected someone outside myself who was the President's wife. I was lost somewhere deep down inside myself.''

What she would turn to next remained a mystery. She gave no immediate thought to pursuing a public career. Her mind was too deadened to entertain guesswork. The physical labor involved in moving out would be good for her, she knew, though the amount of packing to be done was appalling.

In comfortable old shoes and a cheap housedress, she set to work early on Monday morning, ticketing pictures, silver, barrelsful of china, cartons of linens, and the well-worn furniture over which two generations of Roosevelts had scrambled. She would be out before the week was over if she put her mind to it. She sampled some of the twenty-five thousand letters of condolence that poured in, touched by the volume of those which paid tribute to Father for "saving us from despair," but replying would have to wait until the evacuation was completed.

She worked eighteen and sometimes twenty hours a day to finish the job, and none of her children could figure out where she found the strength. Anna could spare little help. She had her own packing to do before finding another home for her children and herself before Colonel Boettiger came back from Europe.

Jimmy would soon fly back to the Philippines to request release from duty as a much-decorated colonel in the Marines. As an executor of Father's estate, he faced a pile of work on his return. Franklin junior, wounded when his ship was bombed at Palermo, Italy, was now in command of a destroyer escort, one of 1,300 vessels engaged in the eighty-three-day-long battle for Okinawa, the final campaign of the war. Johnny, too, was still out there, serving under Admiral Bill Halsey. My own immediate future was rapidly resolved; I was assigned a planning job in the Pentagon.

Mother's pledge to assist him in whatever way she could reconciled Harry Truman to the prospect of her hasty departure. Apart from genuine concern for her well-being, he had reason to keep her close at hand. Father had consistently excluded his Vice-President from most of his councils. To guard against impeachment by a largely antagonistic Congress for misuse of federal funds, he had kept Truman in blank ignorance of the atom bomb, unaware of the very existence of the Manhattan Project. The new President could look for little aid from members of the Cabinet in determining what his predecessor had intended. Father had confided in none of them.

Truman would eventually disband the entire team. Ed Stettinius, a polished product of the Eastern establishment, was far from being Truman's kind of man. He was out by midsummer, together with Henry Morgenthau. The President saw no place in his Administration for a forward-looking Republican like old Henry Stimson as Secretary of War; Stimson would be replaced in September.

Harold Ickes clung on as Secretary of the Interior until the next year in spite of Truman's dislike, and Henry Wallace was kept on at Commerce for the time being because he swung support among liberal Democrats. At the end of June, the new broom in the White House swept away four of Father's appointees in one swoop—Attorney General Francis Biddle, Postmaster General Frank Walker, Secretary of Agriculture Claude Wickard, and Frances Perkins, Secretary of Labor. Mother was especially uneasy about the ousting of Ma Perkins. In her opinion, there was a place for at least one woman in a Cabinet, and she told Truman so.

She could be as frank as she pleased because Truman regarded her as the most reliable source of information about FDR's plans and policies for victory and peace. He shared the almost universal delusion that she was privy to all Father's secrets. He imagined that her memory and knowledge would provide the necessary insights to fill the enormous gaps in his own information. He was grateful for every crumb of intelligence that she could offer to ensure continuity in administration.

At first, she was willing but not particularly eager to be quizzed.

It was her duty to serve, but she must be allowed to remain

behind the scenes. The President also summoned Anna and me on separate occasions for the same purpose of briefing him. The call from the White House came while I was still on leave at Hyde Park. There was a sense of shock at seeing someone other than Father ensconced in the Presidential office, but Truman could not have been more cordial and complimentary about what I had been doing in photoreconnaissance with the USAAF.

He was especially interested in what I had learned of Russia and the Russians in the course of setting up a new airfield at Poltava and in my contacts with Stalin and his comrades at the Big Three conference in Teheran. What kind of people were they? How hard or how easy was it to get along with them? I reported that I'd run into few problems.

Then he told me he planned to send a special envoy to Moscow to tackle the thorny question of exacting reparations from Germany. He would appreciate it if I passed on my observations to Ed Pauley, whose name caused Mother's hackles to rise. So I went over to talk with him. I found him singularly uninterested in anything I could pass on to him about dealing with the Soviets. He did not want to hear my experiences in bargaining with them. Instead, he insisted on displaying the gifts he would be taking with him to smooth his path, mostly lipsticks and nylon stockings. I left wondering whether he envisaged himself as a missionary carrying trade goods for Pacific islanders.

When Truman invited Mother to join the United States delegation in San Francisco for the United Nations founding conference opening on April 25, she had no doubts about his motive. Roosevelt was a prestigious name, capable of adding credentials and luster for the unexpected new President. But acceptance would exceed the bounds of duty, and serving as a figurehead held no attraction for her; hence she declined. She turned down another political suggestion when Harold Ickes, who had castigated her in the past for "interfering" in White House affairs, pressured her to run for the United States Senate on a Democratic ticket that would have made Senator James M. Mead Governor of New York.

She backed away from the limelight. "My children," she told Ickes, "have labored for many years under the baffling necessity of considering the business of living as it affected their father's position, and I want them to feel that in future any running for political office will be done by *them*."

It took Mother four days to conclude the task of moving. Completion brought no sense of accomplishment, only relief. She felt calmer than before, but her vision of the future was no clearer. She was sure of only three things, all of them negative. "I did not want to run an elaborate household again. I did not want to cease trying to be useful in some way. I did not want to feel old."

On the morning of Friday, April 20, she said her farewells to the capital with melancholy and uncertainty but without regret. At ten o'clock that night, she walked into the Washington Square apartment, clad in black, consumed by the illusion that she had committed a wrong which had to be expiated.

Anna's sentiments about leaving were utterly different. She was crushed by the realization that her reign as a power broker had come to an end. Mother had never been enthusiastic about my sister's taking over as the acknowledged hostess of the White House, but in his advancing years Father felt the lack of sympathetic feminine company. He wanted to be comforted, not coaxed and criticized by Mother as he had been all too often. It was his suggestion that brought in Anna and her children from Seattle, where before he entered the army John Boettiger worked as publisher of William Randolph Hearst's isolationist *Post-Intelligencer.* Mother hid her misgivings and the hurt to her pride, but my sister reveled in her new-found status at the side of the most influential human being in the free world, living in what constituted the supreme Allied command post as the war approached its climax. With his timetable so crowded that the rest of the family could see him only by appointment, she was highly selective in granting admission to his study. She exercised far greater influence than Mother ever had, and she became what Mother never truly was—a conduit to the President.

Cabinet members, agency chiefs, generals and admirals all turned to Anna when they sought personal contact with Father, anxious for cooperation in relaying messages to him and his responses back to them. She found enormous satisfaction in passing along his requests and instructions to the foremost men in the land, who had little choice but to defer to her.

Understandably, Father enjoyed being waited on and having his needs attended to; Missy had done much the same in the past, though she lacked Anna's blood relationship and zest for authority. "Sis, you take care of this for me" became a familiar refrain. As often as not, he lunched and dined alone with her, an arrangement she encouraged as a means of conserving his energies. Mother was reduced to telling those who previously had consulted her about Father's predilections, "You'll have to ask Anna about that; she's the only one who would know."

My sister had no appetite for the power of elective office and the responsibilities that accompany it. Influence at the summit and power behind the scenes were what delighted her. Women of similar ambition enliven the pages of history, but only one other Roosevelt was cast in the same mold: Mother's first cousin, Alice Roosevelt Longworth, Uncle Ted's firstborn child, was the same mixture of ambition and irresponsibility as Anna. But after 1908 Cousin Alice could operate in the White House only as an invited guest, the wife of Speaker Nick Longworth, while Anna was entrenched there twenty-four hours a day.

She interposed herself in our parents' day-by-day living, frustrating Mother's dream of reconciliation with Father. Together with Aunt Polly, she fostered the renewed relationship with Lucy Mercer Rutherfurd. Yet Mother refused to acknowledge that this was the reality, not the guilt which she assumed for having failed him.

In this time of trouble after Father's death, the woman she leaned on more than any other living soul was Malvina

Thompson, nominally her secretary, but in fact closer than any relative. Tommy toiled hour by hour with Mother in the evacuation of the White House just as she had tackled countless other jobs during the past twenty years. This short, stout, prematurely gray woman, who seldom received more than a passing mention in a news story or a magazine article, played a role as important as Louis Howe's in the emergence of Eleanor Roosevelt. Louis had coaxed her into big-time politics, taught her how to speak in public, how to sharpen her perceptions and examine facts instead of fancies. That was all part of his long-range strategy for catapulting a man, without the ability to physically walk unaided, into the Presidency in 1932.

Tommy devoted her life to Mother as Louis had dedicated himself to Father. She was Mother's most intimate friend and sternest critic. She handled a majority of the hundred and more letters a day from relations, friends and strangers. She corrected the syntax and grammar of Mother's "My Day" column, which at its peak appeared in some ninety newspapers.

More important, she undertook to correct the flaws she recognized in Mother's character. "Everyone makes mistakes," she would caution Mother when she showed a want of sympathy with the frailties of other people, including those of us children. "You're being narrow-minded," Tommy would say, always speaking her mind if Mother aired some of her prejudices against conduct less upright than her own. "You can't *say* that!" Tommy would protest whenever Mother flared up unduly at what she took to be an act of injustice. "You *must* keep yourself under control."

Tommy was a Bronx railroad engineer's daughter shaky in her shorthand when she first went to work for Mother on the New York State Democratic Committee in the 1920s. Mother's dictation then was as labored as Tommy's wrestling with Pitman's techniques. Though her willpower was as strong as her employer's, the new secretary subordinated everything to her job.

She maintained the filing system and kept the roster of ap-

pointments to the minute-by-minute standard of efficiency
that was demanded. She drew up domestic budgets and often
ran the household in Mother's name. When we children were
afraid of a dressing-down from Mother for our transgressions,
we went to Tommy first to enlist her as our confessor, asking
her to pave the way before we faced parental rebuke. "Tommy, be a doll and just mention that there's another speeding
ticket." "I know I've flunked that exam. Will you break the
news gently to her?"

When we went into the White House in 1933, Tommy virtually cut herself off from all society except the company of the
Roosevelts. "If I lost my job tomorrow, those other people
wouldn't give me house room," she joked. "Anyway, you're
always expected to pay for favors in some way."

She became Mrs. Frank Schneider, but she bore no child.
To us, she was still Tommy, who loved us and, later, our own
sons and daughters, as if we were hers. Frank sometimes visited us in Washington, Hyde Park and New York. Finally the
marriage faltered under the strain of her attachment to us and
they separated.

She had a room in the Washington Square apartment and a
suite allegedly hers at Val-Kill Cottage, which had once been
the furniture factory—a two-story, stucco-covered warren of
rooms and hallways. Tommy's living room did double duty as
her office, and her little kitchen as a bar. In the summertime,
breakfast and brunch were served for guests on her screened
porch. She had a bedroom for herself and another earmarked
for her usually absent husband. Like Mother, Tommy felt no
regret about quitting the White House.

Straightaway after Mother's return to Val-Kill, Father's
will was read to her, Anna, Jimmy and me by the attorney
who had drawn it, Basil O'Connor. The rough-tempered Irish-
man had been his partner in the law practice set up following
Father's reentry into public life with braces on his legs, and
O'Connor continued to the end as his personal lawyer. Mother respected Basil's professional abilities, but she questioned
the inordinate amount of income he earned as president of the

Warm Springs Foundation for the treatment of polio victims and as head of the American Red Cross.

Father left life insurance of $562,142, with the Warm Springs Foundation as beneficiary, and two other policies for Mother. The bulk of his remaining estate, with a net worth of $1,085,486, he left in trust to her, so that she would enjoy the income from it to the end of her life, when the principal was to be shared equally among us children. The legal phrases in the lengthy document that O'Connor rolled off his tongue were confusing to her.

"I am sorry, but I don't quite understand," she kept repeating. "Do you mind going over that again?"

I could hear her saying much the same kind of thing to Father when we sat as a family around the dining room table and he was outlining a new piece of legislation he proposed to send to Congress, or perhaps a Fireside Chat to deliver over the radio. Absorbing or transmitting information, his mind worked fast. Mother was much slower to grasp a point or an argument, and she would interrupt with questions until she was satisfied that she understood.

"I am not *quite* clear about what you are driving at, Franklin. Can you explain that for me?"

"Let's go back to the beginning, Babs," he would say patiently, then cover the ground again to give her full understanding. "This is the plan," and he would spell it out, ABC.

"But I don't see how you can do that," she might break in. "It isn't *consistent* with what you said before," and she would quote his words of a month, a year or a decade ago.

"It's *perfectly* consistent. Don't be a silly goose."

"Then explain to me. Tell me why."

In those days, she was a simon-pure idealist, blind to the practicalities which of necessity weighed heavily in his reasoning. "You have to proceed one step at a *time*," he would answer when she chided him about his pace, for instance, in extending social welfare or broadening the rights of women. "Your goal is *here*," and he would tap the tablecloth, "but

you can't announce that you're heading straight for it. You
may have to go clear around the woods and come in from the
other side."

Maneuvering of this nature was invariably difficult for
Mother to accept. Her idea was always to make a beeline
from one position to another. The experience of widowhood
would add subtlety to her thinking.

The attorney's patience did not equal Father's, but Basil
O'Connor went over the will paragraph by paragraph to clear
up her doubts. Her greatest difficulty lay in making out just
what Father intended to do with the house that had been
Granny's and the Hyde Park acreage, which he had consider-
ably increased. Stripped of the *whereases* that bewildered her,
the document gave Mother and any or all of us children the
right to reside there throughout our lifetimes before the comfortable, airy house and the grounds surrounding it were donated to the government as a national monument. Father
knew, because she had told him so repeatedly, that the prospect held no attraction for her, so he left a letter, spelling out
his thinking.

"I seriously doubt," it said in effect, "whether any one of
you will be able to afford to keep up the place as it has previously been maintained. Therefore I would urge you to hand it
over as soon as possible. Visits I have paid to the homes of
earlier Presidents lead me to believe that the constant arrival
of sightseers could make life difficult for you there. I should
hate to think of you being driven into hiding in the attic or
down in the cellar for the sake of privacy!"

Jimmy, Anna and I agreed on the spot that he was right
about the prohibitive cost of running the property. We were
more than willing to cede our rights of residence. Through
armed forces channels, Mother sent radiograms to Franklin
junior and Johnny to obtain quitclaims from them. Before
long, Basil O'Connor was armed with waivers to present to
the government, free and clear, the mansion, most of its contents and more than thirty acres of land.

Another gargantuan job of housework confronted Mother. Until then, it had been easy to entertain the fancy that Father was off on one of the many trips he took without her and that all she had to do was bide her time before he was home again. Once again, the physical labor consumed in sorting out possessions eased the tension. Every April morning, she slipped away to cut sprigs of lily of the valley to lay at the grave.

Granny had been a hoarder, and so had her only child. He saved everything that came his way, from checkbook stubs to match folders. She had preserved bits of string and ribbon, bolts of cloth and particularly anything associated with Father, including his christening robe and the wild birds he had collected and mounted in a glass case as a boy. On the beds of my home today, we have Irish linens bought by Granny more than half a century ago and handed on by Mother; she found them wrapped in the brown paper in which they had originally been delivered.

Mother had few of the magpie instincts which seemed a mark of the Delanos. The will gave her first pick of the silver, pictures, furniture, linens, china, Granny's furs and jewelry, and almost everything else. She took astonishingly little for herself, only mundane items that could be useful in the future, whatever it held, and others that evoked memories of Father, such as the Turner watercolors. Granny's treasures were divided among Anna and three daughters-in-law.

Sentiment had rarely been evident in Mother before, apart from unquenched love for her father and admiration for Uncle Ted. Suddenly, a new feeling asserted itself. I was fascinated to see photographs of the five of us children, who had been both her joy and her despair, appear in hinged leather frames on her bedroom dressing table. She carried them everywhere she travelled, between Hyde Park and Washington Square, across the country or overseas. We were the family, and she intended to hold us to her heart.

Pictures of Mother and Father in the days of courtship and

years of marriage before Lucy intervened were now kept on permanent display, too, in each of Mother's homes. They had previously been stored out of sight.

Of all the manifestations of change in her emotions, her attitude toward Fala was perhaps the most poignant. He had been strictly Father's dog, a gift from Daisy Suckley. Mother was not interested in Fala. She did not approve of his sleeping at the foot of Father's bed; she felt that he was out of place under Father's chair in the dining room, enjoying tidbits that were slipped to him. At first, Daisy took the black scottie back to stay with her because that was what Grace Tully said his master had wanted. My brother Jimmy sensed how much Fala might mean to Mother.

"She has no one living whom she is personally responsible for," he said. Cousin Daisy gladly returned the dog. Jimmy had guessed correctly. Fala and Mother were soon inseparable. Except on flights abroad, where she went he went, too, in a car or on a train. She walked him through the woods at Val-Kill and around the lamp posts of Washington Square. She fed him, bathed him and had him perform the tricks Father had taught, begging, rolling over, playing dead, with a biscuit as his reward. No one else was allowed a hand in caring for *her* dog.

Her attachment, like all her pleasures, was shadowed by a sense of inadequacy. She was convinced that Fala mourned for the master he could not forget. When the little terrier stretched out on the rug near the dining room door at Val-Kill with a sharp dark eye cocked at each of the entrances, she was sure he was watching for Father, not for herself. When his ears pricked up at the wailing of a police siren, she told herself that he was remembering his days of glory when he rode on Father's lap in a Presidential limousine.

A visit by General Dwight D. Eisenhower reinforced her impression of Fala's pining. Ike, under whose command I served, arrived at Hyde Park from Supreme Headquarters Allied Expeditionary Forces in Paris with three purposes in mind: paying his respects to Mother; laying a wreath on the grave of the President he had come close to worshiping; and meeting Fala—Ike also owned a scottie. The sound of the escort electrified Fala as it heralded Ike's arrival through the gates and up the drive to the front door.

"I knew that he expected to see his master coming," Mother said. In her heart, I think that she did, too. "Fala accepted me," she decided sadly, "but I was just someone to put up with until the master should return."

Some citizens of the community had their own idea for the disposition of the Hyde Park property. A committee of them approached Mother, urging her to lobby in Washington to promote the village as a permanent site for the United Nations. She undertook to write to Harry Hopkins to seek his opinion. From his hospital bed, he told her that he would sound out Clement Attlee, the British Prime Minister; Chiang Kai-shek, the Chinese war leader; Vyacheslav Molotov, the Soviet Foreign Minister; and Charles de Gaulle of France.

"I should think," Harry said, "that they would like to be away from a big city and develop a community of their own. Hyde Park would lend itself ideally for such a development because there is plenty of room for housing, to say nothing of the main buildings." He envisaged the purchase by the government of the Rogers estate next door to provide extra space.

So far as I could judge, Mother was in two minds about the proposal. It would be a fitting memorial to Father to glorify his native village by making it the home of the organization that was his brainchild and, in his opinion, man's best hope for peaceful progress. But the village would be transformed and privacy at Val-Kill lost. Perhaps if the strength of purpose that developed in her afterwards had been born sooner, she would have campaigned harder for Hyde Park when a United Nations commission was inspecting possible locations. But Hopkins was too ill to make the promised contacts. By next January, he would be dead, and Mother was not yet ready to act alone.

She was plagued by financial worries. Probating Father's

will promised to take forever in light of the item-by-item
assessment that would be required because of the impending
handover of the house and land. Granny had been gone almost three years, but Father had been too busy to settle her
estate. For the time being, Mother would have to bear all the
overheads of Hyde Park, including a hefty payroll at the ne-
glected farm, as well as foot the bills at Washington Square.

"It is rather *nightmarish,*" she said as she wrestled with the
problem of making ends meet. She had an inherited income of
$8,000 a year. She also had the proceeds from Father's life in-
surance to tide her over until she was allowed to begin drawing the interest on his estate. She regretted once again that she
had no business training to help her figure out a budget. She
had never lived extravagantly; now frugality was in style as
she pared personal expenses to the bone.

Newspaper editors were eager to start running her column
again. It was not callousness, as the legion of Eleanor-haters
claimed, that drove her to resume dictating "My Day" a week
after Father's funeral; she felt she must earn whatever she
could to pay the bills. The same compulsion led her to return
to the lecture circuits, continue her monthly columns in *Ladies' Home Journal,* and read manuscripts in spare moments
for the Junior Literary Guild at $100 apiece, though she en-
joyed doing that. Self-imposed obligations covered a long,
long list of charities, churches, hospitals and educational institutions. She refused to give them up. She would simply
have to make every penny she could in order to afford her do-
nations to them. There was one source she shunned; she never accepted the $5,000-a-year pension to which she was enti-
tled as a President's widow, but she did take advantage of the
franking privileges which enabled her to answer her mail without the expense of buying postage stamps.

The taxes falling due on Father's estate loomed large in the
nightmare. To preserve the capital sum intact, cash would
have to be raised somehow. We found the solution in Father's
stamp collection. Granny and her husband James, who was
dead when my parents married, had both collected stamps.

Father's interest was originally sparked when Granny gave her schoolboy son her own Chinese and Hong Kong issues. Much of his knowledge of geography came from the evening hours he spent poring over his albums, hundreds of them, with most pages annotated in his handwriting.

The collection ran to approximately 1,250,000 stamps in all, a million of them nothing special, but the balance something else. Father recognized on sight the majority of rarities that had ever been printed anywhere, though $10 was his usual limit as a buyer. He even saved the stamped envelopes containing the crank letters sent to him in the White House, addressed with such endearments as "Dishonorable Franklin Deficit Roosevelt," "F. D. Russianvelt, President of the U.S.A., C.I.O.," and one that especially delighted him, "Chief Shooter at the Moon, White Father of the Pretty Bubbles."

The rarest of the stamps collected in the course of half a century fetched $250,000 at public auction. Other valuable items proved to be the engravers' die proofs of every United States issue since 1894, which sold for $52,955. Taxes due on the estate could be paid painlessly, but Mother continued to fret over her bills, and the Roosevelt-haters fussed, as expected, over the inclusion of the die proofs in his estate, though the Bureau of Engraving and Printing had made similar gifts to every President to be accepted as personal property.

The executors—Basil O'Connor, Jimmy and a New York bank—advised Mother that by June 15 the Hyde Park house must be cleared of everything that was not to be given to the government. She and Tommy kept to this deadline as a matter of pride in accomplishing the near-impossible, scurrying to and fro between the big house, Val-Kill and Washington Square as the occasion demanded in the only car Mother had—Father's blue Ford tourer, which had been hastily stripped of its hand controls and reconverted for normal operating.

May 8 found her in Manhattan, swamped by chanting, dancing crowds celebrating V-E Day. Though her face was unusually drawn and weary, the gaunt, preoccupied figure in the long black coat was instantly recognizable as she was trapped by the throng at the corner of Fifth Avenue and 23rd Street. Mother had scorned the constant Secret Service protection that was extended to her against her will when she was First Lady; she was relieved that she had none these days.

"You are very kind, but I really am *quite* capable of looking after myself," she told the policeman who took her under his wing, but he insisted on finding her a taxicab to take her down to Washington Square. She handed the driver a dollar bill to pay her fare. He would accept it on one condition—that she sign it for him as a souvenir. As she listened to the radio voices of Truman and Churchill, her imagination added Father's to their proclamation of victory in Europe.

The executors had another warning for her. Apart from Val-Kill, the remaining acreage and buildings at Hyde Park must be sold to the highest bidder. She would not tolerate the thought of what anguish this would have caused the man whose importance to her increased as the days passed.

"I could not bear not to try to hold it in the hope that *some* child would want to run it some day," she said. "I'm sure that is what Franklin wanted."

She decided that she would be the highest bidder. She would take some personal capital and buy nearly 900 acres of the land owned by Father. My brother Franklin, thirty-one years old, home on leave and eager to be heard, advised strongly against it. "Capital," he told her, "is a sacred trust." She thought otherwise. One should consecrate oneself to work, not to money, she replied.

I was the child she asked to run this new undertaking as a kind of memorial to Father. I had been mulling over the problem of what I might do when my current stint at the Pentagon came to an end. What would the future hold for a retired brigadier general, aged thirty-four? I had volunteered for the USAAF more than five years ago and counted myself lucky to be alive. Whenever a German fighter pilot gunned down an unarmed photoreconnaissance plane, he was credited with two kills, not one. The losses in my unit were the highest in any branch of the Air Forces—an average of twenty-five percent of our men a month. On most missions flown over North Africa and Hitler's Europe, it was always doubtful that one would make it home.

I was shaky, and both Mother and I knew it, drifting again as I had before in an uncertain sea. For reasons undeterminable to me, I seemed to miss having her close more than my brothers. Perhaps it was because I was the middle child, younger than Anna and Jimmy, older than Franklin and Johnny. They thought there was a bond between us that was stronger than with them, but I had never sensed that. In Jimmy's judgment, I was "the one least able to manage" on my own. Maybe. In any event, I was anxious to make amends.

My talks with her ranged between Val-Kill and the Washington Square apartment. "Would you consider coming back to Hyde Park and working with me?" she asked almost timidly one day. "I don't think I could live there unless you do. I doubt that I would *want* to."

"How could I help?"

"In just about everything. We could be partners, in a way. You could take care of the contract for my column when that's renewed. Then there's my magazine contract, and so many people ask for books to be written. I think, too, that I *might* like to see what could be done in some broadcasts. But perhaps you would want to go back to Texas?"

I had no reason for doing that. The ranch there had been sold at the time of my second divorce.

"Or to California?"

"Mummy," I said, moved as no thirty-four-year-old male had a right to be, "there is nothing in the world I would rather do than work with you." I felt uncannily like the prodigal son. I vowed to myself that I would serve her for the rest of her days.

Neither of us, I knew, had felt such closeness before. My earliest memories were of a distant, sometimes forbidding woman who could seldom find the means of making us chil-

dren understand that she loved us. Warmth and affection in
our lives seemed to come only from Father and Granny.
Mother was the one who disciplined us; she had to badger Father before he would utter a harsh word, and then the reproof
was likely to be gentle. She tried desperately to keep us in
line, but that was out of the question when Granny spoiled us
and we could do no wrong in her eyes.

As Father's career took up more and more of his time,
Mother had to fill a double role in the family. In her opinion,
she had failed miserably, and in our childhood, we would
have agreed with her. Anna, Jimmy and I felt the most ne-
glected. After Franklin junior was born in 1914 and John two
years later, she did her best to make up to them for her failings with the first three of us. Then came the Lucy affair,
which was to distort our parents' marriage beyond repair.

The fact that Mother had turned to me made for a special
joy. I had regarded myself—and who was to argue?—as the
family maverick. I balked at following Father and Jimmy to
Harvard and took off instead to earn a living out West as a
horse wrangler. I had worked in Los Angeles for William Randolph Hearst, whom Father abhorred. I had been unduly willing to make myself useful to entrepreneurs in the oil industry
and the cattle business who wanted an entree to the White
House. As a radio commentator in Texas, I had crossed political swords with my parent more than once.

So it was a moment of some sentiment when Mother invited
me to become her partner in an enterprise designed to maintain as a family trust something that had been dear to Father. I
had never questioned her forgiveness for my mistakes, but at
last something else was clear to me: we children had been
wrong in asking ourselves whether she truly loved us.

She went to great lengths to emphasize to Anna and my
brothers that I was not being treated as a favorite. It went
without saying between Mother and me that we both had to
earn our keep. She spelled out the facts in one of the letters
she sent simultaneously to the five of us as a time-saving device: "I have made no gift to Elliott. . . . I write you this so

that you may clearly see that you will get from the estate all
that you would probably have received in any case, and in addition to make it clear that Elliott is putting in all he makes so
that you will not think any extra gifts have been made to
him."

At that time, there was no discernible jealousy among her
offspring. We were overwhelmed by the loss of the parent we
had adored. We felt that we were tied together by bonds of
mutual affection. One of her biographers, Joseph P. Lash, has
reported "violent quarrels among the children" over "dividing up of the political legacy—which son was to have prece-
dence in running for political office in New York and California."

As one of Mother's many protégés, Joe was in a position to
know better. No such disputes occurred in 1945 or afterwards. There were no "angry shouting matches among the
boys that were more than she could bear." We were four veterans of the armed forces, anxious about returning to civilian
living. Johnny would prove to hold no firm Democratic convictions. Franklin's immediate challenge was to establish himself as a lawyer. Jimmy had to pick up the threads of his insurance business in California. Politics as a mode of life meant
nothing to me. As for Anna, she had no desire whatever to
emerge into public view.

I should be bringing to Hyde Park a new wife—my third, let
it be said. One of my many deeds which Father's enemies
seized on to belabor him with was my first divorce, which
made me history's first White House child to go through the
process. The event did nothing to alter Mother's friendship
with Betty Donner Roosevelt, whom she had welcomed into
the family and treated as a daughter. She extended similar
kindness and affection to every one of the men and women
who were at some time married to her five children, and there
would be a total of seventeen of them in her lifetime.

She showed only understanding and sympathy when my
second wife, the former Ruth Googins, of Texas, divorced me
while I was overseas in 1943. Mother appreciated what dam-

age a long wartime separation could do to a marriage. "Ruth probably needs somebody *else* to help her with her life," she remarked, and she retained a permanent, close friendship with my second wife as she did with the first.

When Faye Emerson and I were married in Arizona in December, 1944, Mother was initially dubious. She had not met Faye. All she knew was that she was a movie actress, and Mother had some Victorian prejudice about the propriety of working in show business. Faye had been with me at the funeral. The more Mother saw of her, the more she admired her intelligence, energy and enormous ambition. "Faye," she concluded, "is *my* type of person." She looked forward to having her as her closest neighbor.

There was a third passenger in the car when Faye and I drove east in early June from our Los Angeles apartment. Blaze, our strapping English bull mastiff, had recently achieved greater notoriety than either of us. I had bought him in England and shipped him to Washington two years previously. After some not-altogether-happy months of White House society, he went to board in my absence at the same nearby military post that stabled Mother's horse, Dot.

Then I wanted Faye to have Blaze as a protector and companion in Los Angeles. From England, I wrote to Anna in her new role as Presidential organizer: any time she could see a way for Blaze to get to California, I should like him to go. She arranged with an assistant to C. R. Smith, a long-time friend of mine who was heading the Air Transport Command, for the dog to travel if space became available in a cargo plane.

Neither Anna nor I had the least idea that Blaze would be granted top priority, but because the call had come from the White House, that is what an assistant imagined was mandated to fill the request. A sailor traveling west on compassionate leave had grounds for complaint when he was bumped off the flight to make room for Blaze, and complain he did. I knew nothing of what was happening until I saw the headlines and heard the news bulletins, but I bore the brunt of the hullabaloo until *l'affaire* Blaze blew over and my duties in the

USAAF could continue, encountering flak only from German antiaircraft guns.

In addition to Mother's cottage, two other buildings made up the Val-Kill property, and she earmarked one of them as our home. The second was currently occupied by two women who in former years had meant a great deal to her; of late, however, the atmosphere between them had grown distinctly frosty. Nancy Cook, who kept her hair cut short and smoked an occasional cigar, and her stately schoolteacher friend, Marion Dickerman, had been associated with Mother in a number of undertakings, not the least of which was the women's division of the New York State Democratic Committee as far back as the 1920's.

If Nancy and Marion, who were not Father's idea of feminine company, had to be around, he wanted them kept at a distance. He was more than happy to give Mother and the two of them a life interest in some of the land he owned at Val-Kill.

"My Missus and some of her female political friends want to build a shack on a stream in the back woods and want, instead of a beautiful marble bath, to have the stream dug out so as to form an old-fashioned swimming hole," Father gibed to a friend. In fact, Father sketched the plans which resulted in a fieldstone cottage, shared as living quarters by the three friends. He also paid for the *al fresco* swimming pool, but Mother footed bills for the cottage.

She dipped into her money once again when Nancy and Marion determined to buy Todhunter School for girls in New York City, where Marion was vice principal. For years Mother taught courses in literature, drama and American history, subjects in which she felt safely grounded.

The most ambitious venture of the three companions was the Val-Kill furniture factory, which called for putting up another building close by—and funneling in most of Mother's radio and writing earnings as well as more of her capital to operate it when profits proved elusive. After the business went onto the rocks during the Depression, Mother sought clear ti-

tle to the premises so that she could convert the factory into a
larger sanctuary for herself. She proposed trading her share in
the fieldstone cottage in return for a release signed by Nancy
and Marion. To Father's outrage and Mother's chagrin, they
said no.

Following our move to Washington in 1933, Mother com-
muted to New York to continue teaching at Todhunter, but
she tapered off her appearances there—to once a week, then
once a month—before she severed her connection completely. She had tried again to obtain clear title to the former factory, this time in exchange for her share in the school. The
settlement Nancy and Marion asked for rankled Mother, but a
fleeting sense of superiority consoled her. "I can never forget," she said, "that these two girls are afraid of the future,
and I am not."

By then, the real estate tangle at Val-Kill had been further
complicated by Father. He, too, yearned for a hideaway in
the woods where he could retire after 1940 to write his memoirs and raise Christmas trees. Again, he drew up the
sketches and began supervising construction of what was
promptly labeled "Roosevelt's Dream House," another stone
cottage located at a respectable distance from the two other
buildings, with a superb front-porch view up and down the
Hudson valley to the distant Catskill Mountains.

His cottage stood empty and not entirely finished. He spent
not a night in the place, which was bare of all furniture when
we arrived at Val-Kill. Yet this was named as the rendezvous
in the memoirs of Dorothy Schiff, former publisher of the
New York Post, who, hopping aboard the bandwagon of those
with whom Father supposedly enjoyed clandestine relation-
ships, claimed to have spent some titillating hours with him
there while Secret Servicemen waited outside. This dalliance,
she averred, took place in 1937. I have a photograph which
shows Father in his little Ford at the site in 1938. "Top Cottage—nearing completion," says the caption in his own hand.

Top Cottage was earmarked for Faye, Blaze and me. Our

arrival provided Mother with an opportunity to bid farewell to Nancy and Marion, who lingered on in Stone Cottage.

"When Elliott came into the place, it became more difficult," Marion told Joe Lash. "One day Nan and I looked up and said, 'When will we go?' " Mother forked out something more than $30,000 for their two-thirds interest. Nancy wrote a good-bye note: "I am leaving the keys in an envelope for you. . . . If you are home before we leave we will come over to see you and say good-bye."

Mother was not to be found. She had learned the time of their departure, set for around three o'clock. "Let's go out, Elliott," she said, "and not come back until they have gone."

It was five o'clock before we returned. One of Mother's attributes was an exceedingly long memory; another was a sense of justice in matters large or small.

3

In face-to-face meetings and in the letters which passed between them, Mother had a wealth of advice to offer the new President. She was sometimes circumspect in her choice of words, as when she hinted at the mediocrity of some of the men he was choosing as counselors:

"I have a feeling it would be helpful if you could build a small group of very eminent, non-political experts in all fields whose duty it would be to watch the world scene and keep you briefed day by day in a map room." Such an arrangement, of course, would minimize the influence of the likes of Jimmy Byrnes.

Or she could be frank and eminently practical as she was within a month of Father's death, when Mr. Truman complained to her that he found handling Winston Churchill a problem almost as prickly as coping with Soviet suspicions of the West:

"Of course, we will have to be patient, and any lasting peace will have to have the Three Great Powers behind it. I think, however, if you can get on a personal basis with Mr.

Churchill you will find it easier. If you talk to him about books and let him quote to you from his marvellous memory everything from Barbara Fritchie to the Nonsense Rhymes and Greek tragedy, you will find him easier to deal with on political subjects. He is a gentleman to whom the personal element means a great deal."

She realized her own shortage of humor and saw the same weakness in Winston when the Russians teased him about things he held sacred, like the preservation of British imperialism and the sanctity of kings. "He takes them deadly seriously," she told the President, "and argues about them when what he ought to do is laugh. That was where Franklin usually won out because when you know when to laugh and when to look upon things as too absurd to take seriously, the other person is ashamed to carry through even if he was serious about it."

She was absorbed by the ebb and flow of hope in San Francisco, where the Allies floundered in a sea of trouble writing the United Nations charter. The Soviet Union demanded a seat at the conference for Poland; the Western powers refused. If Poland were not seated, the Soviets would pull out and the U.N. would be doomed. Then, after Truman delivered a tongue-lashing to Molotov, both sides conceded an inch or two. Some Polish exiles were taken into the Warsaw government, and Poland won its seat.

On June 26, the United Nations Charter was signed, and Mother gave credit where she felt it was deserved. "I think President Truman is doing extremely well," she wrote contentedly to Jimmy the following morning. She did not like one consequence: with this mission completed, Ed Stettinius would be immediately demoted and Byrnes appointed Secretary of State in his place.

There was a subject impossible to discuss in correspondence and probably mentioned only once in her private sessions with Truman: the use of the atomic bomb. The Manhattan Project was still veiled in secrecy. After the mid-July testing at Alamogordo, New Mexico, proved its apocalyptic effectiveness, the question was no longer whether the bomb would work, but how and where to employ it against the Japanese.

The President wanted to learn from Mother what Father had planned. "I do not know," she replied. "I never really discovered what was in his mind. He did not choose to discuss it with me, and I was not inclined to ask. The decisions must be yours, Mr. President." She declined to speculate.

Those civilians and service chiefs who were aware of the bomb's readiness were divided on the issue. One side emphasized that although the Allies in the Pacific war—the USSR remained uncommitted—were closing in on the home islands of Japan, invasion could take a year and cost a million casualties. Also to be reckoned with were the kamikaze pilots, whose suicidal dives onto ships of our fleet were slowing the advance. Such advisers as Byrnes and Admiral Leahy, the President's Chief of Staff, said the answer was to use the bomb to annihilate the maximum number of Japanese.

Opposing opinion held that mass destruction would be unethical as well as unnecessary. In all probability, the civil population could be spared, the argument ran, by a demonstration drop, with Emperor Hirohito invited to attend to see for himself that resistance was hopeless. The favored target was the island of Truk, where the remnants of the Japanese imperial fleet were sheltered. Feelers toward that end went out to Tokyo through the Swedish embassy in Washington.

I felt that because of his concern for mankind Father would inevitably have chosen the more humane course. In all her conversations with me, Mother's attitude did not change, though I differed vehemently with her. It was for Mr. Truman alone to make the decision, she insisted, and for the world to judge whether he had done right or wrong.

With no voice of strong persuasion raised on the other side, Truman accepted the evaluations of Byrnes and Leahy, neither of whom had been sufficiently close to Father to be able to venture an informed guess as to what he would have ordered. One biographer has written that Mother "welcomed" the obliteration of Hiroshima on August 6 with its huge death toll because it cut short the war, but that is a complete misconception; she did not welcome human suffering anywhere.

When, three days after the Hiroshima attack, the same treatment was applied to Nagasaki, her consternation soared. "I was always worried," she used to tell me, "about that *second* bomb."

The sight of Hiroshima horrified her when she visited there eight years later, and in her comments she disassociated herself from the President's act. "The people of the United States," she declared, "believe that our leaders thought long and carefully before they used this dread weapon. We know that they thought first of the welfare of our own people, that they believed the bomb might end the war quickly with less loss of life everywhere than if it had not been dropped."

As she gazed at the ruination, she improvised a prayer: "God grant to men greater wisdom in the future."

She said nothing to criticize Truman in public; she had no wish just then to become a spokesman for liberals. That might have the effect of dividing the Democrats when the country was beset with the problems of converting from war to peace and the danger of recession loomed ahead. She was content to hear Henry Wallace speak out instead because she agreed with much of his thinking.

The day she moved out of the White House, she had written to him, "I feel you are peculiarly fitted to carry on the ideals which were close to my husband's heart and which I know you understand." Her admiration for Wallace lasted long after Father came to the conclusion that shock-haired Hank had muffed his chance as Vice-President in the third term beginning in 1940 and was altogether too callow and unsophisticated to amount to much as a politician.

Taking stock of herself before the summer ended, she saw ever more clearly where her duty lay. She would have to do far more than act as a mere information source concerning Father. She must devote herself to achieving his objectives. "I was one of those who served his purposes," she said after

he died. Those purposes were being disregarded by the new
crew in Washington. The time for seclusion was over. She
would start reasserting herself to serve him again.

After the first evening logs were lit in her living room fireplace, we talked together for hours at Val-Kill, with Tommy
chiming in as often as not. The three of us believed that unity
between the United States, Britain and the USSR was essential. Mother recalled Father's words to her on his return from
Yalta: "It's been a global war, and we've already started making it a global peace."

But what had developed was not so much peace as a cease-
fire. Churchill, out of power in England, was finding a ready
listener in Truman for his arguments that the Soviets were
bent on conquering the world. Stalin smelled an Anglo-American plot to encircle him. What would Father have done in the
circumstances? We both knew that he would have sat down to
talk with the Russian to restore goodwill and mutual confidence. Mother elected to pinch-hit for Father. She was ready
to fly to Moscow to meet Stalin, who was eager to see her.

She was encouraged in her decision by two New Deal
stalwarts who were as alarmed as she by the deterioration in
relations with the USSR. Ed Flynn, Democratic national com-
mitteeman from New York who was on Father's team at Yalta, felt that she should leave at once. After his first and final
mission to Moscow for Truman in May, Harry Hopkins urged
the same course.

"I cannot say I am too happy about the way the atom bomb
is being.handled," he wrote to her later. "In fact, I think we
are doing almost everything we can to break with Russia,
which seems so unnecessary to me."

She would travel, she thought, on the strength of her credentials as a newspaper columnist for United Features Syndicate, not simply as Father's widow. As early as July, she was
in touch with the President: "I haven't spoken to the Syndicate about going at any immediate time because I wanted first
to make sure that it would meet with your approval to have

me go to Russia, either now or in the spring. I would not want in any way to complicate anything that you may be doing."

The response she received from the State Department suggested that she wait until the spring. She was too loyal a citizen to flout the wishes of authority, but she was frustrated by the delay.

"I am obliged to carry out the policy of the Government," she commented that fall. "When my husband was President, although I was the White House hostess, I was, after all, a private citizen, and for that reason I was freer than I am now." She was learning that the price of independence ran higher than she had imagined.

If she was constrained from action, there was an alternative means of getting her point of view into circulation. Father's powerful sense of family feeling made him try to have his children with him, one at a time, whenever that was possible. I had been his intimate at Argentia in Newfoundland, at Casablanca, at Teheran, and twice in Cairo, missing only Yalta. Anna, in the spirit of amity which governed us then, gladly related every detail of what had transpired there.

From watching, listening, exchanging notes and subsequently studying the official transcripts, I had learned what conditions he predicated for the structure of world peace, what conversations had led to them, what bargains and promises had been made. I broached the subject with Mother.

"I was thinking today about something Father said in Cairo: 'America is the only great power that can make peace in the world stick.' He always insisted that the United States would have to lead and help to solve the differences that were bound to crop up."

She glanced up from her knitting, which accompanied every otherwise idle moment, and nodded agreement, with the firelight glinting on her spectacles. The needles clicked, and Tommy's typewriter clattered somewhere else in the cottage.

"I don't think that anybody down there in Washington is very successful at leading any more," I said.

"Do you propose to do anything about it?"

"I don't know. But it's *crystal* clear from everything that Father told me that this country's veering off course."

She had a habit of avoiding committing herself if she could, a hesitancy about expressing a conclusive opinion one way or the other in case it offended anyone in her company, even her children. She paused before she said, "Have you ever considered writing a book?"

"Frankly, no. I've never tried to."

"I think you might want to. A firsthand account of what you saw and heard at the conferences could be *invaluable,* if you could find the time to do it."

"I can give it a try," I said. That winter, encouraged by her at every step of the way, I began the job of producing a book which, when it was published, would turn out to be even more fulminatory than Blaze's flight to California. Meantime, she was pondering another idea for employing me as a kind of understudy. If it was impolitic for her to call on Stalin, why shouldn't I? She would see what could be done about that.

In Harry Truman's political code, fidelity deserved to be rewarded. He owed a debt of gratitude to Mother for her present willingness to say and do nothing of which he disapproved. Hers was a prestigious reputation, greater overseas than in her own country, where scorn for her on the right wing of both political parties was unabated. He asked Byrnes to find some appointment for her that would make good use of her name.

One December morning, the President telephoned her personally in her New York apartment. The first meeting to organize the General Assembly of the United Nations, he reminded her, was due to open in London in January. Would she be willing to serve as a member of the United States delegation?

"Oh, no!" she fluttered. "It would be impossible! How could I be a delegate to help organize the United Nations when I have no *background* or *experience* in international meetings?"

"Don't you worry. There'll be plenty of people to help you."

"But I know nothing about the *procedures* at a meeting of this kind. I'm afraid I'd only be a hindrance."

"I have confidence in you, Mrs. Roosevelt. You'd pick it all up in no time."

Tommy tapped her on the shoulder. "You better think carefully before you turn him down, Mrs. R. You could do that job as well as anybody in the world, if not better."

Mother shook her head. "I am sorry, sir, but I doubt that I am capable——"

The President refused to accept an instant No. "Just you think about it for a while, as a favor to me. You're going to be needed in London. I'm holding that appointment open until we've talked some more."

Mother debated her decision for days. Her deep-rooted insecurity, the inheritance of a sundered childhood, flared up again. She was terrified of failure, yet she could sublimate her terror into a source of strength and deny that it existed. Father had believed the United Nations to be the only path to enduring peace, and she accepted that faith. If she rejected Truman's invitation, she would inflame the guilt she felt over Father.

"In fear and trembling," as she said, she finally accepted. She had no illusions about the President's motive: besides paying off a debt, he calculated that the Roosevelt name would be a business asset for the delegation going to London. "I do feel, however," she told Truman bluntly, "that you were wise in thinking that anyone connected with my husband could, perhaps by their presence, keep the level of his ideals."

Her knowledge of the workings of government was such that she did not appreciate that her appointment was not final until the nomination won approval from the Senate. Truman had old Alben Barkley, the Majority Leader and perennial aspirant for the Vice-Presidency, canvass his colleagues on their reactions. Some of them protested that Mother was a poor choice: she was too muddleheaded, too leftist in her sympathies, too concerned with the plight of Negroes.

When she heard the feedback from Washington, self-doubt surfaced once more. Had she made another wrong decision? The vote in the Senate reassured her; it was unanimous except for the Nay of Theodore Bilbo of Mississippi, to whom Mother was a Bolshevik nigger-lover. He had so many reasons for opposing her, he said, that they would fill a book.

While she continued to marvel at the miraculous outcome, she sat down to see how her new job would affect her income picture. The salary was based on the number of days worked, which would reduce it well below the ostensible $14,300 a year. Washington would pay the travel and hotel bills, plus $12 a day for expenses. Clearly, work as a delegate would cost her more than it brought in, but this was the least of her worries. She was totally in the dark regarding what was expected of her and equally ignorant of procedures to be followed when she got to London.

Nobody told her that she was allowed to take her own secretary with her; she thought she must use State Department staff. She concluded that Tommy, whom she trusted to steer her through any shoal, must be left behind. Mother would have to cope alone with whatever came along, and the prospect dismayed her. She packed her knitting to keep herself occupied.

Having Fala for companionship was out of the question. He had just suffered a close brush with death in a one-sided scrap with Blaze. Our bull mastiff liked to rove in the woods and down the hill while we gradually brought Top Cottage into comfortable shape. One day when Mother was away, he wandered down to her place and met Fala. The scottie was game but sadly outmatched. Tommy came running out of the house to rescue him before he was chewed beyond repair.

Fala had been so mauled and ripped that life looked uncertain. We hurried him off to a veterinarian's, where the outlook remained doubtful for days. For Mother's sake, we had to accept the inevitable. Blaze was kept on a chain for a while. Fala recovered, but eventually Blaze was put away.

Boarding instructions called for Mother to present herself on a Manhattan pier on the night of December 30 to sail in the *Queen Elizabeth* for Southampton. Most of the other voyagers—fellow delegates Stettinius, Texas Senator Tom Connolly and Michigan Senator Arthur Vandenberg, together with their alternates and an army of State Department officials—arrived in spanking style from a special train by motorcade with the customary accompaniment of sirens and flashing red turret lights. The dock swarmed with reporters, radio commentators, photographers and newsreel cameramen, closing in on everyone who approached the gangway as the great, gray liner prepared for sea.

Tommy and Mother drove together to the pier, both heavy-hearted at the parting. They were late, and the excitement had petered out when Mother gave a kiss to Tommy and started walking alone and unnoticed up the gangway, holding back the tears. Then someone on deck spotted her in the floodlights, and she was ushered on board, to slip away immediately to find her stateroom.

On the table there, a pile of blue paper waited for her attention, a State Department policy briefing—much of it stamped SECRET—on United States positions and the work to be done. She forced herself to spend a dutiful hour reading every page, head nodding with fatigue, and finished little wiser than when she started. The meaning of this ream of official gobbledygook was hard to fathom. At eight-thirty, she brushed her teeth and put herself to bed.

The prospect of arriving in England without my father daunted her. The two of them had been invited to make a triumphal tour of the country together by Mr. Churchill the previous spring while he was still Prime Minister and gravely concerned about the return to power of his Conservative Party and himself at the next general election. He did not hesitate to explain his reasoning to Father: the presence of FDR and his First Lady would vastly improve Winston's chances with the voters, to whom he had sold the dream of an Anglo-American partnership in peace as in war.

Winston spread the word, which was premature, that the trip was settled. There was additional cause for his grief at Father's passing when Labor had romped to victory at the polls this past summer. Mother admired the bulldog qualities of Winston, but she liked him better out of office than in. She knew what the British people had thought about Father. She was afraid that they would be disappointed in her.

The ship's clocks were advanced an hour each night as usual on an eastward passage. In consequence Mother, always an early riser, was up and about long before any colleague, to breakfast alone at the captain's table, then lope around the open decks, getting her exercise and mulling over the mysteries of this intimidating job.

Byrnes, head of the delegation, was not aboard. He had a loner's dislike of working in committee, and he elected to fly over later. Tom Connolly, Democrat, and Arthur Vandenberg, Republican, put their heads together to assign the specific tasks to be tackled. There were five alternates—Congressmen Sol Bloom of New York and Charles Eaton of New Jersey; Frank Walker, replaced by Bob Hannegan as Postmaster General; former Senator John Townsend of Delaware; and doughty John Foster Dulles, who would have been Secretary of State now if only Father had not trounced Tom Dewey in last year's election.

The first plain notice of what lay ahead for her came from Arthur Vandenberg. He stopped her in the passageway to her stateroom one day and boomed, "Mrs. Roosevelt, we would like to know if you would serve on Committee Three."

Two instant suspicions crossed her mind. Was a Republican, a devout isolationist until the attack on Pearl Harbor, deciding who was to do what? And why wasn't she as a delegate being consulted in advance? She put those thoughts aside for a moment. "I should be happy to," she answered humbly. "But will you or someone kindly see that I get as much information as possible on Committee Three?'' She had not a clue to what that group might be.

As her knowledge increased, she realized exactly why she had been picked. Committee Three dealt with humanitarian, cultural and educational topics. It was a safe spot for her, where she couldn't do much harm. The male chauvinists—a term she would never bring herself to use—had dismissed the thought of putting a mere woman on any committee dealing with more ponderous questions, like politics, jurisprudence or finance. For the time being, she was too reticent to complain, but she dropped a gentle hint that her colleagues should not count on her being only a figurehead when she told shipboard reporters, ''This is off the record, please, but for the first time in my life, I can say just what I want. It is wonderful to feel *free.*''

The mystifying secret documents appeared as if by magic on the table in her stateroom every day. ''For all I knew,'' she mused, ''they might have originated in outer space.'' Since she could not make head or tail of most of them, she resorted to a better way of teaching herself what was going on. She took her knitting and listened in at every briefing, including press conferences conducted by officers of the State Department and other delegates. It slowly dawned on her that Committee Three just might develop into something more significant than anyone expected.

After the *Queen Elizabeth* docked at Southampton, she sat with white-maned Tom Connolly on the journey up to London, taking in every aspect of the scene passing outside the windows as she had done for Father. Air raid shelters topped with Union Jacks; craters left by bombs, doodlebugs and Hitler's V-2 rockets; wintry fields crossed with barbed wire; and then, as they reached the outskirts of the city, wrecked buildings and neat piles of rubble, sprouting weeds.

She had seen it all once before in wartime, when on a similar dreary day she visited my photoreconnaissance unit and we respected her sensibilities by serving her hot tea to ward off the cold, while we poured whiskey into our cups. She always enjoyed England, though she had a profound distrust of Britain's hand in international affairs. "Great Britain," she once told Truman, "still takes the attitude that she makes the policies on all world questions and we accept them. This has got to be remedied."

Yet in making her what she was, British influence had been considerable. As a teenage orphan, she had been sent off to board at Allenswood, Mademoiselle Marie Souvestre's school for girls in Wimbledon, London, SW, where the young ladies wore straw hats and flannel underwear, shivered under cold showers every morning, made their own beds, played field hockey, and were encouraged to commune with their souls for an hour after lunch. She retained many of the spartan schoolgirl's habits, including a taste for a cup of tea.

"Where's all this destruction I've heard so much about?" old Tom kept huffing. "Things look all right to me." She tried to draw his attention to the clear evidence, but he was not interested: his mind was closed.

When she entered the suite reserved for her at Claridge's elegant hotel on Brook Street, around the corner from the delegation's offices in Grosvenor Square, she protested that it was *much* too fancy, but she was prevailed upon to stay; smaller quarters would scarcely have held all the flowers sent in advance by well-wishers. A mountain of welcoming mail was stacked there, too, and the crowds that gathered at the hotel doors cheered whenever they spotted her, though she would not allow herself to understand why.

She ate supper that Saturday night in the canteen of the United States embassy, two blocks away from the offices, with two of the staff. The next morning she went to her office to organize a daily routine that would have her start writing her column at eight a.m.

The mimeographed secrets arrived each morning on her desk, as impenetrable as ever. One morning, there was a different kind of document, a summons to report at once to the security officer. She was guilty, he warned her when she had tracked him down, of a serious breach: a guard on his nightly rounds had found a "top secret" paper left out on her desk top instead of being locked away. Chills beset her. Shamefaced, she promised that she would make certain henceforth that all papers were locked up and the office door, too, and she would not let her briefcase out of her sight.

Once experience in the job had toughened her, she could not resist poking a little fun at such scoldings. "I frequently noticed," she said, "that information in papers marked 'top secret' appeared in the newspapers even before it reached us."

The United Nations was assembling in the Victorian Gothic vastness of Central Hall, Westminster. She thought it prudent to leave her knitting behind when she set out for the opening session. Ed Stettinius escorted her there, a man of great appeal for her because only loyalty to Father, whose name could bring tears to his eyes, kept him working for the present Administration.

The initial business was to elect Paul-Henri Spaak of Belgium first president of the organization. In the front row next to the Soviet delegation sat Mother, translating earphones adjusted, trying to make herself inconspicuous, with a small team of State Department personnel ranked close behind her, ready to cue her in whispers. From the podium, backed by the U.N. olive branch emblem, Spaak stretched out a plump finger toward her and stirred up an ovation. The assembly rose, applauding, while she blushed and, with a nervous smile, stood in acknowledgment. "Oh, dear!" she muttered, "I really can't think that I *deserve* all this."

She continued to feel uneasy and unwelcome among her American colleagues. She was the lone woman. Unless she proved herself useful, others like her would find United Nations appointments hard to come by in the near future. The feminist in her felt she must pass the test and demonstrate to an unsympathetic Administration that women deserved higher office than they had been given to date by Truman. One more mighty motivation was being reborn, but "I walked on eggs," she said.

Her approach was totally in character and possibly unique: she would try diplomacy by teacup. As soon as she got to know most of the eighteen women among the other countries' representatives, she had them around for tea in her hotel sitting room. To her delight, one Russian turned up, with an interpreter, on the first afternoon. In the weeks to come, the hostess often found that more progress could be made toward reaching an understanding at teatime than on the General Assembly floor.

What she saw there and in the continual round of smoky backroom conferences hardened her judgments of many of the men who allegedly were working for peace. The skepticism of old League of Nations hands, who had watched the collapse of the first world organization, dismayed her. So did the furtive ways of the elder statesmen, with their inbred passion for closed doors and secret understandings.

She was no more impressed by most of her American colleagues, who appeared to be hypnotized by drafting rules and procedures rather than absorbed with the challenge of building a better world. Byrnes, in particular, was turning out to be an even bigger disaster than she had anticipated. He was a glad-hander, who seemingly believed that a smile and a pat on the back were the answers to any problem, shying away from taking any stand on grounds of right or wrong. To Mother's beeline way of thinking, his approach was intolerable.

If only he could be steeled into letting Britain and the Soviet Union see that the United States lived by moral principles and was prepared to do battle here in Westminster for them! She felt compelled "to tell him tactfully that everyone has to get the things they need from us and that is our ace in the hole." He was so elusive that she wondered whether he was deliberately avoiding her, as Father sometimes did when she was crusading. She promptly dismissed the idea. "It isn't that he is leaving me out, for the others complain to me."

She blamed the cynicism and arrogance shown by Vandenberg and Dulles for the prevailing atmosphere of pessimism that American correspondents detected. Vandenberg's tricks especially offended her. He had already leaked one confidential memorandum to reporters. Then he and Dulles boycotted a press conference designed to persuade newsmen that there was no ideological split in the delegation, leaving Mother and Stettinius to field some spitball questions as deftly as they could.

On her approved list, Stettinius' position was secure, like that of Gil Winant, current United States ambassador to the Court of St. James's, another man who wept at a mention of FDR. A place on the list was also reserved for Adlai Stevenson, forty-five years old, once an assistant to Father's Navy Secretary, Frank Knox, and lately head of the American advance guard at this conference. When Adlai and Mother dined together, she rated him most *simpático.*

The smoldering fire that ate away at the foundations of cooperation between the United States and the USSR burst into flame at the unlikeliest place in London—in unimportant, inoffensive Committee Three. The war had left a million refugees living in camps for displaced people—Ukrainians, Byelorussians, Poles, Czechs, Jews and others. The Soviet bloc postulated that anyone of them who refused to go back to his homeland was either a traitor or a quisling. The United States subscribed to the general Western view that every refugee should be guaranteed the right to refuse repatriation without risk of reprisal.

Mother's undiscriminating compassion for human misery put her in wholehearted agreement with the American position, but she spent a futile week trying to concoct a resolution that would bridge the gap between the two sides before she gave up and asked for a vote. Committee Three decided, over Soviet opposition, to present a majority report favoring the Western position to the General Assembly as a whole. The Russians announced that they would carry on the fight there. Speaking for them would be their delegation's leader, the scathing-tongued Andrei Vishinsky, state prosecutor at the Moscow purge trials of the 1930's, and the most skillful legal mind in the USSR.

Mother had worn herself out fulfilling the engagements pressed on her by the admiring British. Public speeches, radio broadcasts, luncheons and dinners at the peak of society, beginning with King George VI and Queen Elizabeth, to whom she had served hot dogs at Hyde Park in 1939—she found the royal couple "nice" but unconscionably sheltered from everyday matters. First, she lost her voice, then London's cheerless winter put her to bed with the flu.

She had barely recovered when her four male colleagues huddled together to choose an American champion to take on Vishinsky. None of them wanted to face him. It appealed to her sense of the ironic when she, the harmless old woman on Committee Three, was approached none too confidently by Mr. Dulles.

"Mrs. Roosevelt, the United States must speak in the debate. Since you are the one who has carried on the controversy in the committee, do you think you could say a few words in the Assembly? Nobody else is really familiar with the subject."

"I will do my best," she replied, trembling at her audacity. She abided by the method taught her by Louis Howe, on which she relied for all the lectures booked for her by the W. Colston Leigh Agency: she would jot down an opening paragraph, then make up the rest as she went along because that way an audience sensed sincerity.

The speech she delivered one February night in Central Hall was a calculated blend of idealism and down-to-earth politicking. Some preliminary head counting had told her that she had to hold the attention of Latin American delegations to the end, so that when a vote was taken they would be there to back the United States.

She pleaded that the United Nations would "frame things which will be broader in outlook, which will consider first the rights of man, which will consider what *makes* man more free—not governments but *man*." And she took care to expound on the virtues of Simón Bolívar, greatest of all heroes of South America's liberation from imperial Spain.

Perhaps some regard for her led Vishinsky to soft-pedal his arguing and keep his sword-sharp wit sheathed, but he could not hope to win against this seemingly innocuous grandmother whom the world respected. When the vote came, the West was the victor, and victory was worth the tremors she had suffered. She went to shake Vishinsky's hand.

"Mrs. Roosevelt, I admire your fighting qualities."

"You are a real fighter, too," she smiled. "Perhaps next time you might try using your abilities on the right side."

It was one a.m. when she got back to Claridge's. She was weary, dragging herself up the staircase to save time waiting for an elevator, when she heard Dulles and Vandenberg following behind. "Mrs. Roosevelt," said Dulles with as much cordiality as he could muster, "we must tell you that we did all we could to keep you off the delegation. We begged the President not to nominate you. But now we feel we must acknowledge that we have worked with you gladly and found you good to work with. And we will be happy to do so again." Mother, to whom a word of praise meant a lot, accepted the compliment gratefully. It would not change her evaluation of either of them, of course.

She fancied that her work with the United Nations was over when she flew from London to Germany on an inspection trip arranged by Gil Winant. She aimed to see for herself some of the refugee camps which until now were only an abstraction to her.

She had been brought up by her Grandmother Hall to accept the standard prejudices of her class in turn-of-the-century America. Catholics were not to be trusted because they owed their first allegiance to the Pope in Rome. Irish politicians by and large were grafters, elected because they bought votes. Jews were cunning money-grabbers of whom every Christian should be wary.

Mother had rid herself of the last of these preconceptions more effectively than the first. She was distinguishable in 1946 as an understanding supporter of Jewish causes, but the temperature of her feeling was no higher than for other en-

thusiasms of hers. What she experienced in Germany began
to alter that. She could pinpoint the moment of change. In the
squalor of a refugee camp at Zilcheim, outside Frankfurt,
where water, food and warmth were in chronically short sup-
ply, a homeless old woman knelt in the mud and clasped
Mother around the legs.

Neither could understand a word of the other's language
save one: "Israel! Israel!" the groveling figure wailed over
and over again. "I knew for the first time," Mother related,
"what that small land meant to so many, many people." One
more reference point was added to the chart of her future.
Zion would have no daughter more faithful.

She came home in a rare mood, as close to self-satisfaction
as I had ever seen her. I noticed a remarkable gain in confidence. She would be sixty-two years old in October, yet she
was still growing up. "I have nothing to do but work," she
said almost gaily. "I have no family responsibilities. I can
take on anything that comes along that seems worthwhile."

She was eager to talk about her experiences. "Mr. Vishinsky," she decided, "really isn't any different from any of
the communists I used to meet in the American Youth Congress." I remembered the morning in the White House when,
at her urging, the gates were opened to four thousand young
marchers, who booed Father as he cautioned them that, while
anyone had the right to call himself a communist, "you have
no American right to subvert the government and Constitution." Mother's disillusionment with the Youth Congress was
completed later that day, when a teatime group she had invited in to meet Father surrounded his wheelchair and shouted
him down.

The devastation she had witnessed in Frankfurt and Berlin
haunted her. "Nothing," she said "could better illustrate the
sickening waste and destructiveness and *futility* of war."
There had been a strong strain of pacifism in her prewar thinking, only temporarily submerged by the stark necessity of
restraining Hitler and the Axis from conquering the world.
Pacifism, she knew now, was not a realistic response to ag-

gression; the answer lay in an international peacekeeping force made up of contingents from the major powers which Father had consistently advocated in his talks with Churchill and Stalin.

Two things happened within a few days of March to decide her next moves. Blunt-spoken Trygve Lie, the Norwegian who, to Mother's satisfaction, had been elected secretary-general of the United Nations, cabled an invitation for her to serve on the first U.N. commission on human rights, as an individual, not as a representative of her country. Meetings would begin in New York next month, reported the solidly practical Mr. Lie, and she would be paid $15 a day plus travel expenses. A return cablegram notified him of her acceptance, and she asked Secretary Byrnes to supply a State Department adviser and a secretary to ease the load on Tommy, whose time would be taken up looking after the rest of Mother's affairs.

Then, at the behest of President Truman, Winston Churchill rode to Fulton, Missouri, to declare cold war on the Soviet Union. On March 5, Former Naval Person, as Father had christened the ex-Prime Minister, denounced the "iron curtain" which, he thundered, the Russians had drawn across Europe. To counter it, he proposed a joint Anglo-American effort "in the air, on the sea, all over the globe, and in science, and in industry, and in moral force." The President led the applause.

Mother had sensed that something like this was in the wind. She had been afraid of Churchill's power of persuasion with Harry Truman, and she and I were equally appalled when we read the newspapers. Stalin was stung into castigating Churchill as "a firebrand of war," who he surmised was eager for an invasion of Eastern Europe—world war number three.

Eight days after the "iron curtain" speech, Former Naval Person called at Hyde Park, as chubby and courtly as ever toward Mother, to place a wreath on the grave. Both of them had long since learned that in public life it seldom serves any purpose to allow a show of private feeling. Not until later, in

London, did a moment of truth arise. "You don't really approve of me, do you, Mrs. Roosevelt?" he grunted. Mother acknowledged that really she didn't.

She felt that he was a political dinosaur, and she hoped the species would be extinguished before he engendered graver danger. At Hyde Park, she mentioned to him her desire to meet Stalin.

"You can't go," Winston said flatly.

"But I want to go, and I think I might be able to accomplish some things *by* going. Perhaps some of the misunderstandings that are growing up could be corrected."

"You could do nothing but cause irreparable damage to relations between your country and mine." When Washington repeated much the same thing to her, she reluctantly agreed for a second time to defer a visit to Moscow.

After he had left, she and I mulled over the significance of what we saw happening on every side. Father had been dead for less than a year.

"How is your book coming along, Elliott?"

"It's coming, but there's obviously some rewriting to be done as a result of that speech at Fulton."

She left to dictate the day's column to Tommy, pacing the floor in the process as usual, face working, hands gesturing. Winston was still on her mind when she declaimed, "We are still loath to give up the old power and attempt to build a new kind of power and security in the world. I am convinced that this timidity is perhaps the greatest danger today."

For herself, she believed that she had conquered timidity. She would commit herself to making the United Nations strong. In doing so, and in talking about the need to audiences everywhere, she came into her own. In her unique fashion, she spoke from her tormented heart in behalf of the common people, who to her meant more than anything else in the affairs of nations. Millions of them in the United States and around the world gave her their love in return, perhaps in greater measure than Father ever enjoyed.

As for me, my intention was that I should finish the book and then go to Moscow.

4

She kept the memory of Father fresh by talking about him to Faye and me. Nothing pleased me better than for her to reminisce about the things the two of them had done together. She chose to remember only the lovely times they had shared, never the estrangement and pain. It was as though she had succeeded in convincing herself that they had known forty years of unblemished happiness from the day they were married.

There was tremendous gaiety in her voice when she recalled the rose-tinted past. "I wore stiff, heavy satin on our wedding day," she would say, "with Grandma Hall's Brussels lace over it. Your father gave me this watch, which he designed himself with my initials and the three little feathers in diamonds like the Roosevelt crest." This was what she wore, dangling from its pin, every day. "He was rather put out when Uncle Ted arrived to give me away and *quite* stole the show. Most of the guests were *much* more interested in meeting the President than in seeing us."

They had two honeymoons, the first under Granny's roof at Hyde Park, the second in Europe after he finished out his year at Columbia Law School. "Oh, my *dears,* the doubts I felt when we embarked in that ship! I was certain I'd be seasick all the way, but the water was calm, and we played piquet, which I invariably lost. I told him he must be *awfully* lucky. 'Babs,' he replied, 'it isn't a matter of luck but plain *skill.*' "

She had an amazing recall of detail, a sign perhaps that she had found comfort in reliving the joy of earlier days during the years when most of it had vanished, just as she preserved every line he ever wrote her that had a crumb of affection in it. "When we got to Brown's Hotel in London, we found they had given us the royal suite on account of Uncle Ted. The sitting room was so enormous I couldn't find anything after I'd put it down. I said, 'Franklin, we simply can't *afford* it,' but that made no difference."

She loved to quote word for word what they told each other, picturing a warmth and devotion that, in fact, became a pretense between them not long after the first of us children was born. "In Scotland, we stayed at Bob Ferguson's mother's old house up in the north. There were lovely gardens on a hillside, I remember. In the night, I heard wild shrieks from Father's bed. He was pointing straight up to the ceiling, saying, 'Don't you see that beam? It's *revolving!*' I had an awful time keeping him from getting up and waking everybody. Then when the maid brought our early morning tea with some thin bread and butter, I asked him if he remembered his nightmare. 'I most certainly do,' he said, 'and I was upset with you, Babs, because you wouldn't get out of the way when that *beam* was going to fall!' "

She kept up the traditions he had established for the family and took on the role he had played in them. Whenever she was home on a sunny Fourth of July, there was a picnic by the swimming pool at Stone Cottage, used only for guests nowadays—we celebrated inside if it rained. Picnics were something she and Father had once enjoyed. All her children and grandchildren within visiting range would be there, munching hot dogs and hamburgers before they listened to her read the Declaration of Independence and the Bill of Rights.

"Congress shall make no law respecting an establishment

of religion, or prohibiting the free exercise thereof; or abridging the freedom of speech, or of the press. . . ." The grandchildren, whom we taught to call her "Grand'mere," might wriggle restlessly before the fluty voice was done, but to us adults the experience was always touching. No one believed more deeply than Mother in every word she recited, and none of it was more important than freedom of the press.

"Father never told me what to write or what not to write," she reminisced, "but naturally I was always aware that whatever I wrote might bring *repercussions,* so I *conserved* myself. I don't feel any such inhibitions now. I write as I please."

Every Thanksgiving Day saw a mighty turkey served as it had been in Father's time with all the trimmings of chestnut stuffing, cranberry sauce, two kinds of potatoes and a variety of vegetables. Mother's culinary skills did not extend beyond scrambling eggs, but she liked to wander in and out of the kitchen, which was far from being a showpiece in its equipment, keeping an eye on the cook's progress. All the family that was within range and as many friends as possible were invited, making elbow space tight around the big table in the cramped dining room.

The first year, as I recall, Franklin and his wife Ethel along with Faye and myself were there. Jimmy and Johnny were in California, and the Boettigers in Seattle, Washington, where Anna's husband was publisher of the local Hearst newspaper. Mother set the style that would endure. She was never bothered if the plates did not match or if there were chips on their edges. The rekindling of affection counted more with her than fine china.

Father had taken great pride—unreasonable pride, we thought when we were young and ravenous—in carving the bird into slices as thin as paper to demonstrate his skill and defer to the tight household budget. It was my turn to attempt the task. I was no match for him. My excuse became a standard for future years when Franklin, Jimmy or Johnny would have a try: "I'd do much better, Mummy, if only the knife was sharp."

This was one day when it was in order to serve a glass of

champagne apiece—usually domestic—because that was what Father had done. When the last piece of pie had been eaten, she pushed back her chair and repeated the toast as he always gave it: "To the United States of America." Then on her own account, she added: "To those we love who are not with us today."

Christmas, too, was an echo of the past. Children were essential, two generations of Roosevelts, augmented by those of her friends. If being there on December 25 presented difficulties, then what about Christmas Eve or a day or so afterwards? Everyone she was fond of must be brought in to share with her somehow. On Christmas Eve, she went to St. James' as before, sitting in the same pew and joining in the same carols that Father used to bellow. "I do believe he actually felt that God would give him guidance when he asked for it," she told us. She was less convinced herself that praying brought about divine intervention.

Christmas Eve also meant a party for the work people on the estate, husbands, wives and their families. Presents for the old retainers would have been picked up on her travels throughout the year—a box of Vermont maple sugar, a salt-and-pepper shaker from Amish Pennsylvania, perhaps a ceramic Big Ben from London. She was an inveterate acquirer of souvenirs, not for herself but as a gift for someone she was thinking of.

On Christmas morning, a stocking she had stuffed with candies, nuts and trinkets waited outside every bedroom door. This *was* a departure from our childhood, when we used to race upstairs to Father's bedroom for a hug from him as he lay against the pillows, then rush to the fireplace for the stockings that were hanging there.

In her study at Val-Kill, the Yule logs would be lit early in the fireplace whose mantel overflowed with cards. We would gather with her before we filed into the dining room. The table in there was aglow with candles, with flowers and place cards written by her with a few lines of verse or a quotation apposite to whomever was to sit there. "To the United States of

America!'' Mother would repeat, and it was time for one of us to pick up the carving set. Ah, if only the blade were keener!

We knew what stood behind the pulled-to doors leading to the living room—a tree cut from the Val-Kill woods, not quite as towering as those that touched the ceiling in Granny's lofty library, but impressive all the same. Mother followed a habit of our grandmother's and piled the gifts for each recipient on separate chairs. She called out each name as she picked up the packages, and whichever of her children had come to her that year would help her hand them out before she moved around, watching them opened, anxious as a mother hen. "I *do* hope you like it. . . . I *think* it's the right size. . . . I thought the *color* would look well on you.''

Her own presents were left unopened until everyone else's had been exclaimed over. Then she would turn to the mound by the door to the porch—the pile grew higher every year. When the company had settled down again and the room was tidied up, she took down the copy of Charles Dickens' *A Christmas Carol* bound in dog-eared leather that had done service in Father's hands at similar moments as long ago as I could remember. Once again we would hear the tale of old Scrooge's redemption at the hands of Bob Cratchit and Tiny Tim, the same, somewhat abridged version told with the same inflections that father had used. Nobody other than Mother was allowed to take over the task. "He made it sound so *significant*,'' she used to say.

New Year's Eve meant going to church for her and coming home to hear over the radio how America was celebrating. On the stroke of midnight, toastmistress would substitute for toastmaster, and we would drink again to the health of our country.

Memorial Day was more a public than a private affair. A dais was raised in the rose garden, with folding chairs set out on the grass for an invited audience to listen to whatever worthy Democrat would be present that particular year to laud FDR and all his works. It was a big event for the village in all manner of ways: for the florists who supplied the wreaths that covered the grave; for the Boy Scout troop that marched in parade and furnished a bugler to play taps; for Postmaster Arthur Smith, luminary of the Roosevelt Home Club, who presided over the ceremonies.

Arthur was cut from the same bolt of homespun cloth as his father, Moses, founder of the club, a tobacco-chewing, dyed-in-the-wool Democrat. As farm supervisor for Granny, Moses had known Father since childhood. His son felt as affronted as Mother when my brother Johnny announced himself a Republican, and Postmaster Smith helped her surreptitiously plaster Johnny's car with Democrat bumper stickers. In a village where Republicans held sway, no defection from the ranks of the faithful could be allowed to pass unnoticed.

On the first anniversary of Father's death, the house and grounds at Hyde Park were formally handed over to the government. Mr. Truman came up for the occasion, and Mother made a speech. Father's spirit, she said, "will always live in this house, in the library and in the rose garden where he wished his grave to be." She felt no more regret about giving up the place than in quitting the White House. It was a relief to be rid of a mansion she had not enjoyed as a home, though she would not say that to the visitors she conducted through its rooms, relating homey little tales about the past.

They came at all seasons to see the house and the grave, sometimes arriving with flowers and departing in tears. The first year brought Princess Juliana of the Netherlands, Soviet Ambassador Andrei Gromyko and his wife—and Madame Chiang Kai-shek. Like other eminences on the international scene who followed them, they had a dual purpose: to honor Father and make use of Mother so far as she was willing. Without exception, she welcomed them to a meal and a talk in her cottage, eager to broaden her knowledge by hearing whatever they had to say. For most, it was a unique chance to establish contact with a woman whose importance within and beyond the United States was increasingly clear. They looked to her for sympathy toward their point of view, for insights into Truman's policies, for reminiscences of Father, for advice on their dealings with Washington.

She was gracious to them all, even to Madame Chiang. Though she was approaching sixty, the wife of the Chinese generalissimo who had been in power for nearly twenty years looked like a porcelain doll. Flawless makeup and long lacquered fingernails spoke of hours a day spent in preserving her beauty. She was asked to lunch, and she stayed well past teatime.

She had a key question to put to Mother. "How on earth could you and your husband tolerate the hostility of the news media and the derogatory comments they made, especially concerning yourself, during all those years when he was the President?"

"Well," Mother answered lightly, "in a free country, a free press can say whatever it chooses. While I *did* have to put up with indignities from certain quarters, I can say that in the long run it does not matter. It is what one does that determines people's *final* judgments."

Madame's gleaming eyes fixed on her hostess. "In our country, we also have a democratic form of government, but we could never allow the press to print untruthful statements about us. If they did, we would have to take action against them." At that point, China's First Lady repeated a gesture I had seen before, when she stayed in the White House and dumbfounded Mother by importing a platoon of servants and her own silk bed sheets. She raised a manicured index finger and drew it slowly across her pale throat.

"Her looks don't change and neither do her autocratic ways, I'm afraid," Mother sighed after the imperial limousine had pulled away. The memory of that afternoon returned some time afterwards. General George C. Marshall, who had succeeded Byrnes as Secretary of State, summoned her and all members of our United Nations delegation to a special briefing on United States policy toward China. Chiang's hold on the country grew weaker by the day. Mao's communists would soon overrun the mainland completely and drive the generalissimo to Taiwan, but our new Secretary of State expressed confidence in Chiang's ability and his regard for democratic process.

Mother was less naive, and said as much. Marshall went over his statement again with military precision. "Is that clear?"

"I'm sorry, sir," she replied, "but that is not the way I read it in the newspapers."

Irritation showed under his forebearance. She was mistaken, he snapped, and he would let her have a State Department position paper for her edification. When it was delivered, she read it through once and then again. She could make no more sense of it than of the other stuff that had been addressed to her ever since her crossing in the *Queen Elizabeth*; she related the sequel when she began updating her memoirs that summer.

She had one of State's best attorneys examine this latest document, hoping that he could explain its meaning. "If this is what they send the President on the subject, God help the President!" said the note he sent in reply. Never one to give up easily, she asked a delegation adviser in to see her and showed him the blue-covered masterpiece. "You must be able to explain this. You must have had a part in writing this paper."

He thumbed through the pages. "Yes, I had," he said, "but obviously it was not intended for you or anybody else to know what it meant."

She was acclaimed chairman of the United Nations Commission on Human Rights as soon as its meetings opened in the library of Hunter College in the Bronx. She braved the subway up from Washington Square every morning—and got lost only once on the journey. She kept the job when sessions were moved to Geneva, then back again closer to home, into temporary United Nations headquarters in Flushing, Long Island. Since she was also to be reconfirmed as an American delegate, she would be wearing two hats, as an individual and as a diplomat. The strain erupted in a case of shingles, a considerable embarrassment because she was impatient of impairment to her health. A scarf around her neck concealed the rash.

She tried to impose good manners on the United Nations in much the same way as on her family, and sometimes she failed at both. Not every diplomat cared to be mothered, particularly if he were a Russian, and her sons by and large were an undisciplined lot who loved to argue.

"There must be a great deal of Uncle Ted in me because I *do* enjoy a good fight," she said, but it was more complicated than that. She liked to take up a battling stance when the Soviets were being more than usually rambunctious, but she was a reluctant fighter until her dander was up.

She abhorred strife at home. Whenever Jimmy, Franklin, Johnny and I got together, we had to be careful to keep the temperature of an argument down in her presence. If the excitement rose too high for comfort, dark disapproval would gather on her brow. "Let us go no farther into *that*. I suggest we change the subject. Shall we talk about——" and the next item on the agenda would be something innocuous and non-controversial. There would be no more quarreling—and no more conversation either.

Unhappily, the same technique could not be applied to the Commission on Human Rights. The unchangeable subject there was how to prepare an international bill of rights, which Mother and her fellows decided was the main task. It broke down into three distinct phases. Foremost was writing a declaration to define literally everything to which mankind has just claim—life; liberty; freedom from servitude and torture; equality before the law; the right to travel, choose a job at adequate pay, join a church, a political party or a union; to enjoy the vote, schooling, social security, rest and leisure time.

The charter, assuming it could ever be completed, would be followed up as the second step by treaties, legally binding on those nations which signed them—mere resolutions of the United Nations carried no such power. The third and final step would be to develop a system for enforcing the covenants.

The challenge was more intimidating than that confronting the Continental Congress, gathered in the summer steam of Philadelphia in 1776 to study what Thomas Jefferson had drafted on his homemade portable desk in a room at Market and Seventh Street. Mother's familiarity with anything like a universal statement of human rights stopped short with her annual reading of the Declaration of Independence at Val-Kill picnics.

In her rare, off-duty moments, I saw a woman who bore little resemblance to the determined Madam Chairman who presided over the commission. There, she set a spanking pace as she sat, gavel close at hand, peering through the thick-framed spectacles which had a built-in hearing aid to compensate for deafness in her right ear. Long-winded, repetitious speechifying was intolerable; she cut it off after a few minutes.

"We must get *on*," she snapped to the not infrequent exasperation of the speakers. She knew very well what some of them were up to. For their own glorification, they were trying to get their rhetoric on record to impress the folks back home in Moscow, London, Paris or elsewhere. She was too old a hand in domestic politics to allow that. She rated the job she had taken on as the most important of her life. In the cause of what was *right,* she was willing to be a slave driver.

In her cottage or at her apartment, she was for the present a different person, shaking her head over her ignorance of parliamentary law and the ins and outs of procedures, resolutions and amendments. "I have to learn as I go along," she said, but few people were quicker at studies than Mother.

She liked to bring back stories of what had been achieved on a particular day then or later. "I got quite *irritated* again with Dr. Pavlov." Alexei Pavlov, a nephew of the Russian scientist who taught dogs to drool at the ringing of a bell, was a member of the Soviet team and a thorn in her side. With bristling black beard and flowing white hair, he was constantly stressing examples of United States discrimination against blacks.

"Today, I really could not *stand* any more. It was not very ladylike, but I couldn't help interrupting him to say, 'Sir, you are hitting below the belt.' I think Father *might* have been more discreet, but I *did* feel better for saying it."

My country, right or wrong was too bigoted a sentiment to appeal to Mother, but she could be rattled when she heard of some wrong that was new to her. Dr. Pavlov caught her out one day. He cited as a typical instance of American brutality a law in Bilbo's Mississippi allowing a man to strike a woman with an ax handle, provided it was no more than two feet long. Mother, who had a working command of French, detected a delegate from Paris murmuring that in France a man was barred from hitting a woman even with a rose.

She wanted the facts of the matter to rebut Pavlov's accusation. A phone call to Washington produced the answer. "As it turned out, there *was* such a law in Mississippi. I felt most uncomfortable. There wasn't much more to say to him on *that* score."

She continued to hope, and more than once to find, that a dispute on the floor of the meetings could be smoothed over by having a group of delegates to tea or dinner on Washington Square. Some Russians were sure to be invited; they were the most fractious of her charges but deserved her friendship nonetheless. She despised any American colleagues who declined to be photographed with a Russian. "I suppose they believe a Russian is automatically a mortal *enemy*, or perhaps they're afraid of the political implications."

She had one anecdote to relate from Washington Square that persuaded her that her efforts with Dr. Pavlov were not entirely in vain. After dinner, he and the other guests listened to a friend of hers give an impromptu recital on her grand piano. "And do you know, as he left he whispered to me, 'You like the music of Tchaikovsky. So do I.'" But she was accorded no further glimpses into his intractable soul.

Her inability to coax him and his like into opening up and
conversing freely with her was something that demanded correction. Molotov was a model of politeness when she spoke
with him or sat beside him at a formal dinner, but he was so
guarded that it was impossible to know him as a man.

Alexander Borisov, a delegate like Pavlov but a later arrival
on the commission, pretended not to understand when she attempted to explain what had been done so far. She found she
could communicate best with Maxim Litvinov, and she put
that down to the fact that he had an English wife. Women, after all, tended to be more *reasonable* than men, in Mother's
view.

Father had succeeded in maintaining a dialogue with Stalin.
Re-establishing those lines of communication was essential if
FDR's aspirations were not to be thwarted. No matter how
hard she tried, she could not find a means of getting Soviet
officials at the United Nations level to talk privately and
frankly with her. The only solution was to make contact with
Stalin, which she was proscribed from doing. She stepped up
her efforts to get me to Moscow.

Growing self-confidence enabled her to exorcise more and
more of the past. The change was heartening to see. She had
been uneasy over Father's fondness for "a little sippy" before dinner, which might extend to two or three martinis
whose proportion of vermouth to gin decreased as time went
by. Now she asked her guests to have a cocktail, as Father
had done. She would have preferred serving nothing more sti-
mulating than a glass of sherry, but she kept her sideboard
stocked with what was needed to slake stronger thirsts. She
usually stuck to a little sherry herself, though once in a while
she would accept a single, watered-down martini if we offered
it.

She personally did not care for alcohol in any form nor con-
done more than one drink each for us. After several minutes
of conviviality, she would say firmly, "We've now *had* our
cocktail; let's go into dinner." I understood her attitude from
the stories of her childhood, which she never tired of relating

as new experiences clarified her perception of the influences that made her what she had been for more than sixty years.

Her mother, born Anna Hall, "was one of the most beautiful women I have ever seen," she used to say, whereas she "must have been a more wrinkled and less attractive baby than the average." Nevertheless, to her father, younger brother of President Theodore, "I was a miracle from heaven." He called her "Little Nell," which was how, in their courting days, she would sign a love letter to Father. Her mother had her own nickname for the gawky daughter who seldom smiled and for two years had orthopedic braces clamped on her legs: she scoffed at her as "Granny."

Mother grew up convinced that she was physically ugly, with a mouthful of teeth so prominent that they gave a look of weakness to her chin. She admitted as much to young Franklin when she put out of her head the wild fancy that this handsome cousin might marry her. "I am plain," she told him. "I have little to bring you."

The inculcated sense of inferiority was not helped by the clothes she was put into as a child—old-fashioned, dowdy dresses that made her ashamed to be in company. To the end of her days, fashion meant nothing to her. She often entertained at Val-Kill in an old pair of grass-stained tennis shoes and a shapeless cotton frock. She refused to part with a topcoat of sturdy Scottish tweed that Father bought her on their honeymoon; the hem was taken up and let down as the only concession to changes in style. "Why, it's a perfectly good coat with *lots* of wear left in it! I see no *reason* to give it up."

In his schooldays, a tumor developed in her father's brain. For most of his thirty-one years of life, he suffered agony, which drove him to drinking, laudanum and morphine to ease the pain. Yet she felt that he alone in the world loved her, and she worshiped him in return. I could imagine the devastation it caused when Father, to whom she had transferred this devotion, found it impossible to live up to her idolizing expectations.

When Mother was eight, Anna Hall Roosevelt died of diphtheria, unmourned by her daughter. She left two sons, three-year-old Elliott and a baby, Gracie Hall. The elder boy was stricken with scarlet fever a year later, and the two surviving children went to live with their widowed Grandma Hall in the dreary Victorian mansion named Oak Terrace at Tivoli, twenty miles beyond Hyde Park on the Hudson River. It was a gloomy household, devoid of affection.

"I was always afraid of something," Mother remembered, "of the dark, of displeasing people, of failure. Anything I accomplished had to be done across a barrier of fear."

The biggest factor in survival was the rare visits of her father. She would slide down the banisters to throw herself into his arms, and he would tell her that someday she would make a home for him again. Her tenth birthday lay two months ahead when she was told the news of his death. After a day of tears, she took refuge in her dream world. "I lived with him more closely, probably, than I had when he was alive."

It was something of a marvel to me that religion had not been driven out of her when it was drilled in so hard at Tivoli. Every Sunday demanded a four-mile jouncing in a big victoria to church and back, which left Mother pale and vomiting. No games, no hot meals and no reading but the Bible was a Sabbath rule.

Two members of the family, at least, followed a different course. Eddie and Vallie, her uncles, were full-blown alcoholics. Both the Hall boys had been young amateur tennis champions in the era when the game burst upon American society. The inheritance of each of them had been squandered on what was then termed "high living," gambling and drink. The terrifying spectacle they made of themselves was linked in her mind with her father's tragedy. That was why a sip of liquor had struck her as a step on the path to damnation, which made this new, more tolerant attitude of hers so astonishing.

The loss of her father and her uncles' self-destruction had one more effect. As a girl, Mother had not known where the money was to come from for the upbringing of herself and

Hall. Grandpa Hall had died intestate; Grandma Hall was helpless in the matter of managing a household.

Only in this year of 1946 was Mother succeeding in conquering an inheritance of fear, shyness and a conviction that in appearance she was unsightly. Happenstance raised the level of her self-esteem another notch.

Drowsy from overwork, she left Val-Kill on a sunny mid-August day to drive alone in the little Ford to Manhattan. On the Saw Mill River Parkway at Yonkers, the sound of the motor lulled her to sleep. The car veered across the highway, slammed into another head on, then sideswiped one more, injuring four other people in the process. Her face collided with her steering wheel, blackening her eyes and breaking off two buck teeth in her upper jaw. I never knew by what miracle that was all the harm she suffered.

In the hospital, she was told, "Those teeth are gone. You will have a permanent bridge to replace them, but don't worry—the replacements can be made to look exactly the same as those you've lost."

Not a bit of it. "I don't want *that,*" Mother said, seizing the opportunity. "I'd like some good, straight teeth to give me a better-looking mouth."

Faye and I drove helter-skelter to see her. She mumbled a greeting, too overcome by embarrassment to part her lips. As soon as a temporary bridge could be installed the following day, she insisted on going home to Val-Kill. When the final dental work was done, she heard compliments from family, friends and United Nations delegates alike on what a handsome woman she had suddenly become. She brushed aside such praise, pretending not to know what they were talking about, but I can testify that in her heart she was delighted.

The little Ford had to be written off. She loathed putting out good money for a new car, and she was peeved when her driver's license was suspended for four months as a result of the crash. Nobody in the family was sorry about that. Machinery of any kind, from an automobile to a can opener, mystified

Mother. She was such an inveterate daydreamer and so chronically clumsy behind a steering wheel that we were relieved because she had to take time off.

With her beautiful new teeth somehow giving a look of greater determination to her jaw, she took herself to Albany and the New York State Democratic convention there in September. It was time to make her presence felt again in domestic politics. She did not yet concur with New Deal veterans like Wallace in openly accusing Mr. Truman of confounding the aspirations of FDR, but initial cordiality toward the President had cooled.

He made altogether too much of the fact that he had been a captain of artillery in France in the First World War, in her estimation, which apparently made him all to eager to succumb to the advice of the military men around him. He had been high-handed in dealing with the threatened railroad strike the past spring, storming at two union bosses, "If you think I'm going to sit here and let you tie up this whole country, you're crazy as hell." He had called Congress into special session to ask for legislation to draft strikers into the army. Before he got to that passage in his speech, he was handed a note, "Agreement signed; strike over." He went ahead and demanded the new law anyway.

Mother took him to task. She watched him from afar like a governess assessing a stubborn student. Father would never have dreamed of handling labor so crudely. Mr. Truman needed some unsolicited advice. "I hope now that your anxiety is somewhat lessened," said her letter, "you will not insist upon a peace-time draft into the army of strikers. That seems to me a dangerous precedent." The President held on to his opinions as firmly as she did hers. He did insist—until the Senate rejected his idea. Relations with Mr. Truman began to cool.

She saw the same, heavy-handed militaristic approach to situations overseas. "Get tough with Russia" depressed her as a slogan. Negotiating FDR style, not this kind of bullying, was the way to reduce tension. She detected Averell Harriman's influence as well as the generals' in Truman's policies.

Harriman was not forgiven for riding roughshod over her good friend Gil Winant when Harriman was in London as a kingpin of lend-lease. Besides, in her judgment, he was all too eager to enjoy the blessings of Tammany Hall. When she came across him in Washington, she scolded the millionaire diplomat as a teacher would a naughty schoolboy.

Byrnes was no better, though it was some satisfaction that he had already handed in his resignation, but it would not take effect until his successor, George Marshall, come back from China next January. Byrnes, jealous because he felt *he* should have been President not Truman, often behaved as if he were. Mother was tickled by one story: when Truman asked for an account of last winter's Moscow conference of foreign ministers which his Secretary of State had attended, Byrnes told him he was planning to talk on the radio about it; Mr. President could listen if he wished.

Byrnes had done his part in undermining Father's plan for peace by refusing to commit the United States to a United Nations police force. This was one of the few topics on which the State Department and the Kremlin saw eye to eye. The Russians did not relish the thought of strangers interfering in their backyard either. Byrnes had been farsighted enough in Moscow to realize that monopolizing the secrets of the atom was calculated to breed suspicion of America in every wartime ally. He reversed himself two months later, and the Soviet vote cast at the United Nations on sharing information was an astounding *Nyet;* the undisclosed reason was that the USSR had felt impelled to launch its own crash program to build bombs.

"I know nothing about politics," Mother liked to say, which was as white a lie as the one she told as a disoriented five-year-old, thrust into a French convent when her father was committed to a sanitarium in the same country. Another little girl swallowed a penny to draw attention to herself, and Mother went to one of the sisters to claim she had done the same. "I was tempted, and I fell," she used to explain to us. "I told a lie, and the nuns knew it. I hadn't swallowed anything. My mother took me off in disgrace. My father was the only one who didn't treat me as a *criminal.*"

She arrived in Albany sensing trouble for her party in November's mid-term elections. The country needed leadership, she thought, which Truman was not providing. The voters felt left out of things, whereas Father, with his knack of explaining in his fireside chats what his objectives were, had given the American people the impression that they were intimately involved in the conduct of their country.

She would not assent, no matter how hard pressed, to running for any office. She declined to be beholden to the Democratic Party or anyone other than herself. She was enjoying the taste of freedom too much. "I am too old," she explained ominously, "to want to be *curtailed* in any way in the expression of my own thinking."

She ascribed some of the Democrats' problems to the President's failure to attract women to his programs. "Among our best workers in all campaigns are the women," she told him. "They will do the dull detail work and fill the uninteresting speaking engagements which none of the men are willing to undertake." The voice of sour, subservient experience when she was mistress of the Governor's cheerless mansion in Albany and then First Lady of the land echoed in her words.

Here she was, a life-long Democrat, currently disenchanted with a Democratic Administration. Friends asked whether it was the moment to revive Father's reverie of the two parties realigned to form a new, overpowering coalition of progressives from each side of the fence. He had once seen it as a distinct probability, with the groundwork laid right after the 1944 election and creation completed within the following four years.

"I think," he had said, "the time has come for the Democratic Party to get rid of the reactionary elements in the South and to attract to it the liberals of the Republican Party. . . . We ought to have two real parties—one liberal and the other conservative." Wendell Willkie, his opponent in

1940, came to hold much the same view. After defeating him at the polls Father enlisted Willkie as a special envoy on missions overseas, holding him in readiness for the bold attempt to build a coalition of liberals as soon as the war was over. FDR gave evidence of his ultimate purpose by appointing two progressive Republicans to his Cabinet, Henry Stimson at the War Department and Frank Knox at Navy. But Willkie was dead six months before Father.

This was one more goal of Father's that Mother was eager to pursue. Eventually, she thought, the projected new party must evolve, but not at present. The circumstances were too critical. Somehow the effort must be made to get Harry Truman turned around and headed forward. The aim should be to put up the best possible candidates. She would work toward that end. "If we do not succeed," she cautioned friends, "we do not have to vote for them." That November produced the first Republican-controlled Congress since 1930. A freshman Democrat, Senator J. William Fulbright, argued that the President should resign, since most of the country was against him.

We watched autumn creep, red and gold, down the Catskills from the porch of the Top Cottage, a soul-satisfying sight. Faye and I retreated behind the big windows of the vaulted living room as the evenings grew cold. It was the one really splendid room in the house. For its sake, Father's design had sacrificed the size of bedrooms and closet space, and there was only one bathroom. "The young generation just washes itself away," he used to joke. The place was finally furnished, with many of his things: his green White House chair, *New Yorker* cartoons that had raised a chuckle, books he had cataloged, blue Chinese screens from the Delanos, a landscape by Winston which he presented to Father at Casablanca.

The manuscript of the book which would be published shortly with the title *As He Saw It* had been completed too. Mother read and approved every line, then added a foreword of her own. To keep her options open and protect her position as a United States diplomat, she took care not to identify herself completely with the opinions she and I shared.

One note of personal regret crept into her words. "As I went to none of these history-making trips which are reported in this book, I could only write of things which were told me. . . . But Elliott was there. I remember how excited he was when he came back, and now it is doubly interesting to read his more complete account of these highly important days."

Then came the typically wary ambiguity: "I am quite sure that many of the people who heard many of the conversations recorded herein, interpreted them differently, according to their own thoughts and beliefs. The records written by all these different individuals are invaluable. This book gives one observer's firsthand account of what went on at the major conferences and will furnish future historians with some of the material which will constitute the final evaluation of history."

In *As He Saw It,* I quoted Father's opinions verbatim. Churchill: "He's scared of letting the Russians get too strong." His own Washington advisers: "Any number of times the men in the State Department have tried to conceal messages to me, delay them, hold them up somehow, just because some of these career diplomats aren't in accord with what they know I think." Threats to peace: "The one thing that could upset the applecart, after the war, is if the world is divided again, Russia against England and us."

In the United States the book stirred up a storm. The conclusion that old-line British imperialism and a new brand of American militarism were making Father's fears come true had me marked down as a tool of the Kremlin by some reviewers. And unforgivably, in their assessment, I had questioned the rectitude of dropping atomic bombs on Japanese civilians. Mr. Truman expressed righteous indignation over that comment, though he soon recovered and was extremely pleasant to me as the years went on.

Mother kept her head low during most of the fracas. "I know you'll understand why I don't want to get involved," she reiterated to me. "My position in the Administration really makes it impossible. Of course, it's *right* for you to express your opinions—"

A scathing attack by another cousin, Joe Alsop—his father had married Mother's cousin Corinne—prompted her to move to my defense. "I am old," she wrote him, "and it makes no difference to me what anybody says or thinks either in praise or blame. But when you are young, I think it makes a difference. I have often differed with my children. I have always tried to recognize the motives which lay behind what they said or did. I make no comparison between any of my children. . . . As you grow older you will realize that there are always two sides to every story and that sometimes people sin, but they rarely sin alone."

She was firmer in a further letter to Joe Alsop. "Since Harry Hopkins, I do not believe that anyone has talked 'frankly' to Mr. Stalin personally. And certainly most of us haven't talked honestly with people like Mr. Gromyko, Mr. Vishinsky etc. I am going to make a great effort to get to know Mr. G. and tell him a few of the things I feel."

I had suspicions that Franklin had fed private information to Joe Alsop and his brother Stewart for use in the Washington column which carried their joint by-line. I put that down to Franklin's caginess in making friends in the right places in anticipation of launching himself into politics wearing Father's mantle. Within the family Mother left nobody in doubt where her sympathies lay. She had not asked for one word to be softened in *As He Saw It*.

The furor was at its height when she came home exultant over a coup she had pulled off at a dinner party with Gardner Cowles, publisher of *Look* magazine. "I think," she told him, "that there's a tremendous story to be told in a *proper* interview with Stalin. Elliott has met him on more than one occasion, including at the time the airfield at Poltava was being built. Perhaps he could go to Moscow for you?"

The contract was duly signed. In the hope that something of this sort might happen, I had been taking an immersion course in Russian for the past six months at Columbia University. I could speak the language haltingly, but I could understand what was said surprisingly well.

I would take Faye with me and fly out in November, armed with a prepared list of questions, which I would augment on the spot. The editors of *Look* devised some of those questions, and Mother contributed more. Since she could not talk frankly with the Soviet marshal, I would be her understudy.

Faye and I were escorted into a huge, green-walled Kremlin office, to be left alone with the marshal and his interpreter for three and a half hours. He rose to welcome us, hand outstretched. "When is your mother coming?" were his opening words.

Book II
The Finding

"I HAD REALLY ONLY THREE ASSETS: I WAS KEENLY
INTERESTED, I ACCEPTED EVERY CHALLENGE AND OP-
PORTUNITY TO LEARN MORE, AND I HAD GREAT ENER-
GY AND SELF-DISCIPLINE."

—ELEANOR ROOSEVELT

5

"Now," Mother said brightly, "we shall have our talk."
We were together in her cottage for the first time since Faye
and I returned, and the knitting needles were already plaining
and purling. "I want to hear all about it. How did you find Mr.
Stalin?"

"Well, he hasn't grown any, of course—he's still inches
shorter than anybody in this family. His hair's turning grayer;
he still smokes a lot of those Russian cigarettes with cardboard holders on the end; wears a smart uniform."

"Who else was there with you?"

"Just Berezhkov, his interpreter. I'd met him before, starting at Teheran. I would question Stalin, and as the meeting
went on, more and more he didn't wait for Berezhkov to
translate. He'd start answering right away. That told me Stalin understands English, but he didn't realize I knew any Russian."

"Could you understand what he was saying?"

"About ninety per cent of it. Only a few words were un-
familiar."

"Were the translations accurate?" As Madam Chairman, she'd had difficulties herself.

"Not entirely, strange to say. The interpreter did shade the meanings of some answers. I was sitting there with a pad and pencil, and I'd drawn a little diagram of the room—*Look* is going to run it. Stalin said, 'Would you like to have a photograph of this office?' I said yes, I'd like that. 'Would you like a picture of this interview?' I said I'd love one, if it could be published in the magazine.''

"Did you get it?'' Mother, the seasoned newspaper columnist, appreciated the value of pictures like that.

"Well, he said, 'We'll see what we can do,' and sent for a special photographer to come in. But no photographer ever turned up. All I had was my sketch, and you know I'm no artist.''

"What was your overall impression of what he told you, Elliott?''

I needed a moment or two to put that in a nutshell. "I had the feeling that he was trying to pass along a message, something along these lines. He felt he was engaged in a losing battle without Father to explore with him likely avenues of coexistence. Stalin also knows darn well that he's failing to maintain the ongoing Big Three relationship that grew up in the war years.''

She said she could understand why. "Do you see anything that might be done to improve the situation?''

"Well, Stalin would like to talk personally with you, of course. He reckons that you could speak up to remind everyone about Father's hopes for peace. I believe he would go along with United Nations control of atomic weapons *and* a United Nations police force. If he said as much himself, he'd be afraid of weakening his own position in the USSR. He'd like somebody outside the communist bloc, like yourself, to speak for him.''

She shook her head. "I couldn't possibly speak in an *authoritative* way without having the opportunity to discuss the whole matter with Mr. Stalin first. Unless I knew what his real thinking was, why, everybody would simply throw cold water on the idea and say that the Russians would never cooperate!"

"Would it help to sound out lower-echelon Russians like Gromyko?"

"They wouldn't know Stalin's real thinking, would they?"

"Do *you* think good faith can be restored without some gesture from both sides?" I asked.

"We have to be firm, but we must also be honest with each other. Otherwise, I don't see how the Russians will ever trust us again." To her way of thinking, the Commission on Human Rights provided a unique forum. There she could personally mix firmness with honesty in the hope that her example would be followed. It was the best she could do if she was not to be granted permission to go herself to Moscow.

She tried to hold middle ground between conflicting points of view as Father had. She did not always succeed, because she was still an apprentice in the art of give and take. Indignation could get the better of her, usually on those occasions when Vishinsky was thrusting in his needle.

Mud was flung at her from left and right. *Izvestia*, Moscow's propaganda sheet, berated her in due course as "a fly darkening the Soviet sun" and "a hypercritical servant of capitalism." The *Literary Gazette* chimed in later; she was a "meddling old woman . . . a garrulous, feeble old woman consumed with an anti-Soviet fever."

Among her own countrymen, the rabid right kept up the abuse she had suffered for the past decade, with Hearst columnist Westbrook Pegler leading the chorus. To him, she was "Eleanor the Great," "the Gab" and—a distressing slur— "the daughter of a dissolute drunkard." Originally she had been startled by the fanatical dislike so many people felt for her, but she was more hardened these days. She could squash Pegler with a surface politeness that reduced him to his place as—well, anything but a *gentleman.*

"I don't know Mr. Pegler well enough to say anything at all about him," she sniped to one reporter. "You see, I have never met him except twice, when he was a guest in my house."

Her method of handling him and his like was something Father had instilled one day in 1943 when she hurried into his office, clutching her principal tormentor's latest outburst. She was just back from twenty-three thousand miles of travel across the Southwest Pacific. With luggage painstakingly weighed to make sure it would check in under the forty-pound limit and toting a portable typewriter so that she could keep up "My Day," she had dropped in at hospitals and mess halls from Honolulu to Australia, a universal aunt to thousands of servicemen.

Pegler jeered. She had taken off, he wrote, solely to gratify her ego and call on friends in uniform. She was in something of a tizzy about it. "It's quite untrue, Franklin, and so *unfair.*"

"Don't upset yourself," he calmed her. "Remember, never enter into a contest with a skunk. All you can do about creatures like him is ignore them. You don't *need* such people. You should be proud they're not on your side."

So she bore the insults with pride, refusing to trim her sails for the sake of the millions of Americans who she knew disagreed with her. That would be as dishonest as being mealymouthed to Mr. Vishinsky when he was in the wrong. Friends used to speculate that she would retire to Val-Kill if the pressures of public life wore her down. She did not seriously consider the possibility, though she liked to talk about it when she indulged in the fantasy that at heart she was only a sweet old *grand'mère* with a shawl around her shoulders and a lace cap on her head.

Nearly two years of widowhood had solidified her thinking. She had a clear idea of what she could accomplish as a standard-bearer for Father. Her influence was unchallenged at the United Nations, where strength of conviction made her the West's most effective spokesman in countering the debating points made by the Soviets. On the home front, she knew that she carried real weight within the Democratic Party, and she was ready to throw it around now that skirmishing was starting for the 1948 Presidential election.

It might be worth testing the wind to check the chances for that coalition of liberals that Father envisaged. She went down to Washington to make the keynote speech at the kickoff meeting of Americans for Democratic Action, which was an updated version of James Loeb junior's Union for Democratic Action, designed to draw together the followers of the noncommunist left. She judged that liberals united from both parties could dominate the land; they ought, therefore, to band together and give up their outdated allegiances as Democrats or Republicans. Persuading them would be no easy matter, but she foresaw it being done in her lifetime. The Democratic Party, left as puny as the present Liberal Party, would then attract only conservatives, mostly Southern, who in the past had voted solidly with right-wing Republicans to thwart Father.

She was happy to have Franklin junior with her at the birth of Americans for Democratic Action, where she made the first contribution—$100—to its coffers and promised to raise $500 more to spark a fund-raising drive. Political ambition was sprouting in my brother's breast. Of all her children, he appeared to be the front-runner. He was the son who had the right full name and looks. He was a practicing lawyer, financially secure in close to ten years of marriage to the former Ethel du Pont of Greenville, Delaware, who was an heiress of the E. I. du Pont de Nemours' arms and chemicals Golconda.

Anna and John Boettiger had left Seattle for Phoenix, Arizona, where they were struggling together in a new publishing venture. Mother had encouraged them to buy a giveaway shoppers' weekly and attempt to upgrade it into a successful, Democratic-oriented daily newspaper in the face of entrenched Republican opposition, morning and afternoon. My sister was a far from silent partner in the enterprise.

The country was plagued by rising prices of almost everything, including newsprint, which aggravated the Boettigers' difficulties. They soon ran into a financial squeeze. Mother had been partial to her son-in-law from the very beginning. She had favored his courtship of Anna after my sister's divorce from Curtis Dall. John's photograph was prominent among those that hung on the walls at Washington Square and Val-Kill. She felt a grave sense of responsibility for the trouble he was in now, so she sent Franklin out to Phoenix to help wherever he could. My brother Jimmy was asked to pitch in too, a little later.

She set about raising extra capital to pour into *The Arizona Times* from her friends and Father's. Henry Morgenthau junior came to the rescue. Bernard Baruch, the self-acclaimed "adviser to Presidents" whose attachment to the White House had multiplied his Wall Street fortune, was another willing Samaritan after she approached him as usual as "my dear friend." "The old gentleman," as she referred to him privately, liked to kiss her cheek and hold her hand when they met in public. For the present, the Boettigers, deep in debt, were fending off collapse.

Jimmy's contacts as a President's son, added to his drive to succeed, made for the prosperity of his California insurance agency. He, too, was engaged in writing a book about Father; *Affectionately, FDR* was notably calmer—and better received in the United States—than *As He Saw It.*

Mother wrote another foreword. "Jimmy needs the money," she said. That would help the current Mrs. James Roosevelt feel more secure. Romelle Schneider, as she was then, had been a nurse at the Mayo Clinic when Jimmy was a patient there in 1941 for surgery to excise stomach ulcers. Father was aghast when my brother told him he intended to seek divorce from his first wife, Betsy Cushing Roosevelt, whom our parent greatly admired.

The end of that marriage spelled the end of Jimmy's career as Father's private secretary. Though the tally of broken marriages among us children already totaled four, it was not a pleasant subject to discuss with either parent. Perhaps the recollection of their own near-disaster was the reason for that.

Her youngest and tallest son, Johnny, had gone into the department store field when he came out of the Navy. Given a job by Walter Kirchner, a friend of mine in Pasadena, he made his way up into a vice-presidency. His interest in public life seemed to rest at absolute zero. What he had in mind was opening a store of his own, with the approval of his wife, the former Anne Sturgis Clark, a spirited Republican.

Mother had come up with another spare-time project for me: editing a volume of Father's personal letters, accumulated from the time he could put pen to paper. It could be a contribution to her chosen mission, depicting the sweep and scale of events of the Roosevelt era as they moved toward their climax. Though the Truman Administration restricted the use of some material—papers that might prejudice relations overseas or libel living associates of FDR—the idea was irresistible when the files of the memorial library were so close to hand.

The Roosevelt partnership, mother and son, had paid $87,000 for 1,100 acres of the 1,365 owned by Father. The woods and fields stretched for the most part on the east side of Route 9, the Albany Post Road, around the Val-Kill cottages. We named the operation Val-Kill Farms; managing it was my allotted concern, as was taking care of the $37,000 mortgage which figured in the purchase price. By Texas standards it was not a major undertaking. At its peak, we had forty head of dairy cattle, a hundred steers, two dozen or so sows and a sizable flock of turkeys. Father had planted evergreens as a cash crop for the future; so we decided to add to the plantation and sell trees at retail Christmas.

Mother was taking on a role which Father latterly could spare precious little time for: as head of the family and protector of us children in our vicissitudes. For the good of the Roosevelt name, we had to be steered along paths of righteousness to the best of her ability and taught to pull together.

This was the era when she circulated another of her letters to her brood in an effort to set a few ground rules for behavior. "I want you to agree that you will never say anything derogatory about each other or make any kind of remarks that can be so construed, and you will never allow people in your presence to say anything which will reflect on the integrity and character of the family."

The five of us paid occasional heed to her admonitions but only lip service to her ideals. We all felt certain that we knew far better than she what made the world go round, which was an error on our part, though it took a while for the truth to sink in. However, those were days when, prompted and pleaded with by Mother, we did stick together and tried to help each other out when the need arose.

Anna's plight was a case in point. The circulation figures of the Phoenix newspaper had to be watched like the temperature chart of a patient in shock. Sales must be forced up before the money ran out and the business died. Shortly before Mother's sixty-third birthday, the Boettigers flew East in their constant search for more cash. My sister confided not in Mother but in Tommy, who of course relayed the news.

Anna was worried about her husband, and her gaunt face was the evidence. The tension was disturbing what she called "his frame of mind," and the stability of their marriage was suffering. The two children by her first husband, Sistie and Buzz, were feeling the effects, too. The Boettigers' visit was a mixed success. Discussions with New York businessmen taught John that if he sold *The Arizona Times* now, he and Anna would emerge with virtually nothing. But Bernie Baruch promised to lay hold of some fixed-price newsprint for them and try to raise another $150,000 which they critically needed. They also heard that sales were climbing, and Boettiger's spirits rose with them.

"We can definitely pull the paper through and make a very good thing of it," he told his wife.

They had left for home when Franklin and I had a Sunday chat at Hyde Park. I was less sanguine than Mother or Anna about the capabilities of Mr. Baruch. "Can you find a bank," I asked my brother, "that would make a loan of, say, $200,000 against my share of the profits we hope to make at Val-Kill? I'd like to offer whatever I can borrow to Anna."

Franklin was more conservative in his thinking. He talked about the risk involved in Phoenix and the chance that profits would not materialize at Val-Kill either. But out of affection for our sister, he telephoned her word of our conversation to boost her morale.

Anna hastened to tell Mother about it in a birthday letter. "Mummy, it was the greatest comfort possible seeing something of you, and you'll never know how much all your help has meant to us. Tell Elliott it's lucky for him he talked to Frankie and not me, or he'd have had a bawling female on his hands. And give Tommy a hug for her always sympathetic and tactful ear!"

Mother, rewarded whenever one child volunteered to lend a hand to another, could not wait until she came up to Val-Kill from 29 Washington Square West. A scribbled note, enclosing Anna's letter, arrived in the mail at Top Cottage. "Dearest Elliott: You are too generous and it's a risk you shouldn't take but I think just the offer did more good than you imagined. You are a reckless darling! Let's stop borrowing in this family and save from now on. I love you both. Mother."

Letters to those she loved—and this included friends as well as us and her close relatives—habitually overflowed with endearments. "Dearest," "darling" and expressions of devotion characterized everything she wrote to them. It was a habit which soon would bring her torment as great as she ever experienced.

"If I have a weakness," she used to say, "it is the need for approbation from people I love." And "we can always do something if we care enough." She went to great pains to keep in intimate touch with each of the five of us. She liked to know everything we were doing or hoped to do, and she would follow through with every bit of help her agile brain could conceive. "I was not wise enough just to love you as children," she would tell us. She felt she had to make amends for what she thought of as her failure in times gone by.

Her driver's license was restored by now, and we were happy for her sake that she made only limited use of it. She was reconciled to having someone else take her where she wanted to go. Around Hyde Park, it was often crew-cropped Tubby Curnan, built like one of the trucks he used to jockey before he enrolled with the Parks Department. His brother Charlie was brought in to cook at Val-Kill when the guest list ran exceptionally long.

Four months off the highways had been good for her. We knew that unless her license had been suspended by the court, she would have been impelled to drive again straight after her accident to prove to herself that she could, and her coordination was so poor that she would inevitably have run into more trouble. As it was, she was apt to keep an eye on her little watch and prod Tubby: "We're three minutes behind schedule. Perhaps we could go a little *faster.*"

She thought that Mr. Truman was going much too fast, too far and in the wrong direction when he asked Congress for $4 billion in aid to Greece and Turkey as a warning to the Soviets that they would be allowed to expand no farther around the Black Sea. If they wanted war, his message implied, the initiative would be theirs. American warships had been sent earlier "on training maneuvers" when the Russians massed troops on the Turkish border "to protect" that country's coastline.

The Truman Doctrine struck Mother as "a most unfortunate way to do things," and she said so to Dean Acheson—Groton, Yale and Harvard Law School—who was acting Secretary of State until Marshall took over. Down to his military moustache, Acheson was a devout Anglophile, and she distrusted him. It was outrageous, she considered, for the United States to attempt to go it alone without so much as consulting the United Nations. What if the USSR followed suit and invaded Greece to "protect" embattled communists there?

Acheson dispatched a senior assistant to win Mother over

to the Administration's standpoint, the latest of a line of courtiers assigned to persuade her that what she felt was right was actually wrong. She had been more malleable in her trainee days as a diplomat when she was so uncertain of the routines to be followed at the United Nations that occasionally Adlai Stevenson had to nudge her into raising a hand in a vote.

This time, she was not to be courted. She told Acheson's emissary as much, underlined her position in her column, and repeated her objections to Truman. "Taking over Mr. Churchill's policies in the Near East in the name of democracy" was not "the way to really create a barrier to communism or promote democracy," she chided the President.

She was fearful that the world was sliding downhill toward a new war, but what she had to say was for Americans only. When Henry Wallace toured Europe denouncing the Truman Doctrine, she was appalled. Such disloyalty to his native land caused her to write him off as a candidate after he quit as Commerce Secretary to make a bid for the Presidency. "He has never been a good politician," she said of this man she had once thought of as Father's most promising disciple, "he has never been able to gauge public opinion, and he has never picked his advisers wisely."

Hard on the heels of the Truman Doctrine came the Marshall Plan, devised by General Marshall as Secretary of State to convince the Western world that this country would do more than jump when the Soviets called the shots. America would combat "hunger, poverty, desperation and chaos" to revive "a working economy in the world." With some strings attached, the Marshall Plan was to distribute more than $12 billion to governments in Europe.

It sounded better to Mother than anything the Administration had come up with to date. Instead of sending emissaries to woo her, Marshall took on the job himself—she was uneasy about where her beloved United Nations fitted in his scheme of things. To her great contentment, he brought her into policy discussions, which neither Byrnes nor Acheson had ever done. Mutual admiration sprang up between Marshall and "the most intelligent, cooperative and effective Mrs. Eleanor Roosevelt," as he called her, while she praised his "integrity and deep convictions." At last, there was someone besides Harry Truman whom she could contact in Washington when she had some thoughts to convey.

One subject on which she peppered both the President and the Secretary with unsolicited advice was the creation of a homeland for the Jews. The old woman's cries of "Israel! Israel!" heard in the camp at Zilcheim left an indelible impression. She was enthused when, in the face of mounting Jewish terrorism, the British decided to turn over the problem of handling Palestine to the United Nations. She fretted over the delay when the United States led a move to set up a special U.N. committee to study possible solutions and report to the General Assembly six months later. General Marshall heard from her about *that.*

She detected the cunning hand of Ed Pauley in all the shilly-shally. Oil was his business, and oil was the reason, in her opinion, that Great Britain was fearful of carving out a country for the Jews in the Middle East: Arab nations might retaliate by cutting off oil exports to Britain and the United States. She cautioned Truman against listening to Pauley's pleas to go slow.

The special committee's report recommended the division of Palestine into one state for the Jews and another for the Arabs, with Jerusalem governed separately as a United Nations trusteeship. Our State Department was enveloped in instant uproar, with most old-liners there urging that the Administration continue looking for an alternative answer for Palestine.

Mother's mind was made up. The Jewish people had already been kept waiting too long and too many of them had perished under Hitler. As a matter of principle, a homeland must be made for them. She was thrilled to find that Marshall saw the issue in the same light. Mr. Truman, on the other hand, could use a little gingering up to inspire him to be more forceful.

One half of the committee's recommendation, as vital to the other as a Siamese twin, became inexplicably lost in the Washington infighting: the simultaneous setting up of an Arab state when Palestine was partitioned.

The State of Israel was all that counted with her. One State Department sympathizer with the Arabs' cause was Robert Lovett—Yale, Harvard and a background in banking. Mother rated him "dangerous" and prayed that he would either quit or be fired.

At Val-Kill Farms, we were cutting trees to sell for Christmas. Since they would be Roosevelt trees, Mother was not looking to reap any vast profit. We would charge one dollar apiece and put them on sale in the poorest neighborhoods of New York City. She was sorry that she would not be around for the selling season, and she would miss by two days the General Assembly vote on partitioning Palestine, but she had to leave November 27 for Human Rights Commission meetings in Geneva, determined to be back in time for Christmas itself.

She found a new soulmate on her flight from New York. Dr. David Gurewitsch, gentle, slender and amiable, had been recommended to her by Joe Lash's wife Trude, already a patient of his whom he had known from student days together in Germany. Soon after Mother left Washington and the shelter of free medical care, she asked him whether he would act as her personal physician. "I am usually in *extremely* good health, so I shouldn't take up *too* much of your time." He had been impressed by Mother from the day they met at a White House reception and he spoke with her for a minute or so. He took her on his rolls, and she had her medical records forwarded to him from the National Naval Medical Center in Bethesda, Maryland.

He needed treatment himself when he fell ill with a resurgence of pulmonary tuberculosis. Mother's immediate response was to invite him to stay in Stone Cottage for as long as it took for rest to cure him. He chose, instead, to be treated at Davos, high in the Swiss Alps, where he had been a patient once before. Having difficulty in getting a seat on a plane, he sought help from Mother by way of Trude Lash, which was how he and Mother came to be making for Geneva together.

The flight was scheduled to last something short of one day in that age of propeller-driven aircraft, but engine trouble delayed them in Newfoundland, the first refuelling stop. A portable radio was available to while away the time. They were back in the air on November 29 when they heard the running broadcast from the General Assembly session in New York. The vote went thirty-three to thirteen for establishing the State of Israel, a necessary two-thirds majority. Without a unanimous Aye from the Soviet bloc, it would have been defeated.

David, born in Zurich of refugees from czarist Russia, was a Jew. Mother joined him in raising hosannas to the opening of a new era in the life of his people.

Fog shrouded the airport when they landed at Shannon, Eire, and kept them there for three days, confined in quarters for transit passengers which were located more than a mile from the restaurant. David was not well enough to cover the distance in wintry weather for his meals. Mother fetched them for him, read to him by the hour as he lay in bed and, as they exchanged confidences in the unworldly setting, opened her heart to him as never before.

He spoke to her about his father, who was fascinated by philosophy before he was ten years old and believed as he reached twenty-six that he had at last solved the riddle of the kinship between man, God and the universe; he was found drowned some months later, leaving a young wife and his unborn son. That struck a chord of compassion in Mother; she, too, had grown up fatherless, and she related her own personal history.

David went on to tell her of his mother. As a youthful widow, she had abandoned the study of philosophy in which she had joined her husband to enter medicine. She made a name as a healer, devising techniques of massage as a means of therapy. Grandparents had raised David, and Mother knew just what that meant from her years in the strict hands of Grandma Hall.

He had experienced a profound sense of dispossession—from home, companionship and affection—and so, Mother eagerly agreed, had she. They were both basically shy, lonely people, driven onward by the concept of duty, not the search for personal happiness. When they finally arrived in Geneva four and a half days after takeoff from New York, a bond of rare friendship had been sealed between them, stronger than Mother had known since her courtship days.

The exhilaration of talking with David bolstered Mother's resolve to finish up the latest round of human rights discussions in accordance with a rigid timetable. She warned all delegates at the Palais des Nations Unies that they would be worked day and night in order to adjourn by eleven p.m. on December 17. She survived on six hours of daily sleep, waking at seven to meet with her colleagues over breakfast, spending every mealtime in more conferences, dictating "My Day" to Tommy well after midnight. Whenever the chance arose, she telephoned Davos to keep in contact with David.

As always, she had to express her emotions in writing to someone she had admitted into her secrets. One letter to him said, "With all my outward assurance I still have some of my old shyness and insecurity and that is probably what makes you feel shy. I've really taken you to my heart, however, so there need never be a question of bother again. You can know that anything I can do will always be a pleasure for me and being with you is a joy."

Some delegates denounced her for merciless bullying, but she did not mind. "We did end our work," she noted primly, "on the evening I had originally designated." I had disappointing news for her when she came home to Val-Kill. Finding the right locations for selling our trees in Harlem and the Lower East Side of New York had proved difficult, and the weather had been wretchedly unseasonable. We hadn't made a nickel on our venture.

Her concern over money asserted itself again. "I'm so

afraid, Elliott, that I shan't be able to keep up with all my expenses," she frowned in one of our three-way chats with Tommy. We checked off the sources of her income for her. Interest on the capital left by Father, invested with the utmost caution, would bring in $30,000 a year. She earned $2,500 a month for her questions-and-answers column in the *Ladies' Home Journal,* whose editors, Bruce and Beatrice Gould, were pressing for a second volume of memoirs from her to follow up the success of *This Is My Story,* which stopped short of the White House years; the Goulds had paid $75,000 for serial rights to that.

What she could expect from "My Day" was problematical, depending on how many newspapers printed it, and the number was slowly declining. On the other hand, demand for her on the lecture circuit was insatiable. She made no fewer than thirty appearances and sometimes as many as a hundred a year, at an average fee of $1,000.

"But it's the *expenses* and all those tax bills that take most of what I earn. I'd like to be able to give my earnings to people and organizations that *deserve* to be helped, but the tax laws won't permit that."

The way to solve that particular problem was to set up a charity fund into which all her lecture fees were channeled, amounting to perhaps a third of her income, to be shared out among tax-exempt charities. But she continued to fear that her capacity to earn money might disappear, depriving all of her causes of her contributions to them.

Her life-style was plain, with little spent to meet her own needs. "I don't want to cut back on what can be done for others," she said. "I shall just have to keep on going. Isn't there something *more* you can think of that I can do, Elliott? What about a radio program?"

"Well," I said slowly, "you could give that a try. Would you like me to see what we could put together?" She thought this was a fine idea. We planned to have a format ready for the coming season.

Early in the New Year, Mr. and Mrs. Gould reignited her desire to travel to the USSR for that elusive meeting with Stalin. They intended to visit the country themselves, and there was some thought that she might go with them, as the Russians instantly suggested. It was Marshall's turn to deter her, and she accepted his counsel in good grace.

President Eduard Benes of Czechoslovakia was also anxious to see her, but time was running out for him. Next month, in a new turn to the cold war, he would bow to communist pressure and bring his nation into the Soviet bloc. Foreign Minister Jan Masaryk, who sat directly behind Mother in the General Assembly, refused to resign. She had been moved by the misery of this son of the founder of Czechoslovakia and his habit of voting with the Russians in every ballot.

"What can you do?" he leaned forward to whisper to her one day. "What else can you do when you've got them right in your own front yard?" In March, he was found dead on the ground beneath an open window in Prague, "a warning," Mother said, "for those who love freedom." Suicide or murder? She would not speculate. Benes himself was dead before the year was over.

Fitting a trip to Moscow or Prague into her present schedule would have required a juggler's skill. She was fast becoming a transatlantic commuter, with Paris the next stop for meetings of the General Assembly there. Packing a suitcase took no more than a few minutes; it was always just one suitcase, none too big at that, which she carried herself. She had an astonishing facility for folding and sandwiching in the bare minimum of garments, enough to allow her to look neatly turned out for any occasion. She took a necklace, some rings, the fob watch and, of course, the photographs in the hinged leather frame.

She wrote again to David. "The people I love mean more to me than all the public things even if you do think that public affairs should be my chief vocation. I only do the public things because there are a few close people whom I love dearly and who matter to me above everything else. There are not so many of them and you are now one of them and I shall just have to try not to bother you too much!"

At the moment, "public things" threatened to overwhelm

her and the rest of mankind. On April 1, the Soviet military government started a land blockade of Berlin by closing off the autobahn and the railroad tracks which ran through the Russian occupation zone of Germany to those of the United States, Britain and France. The tables were shrewdly turned: now responsibility for making any countermove lay in American hands. The cold war could be brought to the boil very shortly.

Hollow-cheeked Lucius Clay, general in charge of our forces in Germany, had set alarm bells pealing in Washington. War, said his cablegram to the Pentagon, "may come with dramatic suddenness." Mother could see the world for which Father fostered such sublime hope being destroyed thirty-six months after he had left it. What would he have done in these circumstances? she asked herself. The answer was obvious. He had advocated similar action before two previous wars erupted. She proposed an American peace mission to meet with the Soviets and the British.

Both the President and the Secretary of State were pressed to follow Father's example. "I do not think I have been as alarmed before," said her letter to Truman, "but I have become very worried and since we always have to sit down together when war comes to an end, I think before we have a third World War, we should sit down together." The President was not convinced. So far as he was concerned, the Marshall Plan and United States military strength provided the only grounds for optimism.

Engaged on all fronts against the Administration, she was at the point of an open break with Truman. Unless the United Nations were provided with enough muscle to impose peace if need be, it would surely disintegrate as the League of Nations had in the 1930's. Why did the United States balk at supplying troops for an international police force? Why was it contemplated that any Americans who volunteered to enlist in such a cause would be stripped of their citizenship? Why the embargo on American arms shipments to the Middle East when equipping the Jews and a United Nations peacekeeping command there "is the only thing which will hold the Arabs in check"? The questions swirled in her head.

She blamed James Forrestal, head of Truman's newly assembled Department of Defense and a man incapable of distinguishing between communism and socialism, more than anyone else for the President's faltering. Forrestal kept insisting that setting up a United Nations army would mean that Soviet soldiers were recruited, too, on a man-for-man basis with Americans, and in that case the United States would be compelled to mobilize halfway for war. "That," Mother stormed, "seems to me utter nonsense."

Tommy's steno pads were filled with diatribes to Washington, dictated as Mother stalked to and fro through her cottage, her apartment or some hotel room overseas, and the typewriter was pounded most of the day. It was to no effect. There was a halfhearted effort by the State Department to canvass some high-level private opinions about a peace mission, but nothing came of that. Forrestal and Lovett argued for shelving the partition of Palestine because the United States was inhibited from enforcing it; instead, they proposed reverting to a United Nations trusteeship over the whole territory.

Mother had reached the limits of her patience. She wrote again to Truman. "I cannot believe that war is the best solution. No one won the last war, and no one will win the next war. While I am in accord that we need force and I am in accord that we need this force to preserve the peace, I do not think that complete preparation for war is the proper approach as yet. . . . I have offered my resignation to the Secretary."

She would be off again in a few more days for London. Her letter horrified Truman. It would be a calamity, he acknowledged, for her to quit. The United Nations, he assured her in a neat reversal of his position, represented mankind's finest hope. Father could not have said it better. Mother did nothing more about resigning.

Visiting London made a pleasant break in the turmoil, all of which was concealed from public knowledge; when she wrote

her new book of reminiscences she made no mention of it.
The British people had little idea that the stooping, smiling
woman who wore a smart hat with a dotted veil and a fox fur
over her two-piece costume was bitterly critical of their government's maneuvers in Palestine.

She was invited to spend a weekend in Windsor Castle,
where King George and his queen personally escorted her to
her chilly suite. The king's mother, tottering Queen Mary,
conducted her on a tour of the royal picture galleries. She reminded my parent of Sara, her own mother-in-law, in her fret-
ting over the way her son had rearranged some of the paintings in their imposing gilded frames.

Mother was impressed by Princess Elizabeth's concern
with young girls who had fallen out with the law, which was
an interest of her own, too. Elizabeth had some idea of Mother's homey personal style—the wedding present that arrived
from Val-Kill for her and Prince Philip the previous November consisted of a dozen bath towels, dusters and tea cloths.

Sir Winston came to the castle to dine one evening. To
Mother's secret amusement, he respectfully declined to join
in an after-dinner game of charades led by Queen Elizabeth.
He had reason to be glum and chomp on a consoling cigar.
Mother had seen him bested in the matter of the statue of Father which she was to unveil in London's Grosvenor Square.
Winston had pushed for a sitting figure to reflect the fact that
Father could not walk. The sculptor, Sir William Reid Dick,
and the Pilgrim's Society, which raised the money, wanted
the man in stone to be standing, head high, face to the wind,
with a cape flowing from his shoulders.

That was the figure which was revealed when Mother, with
King George at her side, pulled a tasseled cord and the covering canvas fell away. There stood a vigorous, young Franklin
Delano Roosevelt as she had known him at the start of their
years together. It was not easy for her to check the tears.

6

The warm afterglow of her visit to England was lost as soon as she came back to work. The General Assembly had been called into special session to debate Palestine's destiny. The United States delegation continued to canvass votes for trusteeship, not partition; the USSR held that partition was the only viable solution. The question of a homeland for the Jews had degenerated into one more conflict in the cold war.

The new Zionist state was due to be proclaimed on May 14, no matter what, when the British evacuated Palestine. Mother received word from Jewish sources that the Soviet Union planned immediate recognition for the republic of Israel. She passed a warning on to Marshall: "The people who spoke to me are afraid that we will lag behind and again follow instead of lead."

Truman had made up his mind to seek a four-year term of his own in the Presidency this coming November even if most commentators rated his chances as virtually nil. His influence was weaker than that of any predecessor since Warren G. Harding. The Republicans looked forward to getting a man of

their choice into the White House for the first time since 1933.
If he was to stand a remote chance of being elected, Harry
Truman had to court every potential supporter, and American
Jews ranked high on the list.

Forty-eight hours before Israel became a reality, American
policy was reversed again. Without letting Mother or anyone
else at the United Nations into his secret, Truman jumped in
three days ahead of the Soviets by granting recognition to Israel on the day of its proclamation, May 14, 1948. Within a
matter of hours the armies of Egypt, Jordan, Syria, Lebanon
and Iraq streamed across the frontiers of the brand-new Jewish homeland.

Mother vented her outrage on Marshall. She reported
"complete consternation" at Lake Success. "More and more
the other delegates seem to believe that our whole policy is
based on antagonism to Russia and that we think in terms of
going it alone."

If anything, her sympathy for the Zionists was magnified by
her affinity for her new friend David and his family—wife
Edna, daughter Grania and, later, baby Maria—whom she
would draw close to herself when he returned from Davos to
resume his medical practice. When Mother turned to writing
her will, David and Grania would both be included as le-
gatees, along with others whom she held so dear that they
were treated as her own children, incapable of wrongdoing.

They made a diverse company, having only one thing in
common: her limitless affection for them. Accepting the order
in which she listed them in her will meant that she placed
Tommy first in her heart.

She felt almost equal fondness for another woman of similar age. Lorena Hickock originally came into her orbit as an
Associated Press reporter mounting watch at the Governor's
mansion in Albany on the summer night in 1932 when Father
won his party's nomination for the Presidency. Almost instantly, the journalist detected a melancholy in Mother that
was inexplicable in light of his triumph. She recalled Mother's

remark in the middle of the campaign: "It's good to be middle-aged. Things don't matter so much."

"Hick," as Mother called her, was assigned to stay at her side during the first White House months and won acceptance as an intimate friend, rewarded with such confidences as, "I never wanted to be a President's wife, and I don't want it now." It was Hick's suggestion that Mother should hold her own press conferences—the first of them predated Father's.

Hick, who never married, found herself so partisan toward the First Lady that she resigned her newspaper job. Mother found work for her to do with the Democratic National Committee and then with Harry Hopkins. On the night Mother and Tommy returned after their evacuation of the White House, Hick was in the Washington Square apartment arranging flowers in welcome.

When illness made the keeping of regular office hours difficult for her, Hick was enrolled into helping Mother put together some of the books for children that publishers begged her to do. Arrangements were made for Hick to have a little house not far from Val-Kill. She was put on salary and given a fair share of royalties before and after publication. Researching the delayed second volume of memoirs was her current occupation. Mother wore a ring that Hick gave her as a seal of their fellowship.

Joe Lash, small in size but imbued with gigantic admiration for her, was another newspaper writer in Mother's most private circle. The affection between them dated back a dozen years, to the stormy days when, with a master's degree from Columbia, he was a leader of the American Youth Congress in its confrontations with Father. Joe, whose politics had grown milder, was sought out by Mother on her wartime excursion to the Southwest Pacific; could Father, less impressionable than she, have had a hand in dispatching Sergeant Lash, as he was then, to the closest place to the ends of the earth—Johnston Island, a speck in the ocean southwest of Pearl Harbor?

After he came out of the services and was job-hunting,

Mother used her persuasions with Dorothy Schiff, a friend on the outer perimeter of our family, to land him at the *New York Post*; he was eventually promoted to be that newspaper's United Nations correspondent. So that Mother might see more of him and Trude, she arranged for another little house in the community of Val-Kill to be theirs at a nominal rent. They fixed it up and proceeded to spend a great deal of time with us, giving him the opportunity to learn much about Mother's outlook and personal feelings. He also contributed the bulk of the labor involved in research for the volumes of Father's letters which were underway.

Mother had known Trude, a social worker and divorcée, longer than Joe. She had been happy to serve as something of a matchmaker in his courtship of Trude. Mrs. Lash and Faye Roosevelt could in no way be considered as look-a-likes, but they both had the drive and energy that appealed so strongly to Mother. She involved herself with Trude in a host of fundraising endeavors for underprivileged groups. The one nearest at hand was Wiltwyck School on the opposite bank of the Hudson, a center for delinquent boys, mostly black and bred in the slums of New York City. Trude was slated to inherit all of Mother's Meissen china in token of appreciation.

Mavris Chaney—"Tiny"—was seen less frequently now that she was Mrs. Martin and living in Los Angeles, but her place in Mother's heart was secure. A wristwatch was one memento she was scheduled to receive under the terms of the will. Tiny, a professional dancer, had been a steady visitor to the old Manhattan apartment on East 11th Street. She was also the unwitting cause of a bygone attack by the "hate Eleanor" league. In her role as protective matriarch, Mother went to considerable lengths to obtain favors and jobs for her chosen ones. She contrived to have Tiny hired in 1941 at something less than $90 a week as an assistant instructor in an Office of Civilian Defense keep-fit program, teaching noontime calisthenics to fellow employees on a Washington rooftop. One Congressman's voice was heard in the chorus of

abuse, demanding why Sally Rand, queen of waving-fan bur-
lesque, had not been engaged in her stead.

Tiny was introduced to Mother by Earl Miller in the first
place, and Earl was turning out to be the unwitting cause of
unimaginable hurt. He had been one of the privileged company for twenty years, longer than anybody except Tommy. Father inherited Trooper Miller, who had served Al Smith as
bodyguard, when we moved into the Governor's mansion in
Albany. Earl was a rugged, muscular specimen, as handsome
as a movie cowboy. Eager to oblige and anxious to succeed,
he was soon promoted sergeant.

At forty-four, Mother's hand with an automobile was no
better than today. Father envisioned the upset that would be
caused if she ran into something or somebody, so he had Miller ride with her when she insisted on using the family car instead of a state limousine. The strapping young sergeant gave
her driving lessons, instilling enough confidence to make her
feel that she had mastered the art.

Step by step, Earl was brought in as a member of our
household. He ate at our table instead of with his comrades in
the kitchen. Mother enlisted him to help with Uncle Vallie
when he turned up roaring drunk one night in Albany; she and
Miller drove him home to Oak Terrace. On another day in Tivoli, Earl and Vallie got into a wrestling match, which could
have only one conclusion; Miller could have felled a horse.

His rough-tongued gallantry was something new to Mother.
He needed no encouragement to confide in her just as David
Gurewitsch did. Miller, born in Schenectady, had known no
home since he was twelve. He had been in turn a circus
acrobat, an amateur champion in the boxing ring, a Navy sea-
man in the First World War and an athletics instructor at the
New York State police academy who starred as a trick horseback rider at the state fairs.

At Warm Springs, he talked "the Boss"—his name for Father—into trying to ride again, but the effort was useless; Father's legs were too weak to grip a saddle. Missy was included

in the classes and Mother too, on her rare visits to the Little
White House. "The Lady," as Earl addressed her, received
his horse, Dot, as a going-away present when we left Albany.
Taking Dot on an early morning canter along the trails of
Washington's Rock Creek Park served a dual purpose: it was
a test of her suppressed fear of horses and part of the sentimental bond with Miller, who was now director of personnel
of the New York State Department of Correction.

The scandalmongers found she made a more vulnerable target than Father. They were forever whispering about Earl,
hinting that he was more than a friend. In one sense, they
were right. Mother loved him because he evoked femininity in
her. She could have been considering this when she declared,
"I think that one of the strongest qualities in every human being is a need to feel needed, to feel essential, to feel important." Their relationship went no deeper into romance than
that.

Earl had the run of her Manhattan apartment like the rest of
her coterie, male and female, and she kept a guest room ready
for him at Val-Kill. She heard his stories about the problems
he had with the first Mrs. Miller, and after his divorce, she
watched his approaches to Missy with tolerant eyes.

Missy had no desire to be married, so he took his first wife's
cousin, Ruth Bellinger, as his bride. Mother lent Val-Kill Cottage for the ceremony, with Anna as a bridesmaid and myself
as best man, and she helped Earl pay for a house in the area.
His second marriage was no more durable than the first, but
Mother continued to give him moral support, casting around
for work for him to do and interests to hold his attention. He
was one of those to whom she wrote regularly, inscribing her
letters with her usual endearments, signing them "with much,
much love" or "a hug and a kiss," and telling of her eagerness to see him again.

Wartime service as a Navy commander concluded, Earl
took another wife, but this bid for happiness was no more successful than the others. Mrs. Miller was suing for divorce.
She had come into possession of a bundle of Mother's letters,

and she had wondered if the terms of settlement would be improved if Mother were to be named as corespondent.

The impact was catastrophic. Mother could not bring herself to believe that anyone might conceive such evil. Day after day, she walked alone through the woods at Val-Kill, shunning even Fala's companionship. She would be gone for hours, enveloped in misery. When she came back, she would take herself to her study and lock the door behind her. She could not force herself to discuss her depression with any of us beyond saying over and over, "How can people *be* like this in the world? I don't know how I can go *on*."

I believed that she was close to suicide, and Tommy was as alarmed as I. The two of us felt powerless when we talked about what might be done to prevent a scandal breaking that promised to destroy Mother unless she could be urged to assert herself. One week followed another, and still there was no change.

Franklin came to the cottage to volunteer his help. As a practicing attorney, he offered to contact Mrs. Miller's counsel. "Let me see if I can determine exactly what documents they're talking about. I'll make a settlement if that's possible." Mother's spirits did not improve.

The crisis was finally resolved, but not through Mrs. Miller's lawyer. A sum of money was passed to retrieve the letters. None of Mother's sons, and most certainly not Franklin, was motivated by fear of damage to his political career if she had been named in court. It was an all too rare occasion when we could make some return for the affection she showered on her children.

Franklin and I both went carefully through every recovered page. We agreed that they signified nothing beyond her transparent fondness for Earl. They were almost childish in their sentimentality. There was no reason to doubt that a judge would have come to the same conclusion once we had rounded up and produced some of the hundreds of letters couched in similar terms she had written over the years to other people.

Mother had suffered needlessly as the victim of a greedy legal game. When her shattered confidence was slowly repaired, she would say so convincingly that any stranger would believe her, "I long ago reached the point where there is no living person whom I fear and few challenges that I am not willing to face." Tommy and I knew better. "What am I living for?" was a question that would return to haunt her. David Gurewitsch was one of those who heard it repeated as time went by.

She persisted in her faith in Miller, holding him completely blameless and speaking never a word against him. When he moved to Florida, the correspondence between them continued. In her will, she left him $500 and a diamond ring.

The year 1948 was darkened for her by the shadow of the Millers' divorce. In her anguish, she planned to take no part in any political campaigning, not even for Adlai. Last fall, she had prompted him into running for office as Governor of Illinois. She detected in Stevenson an ability akin to her own—to grow and keep on growing in response to challenge.

Tom Dewey was a certainty to be nominated again as the Republicans' Presidential hero. She accepted Father's estimate of the slick little lawyer, though she shrank from repeating his description of his 1944 opponent as "a son of a bitch." But she could stir up no enthusiasm for Truman either. He struck her as gullible, weak and vacillating; his record on Israel was proof of that to her.

There was no sign that his abilities had grown since she watched him sworn in and he exclaimed afterwards that he felt "like I'd been hit by a bale of hay." He was a captive, she thought, of his old cronies from Boss Pendergast's regime in Kansas City, incapable of attracting men of stature into his entourage. Consequently, he had to rely on inferior people in sensitive appointments, like bemedaled Harry Vaughan, slippery Ed Pauley, and John Snyder, the small-town banker who ruled at the Treasury. It was time for a change, but was there anyone who deserved liberal support? She decided to sit out this election.

The President, looking for her seal of approval for his candidacy, asked her down to Washington. She was not to be courted. "I have yet to make up my mind," she told him, a bitter response from the woman he had cultivated as an ally and praised as "the First Lady of the World." A frivolous move was made that summer to promote her as his next Vice-President. Yes, Truman told a press conference, she would be acceptable. "What else do you want me to say?" he added, grinning. The moment Mother heard what was happening, she announced sharply that she refused to run for any office in the land.

Jimmy and I felt certain that Dwight D. Eisenhower would make an ideal candidate for the Democrats. He could be depended on, we believed, to restore the policies and approaches of Father, whom Ike had so greatly admired. From personal contacts with him, I knew that his ambitions ranged beyond a military career. Harry Truman must have guessed that, too, when in Berlin in 1945 he offered to help Ike achieve whatever he wanted, not excluding the Presidency in this coming election.

My brother and I broached the subject of Ike as a potential Democrat to Mother. "I think one would need to know where he stands on the *issues*," she said. "Are you sure that he would be willing to be drafted? Of course, he *might* be able to unify the party——" The conversation left Jimmy and me in agreement that Mother was not unwilling to see Ike replace Harry Truman in the White House.

She was more outspoken about her favorite for the Vice-Presidency. Father's fate made the choice significant. Justice Bill Douglas had been his original preference for running mate in 1944. Father had steered clear of the party convention that year and let Bob Hannegan handle the selection of a Vice-President most readily acceptable to the delegates. He gave Hannegan two penciled notes for use as ammunition, the first listing Douglas ahead of Truman, the second reversing the order of choosing. Mother put Douglas first again this time around.

She sent him a telegram. YOU WOULD BE OF GREAT VALUE
AND GIVE SOME CONFIDENCE IN THE PARTY TO LIBERALS IF
YOU ACCEPT. . . . YOUR ACCEPTANCE WOULD GIVE HOPE TO
MANY FOR THE FUTURE OF A LIBERAL DEMOCRATIC PARTY.
Mr. Truman would be dull-witted indeed if he did not catch
the implication of her words.

Douglas was not willing. Why should he be when Henry
Wallace's left-wing peace party would inevitably split the
Democratic vote and Truman's proposals on civil rights so en-
raged the South that this Democratic fiefdom would defect
and run Governor Strom Thurmond of South Carolina as a
Dixiecrat?

I was out of range as a target for Truman's arrows; Jimmy
was not. Back in California, he was drumming up support for
drafting Ike. The President buttonholed him during a trip he
was making there. "Here I am," he barked, "trying to do everything I can to carry out your father's policies. You've got
no business trying to pull the rug out from under me."

The series of radio programs was taking shape. There
would be five afternoon shows a week, identified just as
"Eleanor Roosevelt." She could record them in two hectic
sessions, interviewing the foremost personalities on the international scene.

The plan was to try it on a single outlet as a beginning, then
syndicate to as many stations as wanted to buy. The initial
contract was signed with the National Broadcasting Corpora-
tion for New York City listening. Mother was nervous as ever
about taking on something new. As always, the more she
trembled at a prospect, the greater the effort she put in. She
took to radio as an encouragement to me and also for the sake
of Anna. All Mother's pay was funneled to her daughter to
help with her debts.

The plight of the Boettigers' newspaper grew worse in spite
of the efforts made to salvage it. John's fluctuating moods
were settling down into steady despair. The marriage could
not hold up under the strain much longer.

Agonizing over personal problems was not a Roosevelt

trait. On the whole, we preferred either to come up with an answer or at least make light of trouble if we could. Mother, however, was not amused when her Aunt Maude Gray, Grandma Hall's ancient daughter with the red-dyed hair, joked that "Totty"—an old nickname for Mother—ought to marry Bernie Baruch. He would be dead after a week, Maude cackled, and then her niece could bail out Anna from the proceeds of his estate.

Franklin also liked the sound of "Draft Eisenhower!" and moved into the leadership of the action in New York. That brought another emissary from Washington to Mother's doorstep, asking with the utmost delicacy what her son was up to. She let Mr. Truman know what she thought about that encounter. "I would not presume to dictate to my children or to anyone else what their actions should be. I have not and I do not intend to have any part in pre-convention activities."

She maintained professional friendships with an astonishing variety of people: international statesmen, politicians of various colorations, union bosses, philanthropists. Dave Dubinsky of the International Ladies Garment Workers Union was one of her friends, and Walter Reuther of the United Auto Workers another. A donor to a charity she supported could claim her as a friend, like Harry Brandt, a movie-theater mogul who gave to the Cancer Society. Concern for black equality kept her in touch with leaders such as Mary McCloud Bethune and Walter White of the National Association for the Advancement of Colored People.

She enjoyed company as diverse as that of Fannie Hurst, novelist and latter-day advocate of something akin to transcendental meditation, and Lady Stella Reading, wife of the British ambassador to Washington in the era of Lucy Mercer. Lady Stella, organizer of her country's Women's Voluntary Services during the war, was invariably among the first to welcome Mother on her trips to England. The hospitality was returned on our side of the ocean.

"Oh, how *lovely* to see you!" Mother would beam, and it was meant sincerely, which was not always the case when some others rang the doorbell. She and Stella were one of a kind in size and energy. My sometimes irreverent fancy was tickled to see these two imposing ladies advance on each other to join in majestic embrace.

Her affiliations with the unions as well as influence with the liberals made Mother's endorsement vital for the President. He needed not only workingmen's votes but cash contributions, too, when campaign money was at such a low ebb that there was danger of funds running out before election day.

In our household, I did not go so far as Mother in backing organized labor's drive for power by way of the closed shop. We thrashed out our differences in habitual style one day—she delighted in any exchange of opinions provided the rules of good manners were observed.

"How can you work for the idea of the closed shop," I asked her, "when it means a man must belong to a specified union to hold on to his job?"

"Well, for the *most* part it's healthy because then he has an organization behind him to fight for his *welfare.*"

"But you carry this too far. In many cases, a closed shop excludes people who are members of a different union that they firmly believe in. One union picks up a total of fifty-one per cent of the votes in a company election and then takes over, driving out all its rivals. That isn't democracy."

"Yes," Mother nodded, "I understand you. But nothing is *perfect.* In my belief, if a majority of people vote to belong to a particular union, then the minority should go along and have the one union represent every worker in the company, so that management isn't in a position to play one against the other."

"Draft Eisenhower!" died aborning just before the primaries when Ike, principles on parade, wrote to a New Hampshire newspaper. "The necessary and wise subordination of the military to civil power will be best sustained," he declared, "when life-long professional soldiers, in the absence of some obvious and overriding reasons, abstain from seeking high political office. . . . Nothing in the international or domestic situation especially qualifies for the most important office in the world a man whose adult years have been spent in the military forces.''

I was not one of those who cried "Amen!" Ike, in my estimation, would make a better President than anyone else in sight. Mother clung to her seat on the fence, and there was nothing Truman could do to coax her down.

Somewhere along the line, I wanted her to have something that she had declined in the past—a likeness of herself painted by a top-notch portraitist. Father once had the same idea as a surprise for her, and on his behalf an artist was commissioned to follow her around Hyde Park and Manhattan, making surreptitious sketches in preparation for the picture. When it was presented to her at a family gathering, she burst into tears and ran up to her bedroom, crying, "It's hideous, *hideous*! I hate it!" Father thereupon kept it hanging over his study door.

Now that her looks were so singularly improved by the beautiful new teeth, I thought it time to try again. She promised to sit for Douglas Chandor, who had a deserved reputation for portraying handsome ladies, and he and I agreed on a fee of $2,000. She found no fault with the painting when it was delivered, only with the bill. Chandor was so well satisfied with the finished work that the price had risen to $10,000.

Mother would not dream of allowing me to pay. "It's too expensive, Elliott, and you know it. As a matter of *principle*, I cannot permit you to accept.'' So one more effort to give her something which she might be pleased to hang on her walls came to nothing. Three more Presidents had to come and go before the portrait found a home. Lady Bird Johnson bought it from Mrs. Chandor for display in the White House. I am not sure what Pat Nixon did with it.

The General Assembly was scheduled to meet in Paris toward the end of September. Mother took off, leaving Truman still in the dark over whether he might look forward to her endorsement. The Democrats who remained after the drift to Wallace from the left of the party and to Thurmond from the right had reluctantly nominated Truman, with Alben Barkley for Vice-President. Only the one-time "Senator from Pendergast" talked with any conviction about beating Tom Dewey.

Truman devised his strategy with no help from Mother or any of her followers. The high-sounding Republican platform contained many an FDR measure: extended social security, broadened civil rights, federal housing, and a national health scheme. The President called back the Congress that had blocked him for the past two years into special session on July 26—"Turnip Day in Missouri," as he noted cheerfully.

He confronted the lawmakers with bills to hold down prices and meet the critical shortage of housing. Congress had to put up or shut up; either pass laws that would undercut the Republicans and strengthen his chances, or once again sit tight and ignore him. The legislators chose to sit tight—and they delivered themselves into his hands. The strategy of his campaigning was made to order. David would battle Goliath, his target "the no good, do nothing Eightieth Congress" that balked at improving conditions for the American people.

He set off to reach as many of those people as he could at the lowest possible cost, hoping to God that the money would trickle in from somewhere. The drab-green Presidential special rolled out of its railroad siding, and Harry Truman was on his way, lashing the enemy at every whistle stop. In Albuquerque, New Mexico, a voice in the crowd bellowed, "Give 'em hell, Harry!"—which described exactly what he was doing. But twice on his travels it was nip and tuck whether there would be enough cash to continue.

Just before she left for Paris, Mother had dashed off one column giving lukewarm backing to the Democrats without mentioning the candidate by name. A day or so after arrival, she received a telephone call from Frances Perkins, none too happy that in party councils she, the first woman Cabinet member in the country's history, was put in the shade by Mother.

Frances had some stinging news to deliver: Drew Pearson, Washington columnist and radio commentator, was saying that since Mother had not spoken up for Truman, it could be assumed that she was a secret adherent of Dewey. What answer did she intend to make about that?

Mother pondered for a moment. Dewey was bound to win, she thought, but perhaps there was a possibility of saving the best of the liberals in the November landslide; Adlai, for example, and Helen Gahagan Douglas, California New Dealer who had won a Congressional seat in 1944 and was a frequent White House guest with her actor husband, Melvyn.

Another consideration entered into Mother's thinking. In almost every respect, she and the President were polar opposites. He had been born on a poor Missouri farm; her background had been moneyed for generations after Claes Martenszen Van Roosevelt landed from Holland in New Amsterdam in the 1640's. Truman was a product of the Kansas City political machine; and she despised bossism and everything that went with it. He was brash and outgoing; she was a guilt-ridden introvert. But he had courage in abundance, a quality Mother respected in anyone, and no man was putting up a gamer fight than Truman.

From Paris, she finally sent him an open letter: "I am unqualifiedly for you as the Democratic candidate for the Presidency." Liberals and labor would take note, but she had no faith in his winning. "There are two things that I wish to avoid above all else," she said in private. "One is war, the second is a Republican victory." Only a month remained to voting day.

Meantime, there was more congenial work to be done, and fresh disappointment in store. "I believe," Marshall told her before their departure for the French capital, "that this session of the General Assembly will be remembered as the human rights session." Nearly two years of drafting, wrangling and patching had brought the Universal Declaration of Human Rights to the verge of completion, together with the covenant which, on signing, would legally bind a government to observe the terms of the declaration.

Mother was a changed woman as a result of the past two

years. She had learned the business of give-and-take which she previously scorned as manifesting lack of precious principle. She was flexible in argument now where she had been rigid. She recognized that every question was many-sided, not a clear-cut matter of right or wrong. If Father had lived, she would no longer have rushed to contradict him when he traced out his point on a tablecloth and tried to explain, "You may have to go clear around the woods and come in from the other side."

The lessons had not been easy. Some meetings left her dazed by the complexity of the task. At others, she would remove her spectacles, which automatically deprived her of her hearing aid, and catnap for a while, relying on a friendly nudge to awaken her if a television camera peered in her direction. As Madam Chairman, she would slam down her gavel so hard it made the water pitcher jump, as when she shrilled at Dr. Pavlov, "We are here to devise ways of safeguarding human rights. We are *not* here to attack each other's governments, and I hope when we return on Monday the delegate of the Soviet Union will remember that." One more crash of the gavel. "Meeting *adjourned!*"

She had presided on the rostrum and sometimes over the teacups to iron out misunderstandings and thrust ahead. When the conversation got too deep for her, she just kept on pouring tea. She listened to China's Dr. Peng-Chun Chang, who had as many proverbs to quote as Mao Tse-tung, suggest they study the philosophies of Confucius for a month or two and profit from the sage's teaching that the road to salvation lay only within the human heart.

Lebanon's Dr. Charles Malik advocated the doctrines of Saint Thomas Aquinas, the "angelic doctor," who set forth the fundamentals of thirteenth-century Catholicism. Moslems argued that the wording of the article covering religious freedom contradicted what the Koran stipulated. The British, speaking for the Labor government in London, reflected that freedom from want and total personal liberty were irreconcilable. Eighteen nations were represented on the Commission on Human Rights. No two of them thought in the same terms, with the exception of the Soviet bloc, which kept up a concerted drumfire of propaganda against the West.

She also had problems with the lawyers on the secretariat. She felt on safe ground during the legal haggling over how the declaration should be phrased. Everything must be stated in the simplest terms, she ruled repeatedly. That other declaration, written in 1776, was the model to follow. But what truths could this contentious committee hold to be "self-evident"?

"That all men are created equal"? Not a bit of it. Madame Hansa Mehta, representing India, objected to this as flagrant discrimination against women. "Nobody in *my* country sees it that way," Mother explained, but Madam Chairman lost the round. The final draft began, "Whereas recognition of the inherent dignity and of the equal and inalienable rights of all members of the human family is the foundation of freedom, justice and peace in the world. . . ."

Madame Mehta had more reservations about Article 26 dealing with the right to education. A preliminary draft declared that this extended to primary, secondary and higher levels of schooling. Another objection from Madame Mehta. "Our economy is strained," she said, "and we are trying only to give all children a primary education. What would happen if we suddenly attempted to provide secondary and higher education too?" She wanted an amendment: each country should be privileged to set its own gradual pace.

Mother shook her head. "The trouble with that is that I do not believe the United States Senate would ever ratify a treaty so vaguely worded. The senators would ask, 'What does gradually *mean*—five years or ten or a hundred?' I just don't believe they would accept it."

The separate rights guaranteed by the American Constitution for the forty-eight states (Alaska and Hawaii were not in the Union yet) were a stumbling block. She was compelled to give an impromptu course in constitutional history to allay many delegations' resentment at being asked to agree to blanket commitments while the United States seemed always to

be searching for loopholes to protect these mysterious
"states' rights."

The final draft of Committee Three's declaration was ready
for submission to the entire General Assembly in Paris. She
was foolish enough, she said afterwards, to imagine all would
be plain sailing from now on. She had not reckoned with the
Communists, who had the committee reconsider the document, every paragraph, every word, every comma. Two more
months would be spent before each *whereas* and all the thirty
articles were reapproved. The late nights and early mornings
demanded by Mother to meet her deadlines wore out Tommy.

At the bidding of Lucius Clay, Mother took one day off for
a flying visit to Germany. There had been a sudden about-face
in United States policy toward the West Germans. The Soviet
blockade of Berlin made it essential, in Washington's assessment, to have German support and let the crimes of Hitler and
his Nazis fade into history. The airlift over the Russian zone
had been Truman's answer to the Russians. In 321 days of
American and British missions, well over two million tons of
food and coal were delivered to Berliners.

Mother's presence was requested in Stuttgart as part of the
process of wooing West Germany. Clay wanted her to talk to
a group of women doctors. Some careful thinking preceded
her reply. Her wartime speeches denouncing Nazi persecu-
tion of Jews had engulfed her in abuse from German propa-
gandists. Both my parents enjoyed top priority on Hitler's
death list. She had no illusions about the loathing the Germans
must have for the American occupation army, but she agreed
to face the Stuttgart audience. It would be cowardly to refuse.

She sensed bitterness in the air when she was escorted in,
exactly as she had anticipated. It did not bother her or tempt
her to tone down her words. She began by condemning the
deeds of the Nazis every bit as vehemently as in the past. "I
had no intention of letting their coldness prevent me from saying certain things I had in my mind," she said afterwards.

Her view of Germany was another legacy from Father. After two world wars, the Germans must be kept from starting a third. She used to remind us children of the conditions he had laid down for them under an Allied occupation: "No aircraft of any kind, not even a glider. No uniforms. No marching." She was incapable of adjusting that view after Henry Morgenthau reported what Father had said to him at Warm Springs on the night of April 11, 1945. Henry left convinced of FDR's determination "not to allow any sentimental considerations to modify the conditions necessary to prevent Germany and the German people from becoming aggressive again." The drifting away from Father's steely concept, more obvious these days than before, was something else she attributed to Churchill's influence.

Her criticism was laid on hard and strong in the Stuttgart hall, and the atmosphere grew icy. "The German *people*," she reiterated, "must bear their share of the blame." Her feelings relieved, she turned to subjects more palatable to the audience's appetite: the fortitude the Germans were showing in Berlin; their defiance of Communist power; their future under newfound democracy; the United Nations' role in assuring peace. "And now I extend to you the hand of friendship and cooperation!" The restraint of the applause did not surprise her; it was preferable to "Sieg Heil!"

Like the pollsters, Tom Dewey and every living Republican, she was amazed the morning after election day to hear that Truman was the winner and that Congress had Democratic majorities once again. Helen Gahagan Douglas was in for another term, and Adlai was the astonished Governor-elect of Illinois. Mother had wondered whether a Republican victory would spell the end of her work as a United Nations envoy. Bearing no ill will for her long-delayed endorsement, the President set her doubts at rest by reappointing her.

She was seldom given to rejoicing. Once a goal had been set, an earthquake was needed to alter it. What mattered was having four more years of trying to steer Truman closer to her paths. Liberals must not let lucky Congressmen forget what they owed to the progressives and organized labor. Still in Paris, she turned over in her mind how to explain her long-term views to the President at their next meeting.

"Our real battlefield today is Asia," she would tell him on her return, "and our real battle is the one between democracy and communism." The downtrodden peoples of the world, prey to the communists, must be supplied with tangible proof that "democracy really brings about happier and better conditions."

The human rights declaration came up for General Assembly vote at last at three o'clock in the morning at the Palais de Chaillot on December 10. A future Secretary-General, Burma's U Thant, would characterize it as "the Magna Carta of Mankind." Alexander Solzhenitsyn was to praise it as the best document the United Nations ever produced. It was largely Mother's doing.

"I used to think I had reached the limits of my patience in bringing up five children," she used to joke afterwards, "but I was mistaken. It took *much* more patience to preside over the Commission on Human Rights."

In language that the delegates had chewed over since 1946, "The General Assembly proclaims the Universal Declaration of Human Rights as a common standard of achievement for all peoples and all nations, to the end that every individual and every organ of society, keeping this Declaration constantly in mind, shall strive by teaching and education to promote respect for these rights and freedoms and by progressive measures, national and international, to secure their universal and effective recognition and observance, both among the peoples of Member States themselves and among the peoples of territories under their jurisdiction."

The heart that knew little rejoicing was not entirely satisfied with the outcome of the balloting—the perfectionist yearned for a unanimous Aye. Instead, forty-eight countries approved; two delegations stayed away; and the Soviet bloc led eight abstentions, contending that echoes of America's Bill of Rights sounded too loudly in this document at the expense of

the gospel according to Karl Marx. How to enforce this new
Magna Carta remained uncertain; no covenant was ready yet.
But when the votes were tallied, Madam Chairman of Committee Three glowed pink with pride as every delegate rose to
cheer her.

Christmas at Val-Kill was happy that year. She had survived the pain of the Millers' squabble. She had achieved the
most important goal she had ever aimed for in public life. And
for the moment harmony within the family promised to continue undisturbed. For the time being, she had succeeded
where she was certain she had previously failed—in becoming
a real mother to all of us. The mockery of it was that by our
own doing, we would see her fail at that once more.

One more event marked 1948, though she said not a word
about it. On August 1, after months of illness, Lucy died at
the age of fifty-seven in New York's Memorial Hospital, leaving one child, Barbara, married and living in Boston.

7

Val-Kill was Mother's sanctuary, where anxiety could temporarily be put aside and she could talk contentedly with family and friends in terms of what she pretended to be, a woman with no doubts about anything, too busy to spare a moment for regrets or remorse.

She was up every morning by seven o'clock to start the day with exercises on the bedroom floor. Their purpose was to keep her stomach muscles trim and control what she termed "my pot." Contrary to rumors of White House days, yoga was not part of the workout. She would lie on her back and count how many times she could raise and lower her upper body. In the course of time, she found she had to tuck her toes under the bed to continue doing sit-ups.

The daily dozen was followed by a cold shower, carrying out the spartan hygiene learned as a boarder at Mademoiselle Souvestre's. The pattern of schoolgirl habit did not change. She dressed at the same speed with which she once had scrambled into uniform in time for morning assembly.

Mother used no cosmetics beyond a light dusting of talcum

powder. She had the least vanity of any woman I have ever met, but she was sensitive about the neatness of her appearance. The only strain of pride in her dated back to schooldays, too. She was pleased to feel that she had enjoyed a *sound* education, with the accent on the classics of English literature— Shakespeare, Dickens, the poets and essayists who were studied in class at Allenswood.

"You ought to do something about your hair, Eleanor" was a continual complaint from Aunt Polly, whose well-defined widow's peak owed something to the sharp triangle painted with eyeshadow on her forehead. Her hair was an annoyance to Mother. She had to admit that the wispy gray strands did look untidy all too often. She kept them long and pinned up in a bun, yet the ends seemed perpetually eager to stray. She tried experimenting with a number of hairdressers and as many different styles, asking them to cut short, medium long or give her a permanent wave.

"I can't possibly come back to you for another ten days," she would tell them. "Can you suggest something that will stay neat and *presentable*"—a favorite word.

Still in her bathroom, she would pop down a daily ration of health pills—doses of vitamins A, B and especially C as prescribed by Dr. Gurewitsch. She did not know much about the vaunted benefits of vitamin E, but she firmly believed in the efficacy of garlic tablets in improving the memory.

By eight o'clock, she would be downstairs for breakfast, expecting everyone under her roof to keep to the same timetable. The meal was what the travel agents describe as English-style, starting with orange juice—Mother preferred lemon—and progressing to bacon and egg, toast and marmalade. Her own coffee was half diluted with warm milk, another legacy of the years with Mademoiselle Souvestre.

Straight after breakfast, she headed into the kitchen to write out the day's menu for the cook. Imaginative meal-planning was not a forte of Mother's. Luncheons and dinners were likely to be a stereotyped choice between steak, lamb chops or chicken.

If this were the morning of the week for changing the bed
linen, she would make her way upstairs to the closet to pull
out the sheets and pillowcases, which made an impressive pile
when more than a dozen overnight guests might be staying in
the three cottages. Bed-making was left to the maid or to
Tommy if there was no maid on call.

With the household taken care of for the present, Mother
would pace into Tommy's sitting room-office to start on the
day's mail, whose volume never decreased. Most of the
morning would be gone before that job was finished. She liked
to do some of the marketing herself sometimes, taking off
down the hill to the general store in the village or shopping at
roadside stands along Route 9 for fresh fruit and vegetables to
bring back in the trunk of the car.

When the weather was warm enough, she would fit in a
swim in the outdoor pool, occasionally taking an uneasy dive
off the board, with a frown on her face and her nose squeezed
between a finger and thumb. She had been doing this for more
than half a century, ever since Uncle Ted inspired his trembling ten-year-old niece to screw up her courage and jump off
the dock at Oyster Bay, Long Island, then ducked her when
she came up spluttering. Like it or not, diving was good for
character.

Taking it easy for a while after lunch was something of a
tradition at Val-Kill for everyone but Mother. She went to
work again with Tommy, checking over the copy for "My
Day" before a messenger arrived around two o'clock to pick
it up for delivery to United Features and then tackling a new
column. As soon as there were flowers in bloom, she would go
out to snip a basketful, enough to fill a vase in each guest
room and elsewhere around the house, with some blooms left
over to take to Washington Square to present to friends. Florists' elaborate bouquets had no appeal for her, but a gift of a
few garden roses or a bunch of black-eyed susans picked in
the fields were sure to please.

Tea was served every afternoon, with Mother pouring. A
silver pot and the Meissen china were reserved for distin-

guished guests, but no matter who was there, she would spark some lively debating until duty called and she returned to her chores with Tommy.

Unless the rain was hard or the snow deep, she took an hour's walk through the woods every day. Fala was her only companion if she had something to turn over in her mind, or a guest or two would be included if she wanted a chance to hold an uninterrupted conversation. In wool socks and a pair of roomy shoes, she strode along the trails at such speed that companions found it hard to keep up with her.

Dinner called for changing her dress and putting on a piece of jewelry or two. She had such internal solitude that she disliked dining alone; there were always several at table. The discussions were in the hands of Madam Chairman, bearing in mind what was most likely to interest the company and provide her with the opportunity to explore her guests' opinions. Coffee and liqueurs, one more sign of her expanding tolerance, were served to maintain the talking until about eleven o'clock. We were then provided with a firm hint. "Well, my children, it's going to be a hard day tomorrow, so it might be a good idea if we thought about retiring." Anyone up to the age of fifty might be addressed as a member of the younger generation. Should the exchange of views be brisk, bedtime was deferred as late as one o'clock.

She would climb the stairs to brush her hair and tie it back in a pony tail with a blue ribbon, as she had when she was her father's Little Nell. A plain, floor-length nightgown, cotton in summer and wool in winter, was bedtime wear; she wore an old blue robe over it and equally ancient slippers while she brushed her teeth.

By the bed with its uncompromising, hard mattress, she knelt to say her nightly prayers. "Our Father, who has set a restlessness in our hearts and made us all seekers after that which we can never fully find, forbid us to be satisfied with what we make of life. Draw us from base content and set our eyes on faroff goals. Keep us at tasks too hard for us that we may be driven to Thee for strength. Deliver us from fretful-

ness and self-pitying; make us sure of the good we cannot see
and of the hidden good in the world. Open our eyes to simple
beauty all around us and our hearts to the loveliness men hide
from us because we do not try to understand them. Save us
from ourselves and show us a vision of the world made new.''

During the week, when she worked in New York, her personal routine was much the same, though there was no swimming and Fala was walked on a leash around Washington
Square. Faye and I rented an apartment of our own on the
north side. A limousine whisked Mother to and from Lake
Success, while the great glass-fronted oblong that was to be
United Nations headquarters, paid for by the $65 million loan
authorized by Truman the previous summer, took shape
alongside the East River at the foot of Forty-second Street.

The principal labor facing Mother and the Commission on
Human Rights these days was drafting the covenant. Or
should it be two covenants for the sake of expediency, one a
contract encompassing humanity's social and working life,
the other covering politics and civil freedoms? She and most
of her American confrères thought the dividing would pro-
duce better speed, but the Soviets and others immediately disagreed. Splitting off social and economic rights, they argued,
would tempt some governments to ignore them and accept
only the less important obligations concerning political and
civil liberty.

She could see no end to the squabbling. Madam Chairman
would just have to bear with it again. But the declaration
alone was to be a kind of monument. When the time came for
emerging Third World nations in Africa and other new states
such as Cyprus, Jamaica and Trinidad to write constitutions
for themselves, they would include human rights as the declaration spelled them out. The impact of what she and Committee Three accomplished was, she concluded, ''much greater
than most Americans suspect.''

At United Nations headquarters, she was a stellar attraction for sightseers. Visitors on guided tours chattered with ex-

citement when they caught a glimpse of her pacing down the halls or standing in line to lunch at the cafeteria. The same thing happened on planes and trains or if she stopped the car to use a washroom.

"I can't understand all this *attention*," she used to say to us. "I'm quite sure I don't deserve it." But without question she was a public figure of towering dimensions, and beginning to accept the fact that she was famous.

The day was approaching when the Roosevelts would have to leave Washington Square. The radio show caught on fast. Roosevelt Enterprises, Incorporated, had two hundred stations on the line before we were through. Her apartment was no place for running a business, nor was Faye's and mine. If Tommy was out, Mother had to answer her own telephone—occasionally if she was busy in a disguised voice as "Mrs. Roosevelt's secretary." When Anna Polenz, the one maid, was off somewhere, Mother would greet callers at the front door.

One evening, a harassed woman came looking for the maid to see whether she would fill in for a babysitter who had let her down. It happened to be the maid's day off, so Mother pinch-hit in her servant's place, taking charge of the infant when its mother left, changing diapers, feeding a night-time bottle, tucking the baby into bed, then carefully putting the rubber nipple to soak before the parent returned.

I felt that goodness of heart could make Mother dangerously accessible when threats against her life from the Roosevelt-haters turned up regularly in the mail and over the telephone. Somewhere safer and, I hoped, better equipped had to be found for the important partner in our booming business.

We moved into the Park Sheraton Hotel on West 56th Street, not far from Central Park. Mother was cheerful about the suite we shared. The bedroom was hers, while I slept on a daybed in the sitting room, which was a poor arrangement when we worked late and callers showed up early. Tommy had a room next door and hated it. Leaving the apartment had been a wrench for her, though it was Mother's hope that Tommy, visibly aging, would find life easier in these new quarters. Roosevelt Enterprises had an office on another floor.

We recorded programs four and five at a time in the dining room to a tight schedule. It made for hectic days of guests arriving and departing on the button. Mother handled them with practiced skill, unruffled as she ushered them off with, "Oh, dear! I have enjoyed this *so* much, but that must be my *next* appointment."

She was eager to venture into an allied activity. I was negotiating a contract with NBC television, again with part of her pay check destined to help Anna in Phoenix. The format was easy to find. We would duplicate the scene I had witnessed on countless occasions at Val-Kill and invite world celebrities—Albert Einstein, for example—to come to the hotel on Sunday afternoons and converse with Mother on live television while she poured the tea in front of cameras in the ballroom. The set would look like the corner of a paneled library—a silver teapot and fine china would be used as props. During the run of these hour-long shows, I asked Winston if he would join her over the teacups. He sent his regrets.

Meantime, she had another commission for me. Would I consent to act as her literary agent? The manuscript of the second volume of her reminiscences was, we considered, in publishable form. Admittedly, she had winnowed her recollections with some care as she carried her story forward from 1924 to Father's death. A reader would have no clue to the existence of Lucy Mercer Rutherfurd or know that my parents had ever exchanged an angry word.

Mother reverted to her practice of leaving her meaning clear to those of us who were aware of the untold story and could read between the lines. "I do not claim to be entirely objective about him," she wrote of Father, "but there are some things I know that I feel sure nobody else can know." He was "particularly susceptible to people," and "he made an effort to give each person who came in contact with him the feeling that he understood what his particular interest was." Without a doubt, she was thinking of Lucy when she set down those words.

Bruce Gould was sadly disappointed with her evasions, though she had undertaken the revision of some sections of manuscript at his urging. *This I Remember,* as the book was to be called, was vastly inferior to *This Is My Story,* he thought, but she did not see how she could find time to go along with his suggestion and tackle the whole job again with a ghostwriter.

George Bye, her current agent, was inclined to side with Gould as many an agent would rather than risk a run-in with one of the most influential editors of the day. Tommy and I had audience with the editor of *Ladies' Home Journal* in his Rockefeller Plaza sanctum. His magazine's most eager rival in the race for circulation was *McCall's,* edited by Otis L. Wiese, more accommodating than Gould, whose standards were uncompromising.

The outcome was that Wiese bought *This I Remember* for $150,000 sight unseen, with no changes asked for, and took over Mother's monthly questions-and-answers feature at $3,000 an installment—$500 more than the *Journal* had been paying—under a five-year contract that was renewed throughout her life. Bruce Gould had few regrets. *McCall's* did pick up circulation, but not enough to catch up with his magazine, and he still thought Mother's memoirs were substandard. While the iron was hot, I approached United Features Syndicate, and the rates for "My Day" went up too.

It seemed certain that 1949 would be Mother's most secure financial year yet, with half the money from Wiese allotted to Tommy. Her gratification was short-lived. A fresh set of cracks was appearing in the roof that Mother raised with such effort over our family.

Franklin decided he would be first out of the box in running for political office. Granny in her day had taken it for granted that according to primogeniture her eldest grandson, Jimmy, would succeed Father at the top of the pyramid. Father had similar hopes until ill health and divorce from Betsy cut short

Jimmy's possible White House career. In California, he was taking his time about returning to the national scene.

The track was clear for Franklin. He had the name, energy, a commanding presence, and he would be thirty-five years old in August. He was falling behind the timetable achieved by Father: New York State senator at twenty-eight and nominated for Vice-President ten years later.

Mother was thrilled when Franklin announced that he would seek Sol Bloom's seat in the House of Representatives when the owlish little Congressman retired in May. What was more, my brother would run as a liberal Democrat on Manhattan's West Side against a candidate of Tammany Hall. "It's a *very* fine thing for Franklin to do, to fight the machine," she told me. "I think he's making *exactly* the right move. I'm sure he will do well. How wonderful it would be to have him in Washington, standing up for the same things as Father!"

"I guess he'll probably make it. He'll put up a darn good fight, anyway. I'll go and help if he wants me."

Her face clouded over for a moment. "I'm rather disturbed about his marriage. I gather that he and Ethel are having *difficulties*. I believe that he may be interested in another young lady. I do hope that everything will be straightened out."

It was not. Early in April, Ethel appeared in Reno, seeking divorce, the sixth involving one of Mother's children so far. An aspiring politician is bound to weigh the potential damage caused by a marital breakup at an election time, but this event was dealt with calmly and free of scandal. On May 18, Franklin won handily over Tammany's man, and on May 22 Ethel was granted what she wanted.

He had asked my help in the campaign, and he asked it again in letting Mother know that a new bride was in the offing. Susan Perrin lived with her parents on Long Island, not far from the house into which Franklin and Ethel moved after he came back from the war. Miss Perrin had performed sterling work for my brother during his run for Congress.

Mother was not surprised. Her affection for Franklin did not falter. "If he made a mistake and he and Ethel grew apart from each other, I don't think anyone should be *blamed,*" she said.

She was happy to attend the September wedding in Susan's mother's New York apartment and stay on for the reception, careful not to overshadow bride or groom as Uncle Ted had done on her wedding day. Mother had a new daughter-in-law to befriend and draw into the family that was so eternally restless in its emotional involvements.

An infinitely more wounding blow had struck her by then. The Boettigers' newspaper was on its last legs in spite of everything she had done to save it. "You must pitch in and do all you can to help each other," she exhorted us as an article of faith. Jimmy personally had raised money like Mother, including some of his own, and cosigned notes for further loans to Anna and her husband.

But there was no longer a chance of fending off *The Arizona Times'* collapse. Losing the struggle disrupted John Boettiger's thinking. He deserted Anna, who was left to close down the house in Phoenix at the same time that debts swamped her. Her plight worsened as her health failed. The pallor and loss of weight were finally diagnosed as "desert fever" when X-rays revealed a condition of the lungs not unlike tuberculosis. She was admitted to a California hospital and stayed bedridden for months.

It was then that Mother truly took Anna back into her heart. The part my sister had played in helping to reinstall Lucy and frustrate my parents' reconciliation was completely obliterated. Money to live on, to pay the medical bills and to reduce the debts came from Mother's pocket. She made no attempt to censure either Anna or John Boettiger, for whom her deep affection turned to pity. Life was too hard for its victims to be condemned, no matter what they did.

Her youngest child was also in difficulty. The Beverly Hills store that my brother Johnny opened after leaving Walter Kirchner had gone under, and he was unemployed. He had tried to find other jobs, his letter said, but with no success. Could Mother do anything for him? Her first obligation, as she saw it, was to make living easier for all of us and try to put us firmly on the road to personal happiness.

"Wouldn't it be possible, Elliott, to take him into our office and offer him work as an assistant while he looks around for something he might prefer to do?"

"No problem. We're in good financial shape. I'd be delighted to have him."

"Perhaps he and his family would like to live in Stone Cottage. That would be quite *convenient* for him to travel from there to New York, and maybe he could have a small apartment in the city to stay in during the week."

And so it was arranged. We brought Johnny, his family and furniture from Pasadena, she turned over Stone Cottage to him, and he was taken into Roosevelt Enterprises at a salary of $2,000 a month. Eventually, he would be given a half interest in the Hyde Park property I owned.

Johnny and his wife Anne quickly became fixtures on the Val-Kill scene, and he settled down at Roosevelt Enterprises, more than earning his keep. Mother, the protector of her brood, felt reassured again with three of her sons close by and Jimmy warming up in Democratic Party affairs in California, planning to run for Governor next year. Everyone was provided for except Anna, and Mother would make sure that the rest of us would continue to care for her.

Self-doubt was being buried deeper and deeper. Mother felt increasingly like Uncle Ted in the enjoyment of a good fight. It was not beyond the stretch of imagination to conclude that she provoked her tussle that summer with Francis Cardinal Spellman, the rotund prelate of New York who had been an irritant to her for years and years.

The roots of Mother's antagonism to the Catholic Church, which was thinly disguised for public purposes, could be traced like so much else in her character to her childhood. To her mind, Catholicism and political corruption were inextricably entangled. She was barely in her teens when fresh scandal erupted around Tammany Hall, where the John Kellys, Tom Gradys and a cabal of other Irish Catholics had held court for the past half century while they perfected a machine organization to control the city and state of New York and put government up for sale at the bargain counter.

Her reading of history persuaded her that almost from the day of its founding in 1789, the fraternal Tammany Society had been a lair of predators. Tammany had sold the New York State vote to the Republicans in 1888 to get Grover Cleveland out of the White House and Benjamin Harrison in. It had survived the reign of Boss Tweed, jailed for bribery, but as an impressionable orphan Mother must have heard the rumblings in Grandma Hall's Republican household over the latest uproar. Tammany had been caught peddling favors again.

She was twenty-six when Father, a young State senator in Albany, led a revolt against Tammany's choice of one of its drones to fill a U.S. Senate seat. "This fellow is still young," growled Boss Tim Sullivan. "Wouldn't it be safer to drown him before he grows up?" The punishment meted out to one of Father's followers who ran a little rural newspaper was her first direct lesson in Tammany tactics. The official notices whose publication provided most of his income came his way no more, and he was driven out of business.

"My blood boiled," Mother remembered. "I realized that you might be a slave and not a public servant if your bread and butter could be taken from you."

The one Irish Catholic she worked for with any show of enthusiasm was Al Smith, and then only because he could be used to coax Father back into public life after his attack of polio when Granny was cajoling him to retire into an invalid's life at Hyde Park. Smith was a link with the past, when Father had been physically unimpaired. He had seconded the cigar-chomping East Sider's nomination for the Presidency in 1920 but to no avail. The Democrats picked James M. Cox, who chose Father as his running mate, though Boss Murphy acknowledged, "I don't like Roosevelt." Tammany found Father as artful as a mongoose circling a snake.

Not Cox and Roosevelt but the Warren Harding–Cal Coolidge ticket was elected, of course. Polio and his struggle to walk kept Father in the wings until, thanks primarily to Louis Howe, he was ready to reappear on stage and again nominate Smith, the "Happy Warrior," for the White House.

Mother's feelings were decidedly mixed. Catholics, she was convinced, owed basic allegiance to their church, not to their country. A Catholic President would spell unknown peril for the United States, but the risk must be taken for the sake of reactivating Father. Anyway, she fancied Smith's chances of winning his party's nod were no brighter than before. Her instinct was right. John W. Davis, starchy Wall Street lawyer, was the sacrificial lamb selected by the Democrats for preordained slaughter by Cal Coolidge.

She felt happier about campaigning for Al, a Tammany man to his manicured fingertips, when he ran that same fall for the governorship of New York against her cousin Ted, Theodore's eldest son. If a Catholic *had* to hold public office, far better and safer in Albany than in Washington. Ted had served as Assistant Navy Secretary under Harding. The private sale of federal oil reserves in Wyoming's Teapot Dome fields during Harding's brief but cankerous term was a sizzling campaign issue. Mother let herself be talked into trailing Cousin Ted around the state in a car on whose roof a huge teapot spouted steam. Smith won the election, but she was ashamed of stooping so low to render him aid. She vowed never to repeat such unprincipled tricks.

On his third bid for the Presidency, Al was finally nominated in 1928 to take the field against Herbert Hoover. Smith beseeched Father, a proven political attraction, to try for the job he was vacating, mainly to help Al carry New York State. In a landslide Republican year, Father was elected Governor by 25,564 skimpy ballots. Smith lost his home State by more than 100,000, and Hoover was declared the winner by 444 electoral votes to Al's 87.

Once Father was installed in Albany, Mother's enthusiasm for Smith faded fast. She had compromised with her prejudices too long. Al, she was to confide obliquely in her mem-

Mother, as she looked in 1945, the year of father's death.

UPI (Acme) photo

Winston Churchill comes to Hyde Park to pay his respects at the grave of his old friend Franklin Delano Roosevelt, on March 12, 1946. He is accompanied by mother.

Mother joins Senator Connally, Senator Vandenburg, and Secretary of State Stettinius in preparing to board the liner *Queen Elizabeth* on the way as delegates to the first United Nations regular meeting in London, 1946.

UPI (Acme) photo

UPI (Acme) photo

President Truman had great respect and affection for mother, despite their frequent differences over foreign policy. Here they confer in early 1946.

Mother often faced the intransigence of Soviet Foreign Minister Viacheslav Molotov and UN delegate Andrei Gromyko (center) at the UN, as in this picture taken in late 1946.

UPI (Acme) photo

Mother holds up for inspection her greatest contribution to the advancement of mankind—the United Nations Declaration of Universal Human Rights. The document was ratified at Lake Success, New York, in 1949.

Mother addresses the General Assembly of the United Nations in October, 1952.

Franklin D. Roosevelt Library

Mother devoted much time to helping Israel to raise development funds. In 1952 she traveled througout Israel to view agricultural and industrial projects. Here she inspects the Jordan River project.

Mother met with Golda Meir in January, 1949, when both were serving at the United Nations.

Photo by Leo Rosenthal

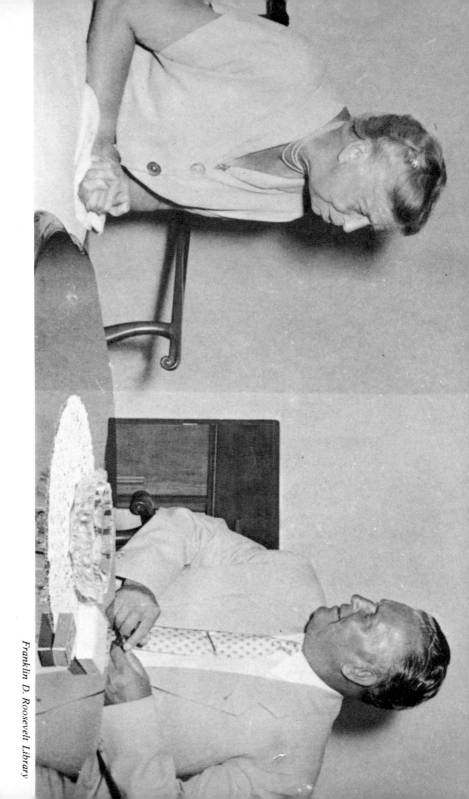

In 1953 Mother visited Yugoslavia and met with Marshal Tito at Brioni, his summer capital.

Franklin D. Roosevelt Library

Mother considered Adlai Stevenson to be by far the most qualified man to be President in 1952, 1956, and 1960. Here she joins him at the 1956 Democratic National Convention in Chicago.

Mother on her trip to Japan in 1953 visits the Memorial Tower at Hiroshima.

Even in 1960, mother spurned assistance in carrying her belongings while traveling. Here she is at the Washington airport in 1960.

oirs, "had certain shortcomings" because he "had spent the greater part of his life in one state, and practically in one city." She applauded Father, whom Smith had imagined he could dominate, when he cut off the patronage which Al had dispensed so liberally and cold-shouldered Al's cronies. A fitful creature whenever she tried to figure out her destiny in those days, Mother declared that she would never again talk politics in public.

She failed to see why Governor Roosevelt, with his eyes already fixed on the Presidency, was so reluctant to confront Tammany head on. Surely this was an obligation he should feel compelled to recognize. She wondered whether he had been converted to her straight-line approach when, in his second Albany term, he took aim at another son of the Society in the person of Jimmy Walker, Irish Catholic dandy and mayor of New York City. Father needed Tammany's support in an attempt at the White House, but on balance he needed a spotless record more.

He went clear around the woods to attain both objectives by first uncovering corruption, then condoning Walker's resignation so that Tammany's grand sachems could not accuse him of firing their fellow chieftain.

Father's pragmatism saved him from bigotry. What counted was converting the maximum number of voters—be they Catholics, Jews or Anabaptists—to his way of thinking. He made a point of having Catholic secretaries in Missy and her deputy, Grace Tully, appreciating that they would be sure to find time on his calendar for appointments with Francis Spellman and his colleagues in the hierarchy. FDR was unshaken in his conviction that, face to face, he could bring any man or woman around to agreeing with him at least in part.

Mother disapproved. In her private opinion, cardinals, bishops, monsignors and the Vatican were in league with Tammany and cradle-Catholic politicians. Her bias was so embedded that in this area she was incapable of modeling her thinking on Father's.

There may have been an additional reason for her inflexibility. The untroubled face she presented to the world, her disregard of frills and furbelows, the fact that she stood close to six feet tall—from these Mother appeared to have no more than an ounce or two of femininity in her. But emotionally, she was vulnerable, and Mrs. Rutherfurd had been a Catholic.

One objective for which Cardinal Spellman and his church lobbied was winning government funds for parochial schools. Mother was adamant against any such tampering with Article One of the Bill of Rights: "Congress shall make no law respecting an establishment of religion. . . ." Church and state must remain separate entities as the founding fathers intended.

When the latest attempt was made in Congress to funnel public funds into Catholic institutions, she used her newspaper column late in June, 1949, to belabor it. She was frankly weary, she admitted at Val-Kill, of being criticized by Catholic prelates and laymen alike for her open-mindedness about divorce; her support of the Spanish loyalists in the 1936–1939 civil war and her success in the United Nations in blocking concessions for the Catholic victor in that war, Francisco Franco; her gentle words about birth control in her magazine articles; and her liberalism in general.

The cardinal allowed a month to pass before he counterattacked. In the interim, another court action added to her woes. John Boettiger filed for a divorce, and Anna promptly instructed her attorneys to bring a countersuit. One more Roosevelt marriage had failed.

The cardinal's open letter was released to the news media on July 22, the morning after it arrived by special delivery. Mother suspected that it had been composed at least in part in the Vatican. Her column, he fumed, could only be construed as a personal attack upon himself; she had deliberately misunderstood the position of the Church. All he sought from taxpayers' money was textbooks, some medical care and school busing. "And even though you may use your columns to attack me and accuse me of starting a controversy, I shall not again publicly acknowledge you. For, whatever you may say in the future, your record of anti-Catholicism stands for all to see—a record which you yourself wrote in the pages of history which cannot be recalled—documents of discrimination unworthy of an American mother!"

She needed nobody's help but Tommy's in firing off her reply that same day. I had never seen her lose control of anger until now. Within the family, she never raised her voice, no matter what the provocation, but today she was fuming. She fluttered with rage as she dictated. Readers of "My Day" were told that a personal letter would be forthcoming for the cardinal, who, she observed, had expressed himself "in what to him seems a Christian and kindly manner and I wish to do the same."

Did she ever! Her answers to correspondents were sometimes rattled off or left largely to Tommy. In this case, Mother employed the skills acquired over years of writing columns, books and magazine pieces to goad the ecclesiastic in her letter to him.

She could not say that "in European countries the control by the Roman Catholic Church of great areas of land has always led to happiness for the people of those countries. . . . Spiritual leadership should remain spiritual leadership and the temporal power should not become too important in any Church. . . . I assure you that I had no sense of being 'an unworthy American mother.' The final judgment, my dear Cardinal Spellman, of the worthiness of all human beings is in the hands of God."

Through the rest of July and into August, the confrontation was headlined in the press and in a whirlwind of letters exchanged between adherents on either side as if this were a championship bout, His Eminence versus First Lady. The mail sacks dropped off at Val-Kill were stuffed full of letters as always when Mother was making news again. Most of them backed her stand. She continued to seethe, with only brief relief when Anna's lawyers prevailed and the judge awarded her the decision over John Boettiger.

Analyzing the Spellman situation, Mother aired her suspicions. She detected maneuvering by the Vatican. "I do believe, Elliott, that what they are *really* after is to get an American ambassador appointed to Madrid. They are trying to *discredit* me with the United Nations."

A second impression darkened her mind. "I think they felt the time had come to form a Catholic party in this country and hoped it could be accomplished. It was a disappointment to them that it did not turn out quite the way they hoped."

Priests at Sunday masses, acting as though on signal, berated Mother from their pulpits. One dissonant voice was that of Bishop Bernard Sheil of Chicago, who spoke up for her. He had rendered similar service a decade earlier when he took to NBC radio to rally Catholic support for Father in repealing the embargo on arms shipments to Europe, which was frustrating Britain and France in facing Hitler Germany. Many Irish Americans were opposed then and afterwards to anything that would aid the detested British.

She stood her ground through the hot summer weeks. It fell to Ed Flynn, who she trusted to tell the truth as he saw it, to break the deadlock. By this time, the resurgence of blind hostility between the defenders on both sides had reached the point where Mother hinted to Truman that she would be willing to step down as United Nations ambassador. The President would hear of no such thing.

Flynn, of Irish blood and Catholic faith, contacted Pope Pius. The initial step toward an armistice was the drafting of a further letter to be signed by the cardinal at the Holy Father's suggestion. Ed the peacemaker approached Mother to find out whether she would approve the text in advance. *"I'm* not the one," she assured him stiffly, "who said I would have nothing to do with the cardinal." Her message was relayed to the chancery on Madison Avenue.

The telephone in Val-Kill Cottage brought a personal call for her from Spellman that evening. Might he send an emissary to show her the draft tomorrow morning? Why of *course!* she replied, equally urbane; she would be most happy to receive him.

The breakfast dishes had scarcely been carried away when an amiable priest presented himself at her door. She meantime had drafted a statement of her own, to be made public simultaneously with the cardinal's. She and her visitor went over both documents together, changing a word here, clearing up a point there. If the priest told her his name, she did not catch it. All she remembered about him was how he praised the schooling afforded French-Canadian children by Mother Church in Catholic Québec.

Once the statements were issued, the general conclusion was that the fracas was over. Without mentioning Mother, the cardinal spoke of "great confusion and regrettable misunderstandings"; she accepted his words as "clarifying and fair." He felt it advisable to demonstrate personally that all was forgiven when he let it be known that he would like to visit her. She invited him to lunch at his convenience.

One sultry day in August, she was at her desk, wondering how to fit in a swim, when Tommy hurried in. "Mrs. R., Cardinal Spellman is on the porch, and he wants to see you."

"Well, well!" Mother said in feigned surprise as she went to take his hand. He had stopped by, he explained, on his way from New York to dedicate a chapel in Peekskill—some miles to the south, nearer Manhattan than Hyde Park. A pair of anonymous monsignors attended him.

I sat through the meeting fascinated by the manner in which the two champions faced each other. There was not a trace of hostility. Such sweet charitability prevailed that a stranger would take them to be the greatest of friends. They agreed that each had the right to a point of view which the other could respect. Olive branches stretched out from both sides; they promised each other there would be no further quarreling in public.

Mother had one not-so-gentle thrust to deliver before he departed. "Sir, it is rumored that you are opposed to Governor Lehman." A Jew, family friend and Father's Lieutenant-Governor in Albany, he would soon be running against John Foster Dulles for the seat in the United States Senate left empty by Robert Wagner. "If the Catholic vote goes against him, a lot of liberals, Protestants and Jews will resent that, and it will be impossible for a Catholic to be elected in New York for years to come."

Keen eyes gleamed behind the polished spectacles; a patient smile crossed the close-shaven cheeks. "Oh, Mrs. Roosevelt, I am not opposed to Governor Lehman. I'll be in touch with Ed Flynn about that." A monsignor jotted down a note.

The big black car crunched away down the gravel road. *"So insincere!"* Mother sighed. She was worried about Herbert Lehman, who had proclaimed himself her ally in the controversy with the cardinal and for his pains had been warned by more than one priest not to count on the Catholic vote.

His Eminence had not convinced Mother that he bore no grudges. Close on the heels of his visit, she wrote to Lehman about the threat of Catholic ballots being swung to Dulles: "It seems too stupid to be true, but the Cardinal has been doing stupid things of late."

Two months later, still afraid that Lehman would suffer from the priests' influence with their flocks to pay him out for his fealty to her, she pressed Truman to rally the Democrats to the Governor's aid. She could not decide whether Herbert's election victory was the result of Truman's backing or evidence that the Catholic Church swung less weight with its congregation than she imagined.

In those years of distrust throughout America, Mother got caught up in the witch hunt conducted in the name of "loyalty" that intensified after the Soviets' first atomic bomb was exploded in September. Most of the country credited the terrifying achievement to espionage—the spying of Klaus Fuchs in Britain and of Ethel and Julius Rosenberg in the United States.

The idea that Russian science had caught up in the cold war was too appalling to contemplate. The House Un-American Activities Committee gleefully shredded the Constitution and hurried to work. In the Senate, Joseph McCarthy—another product of Irish background and Catholic faith, as Mother noted—was looking around for ways of restoring himself in the graces of his Wisconsin constituents after the Washington press gallery voted him the worst Senator on Capitol Hill.

In Congressional committee hearings, Mother's name became a football to be booted around while accusations fell thick as autumn leaves: she had aided Hans Eisler, German communist, to enter the United States; she had abetted the American Youth Congress in undermining our society; she was nothing but a tool of the USSR. All of this, it must be said, came when in the world forum of the General Assembly she had emerged as the preeminent critic of Soviet obstruction.

Truman taunted the House committee as "the most un-American activity in the whole government." Mother went further. "I feel we have capitulated to our fear of Communism," she declared, "and instead of fighting to improve democracy, we are doing what the Soviets would do in trying to repress anything we are afraid might not command public support."

She did her utmost to get subpoenaed as a witness or alternatively obtain permission to appear as a voluntary witness to refute the charges which commanded the headlines. "It is *totally* unfair," she complained to me over and over again, "not being able to get a statement into the record and covered adequately by the press."

The headline-hunters in Congress ignored her pleas to be allowed the floor. They wanted only the slurs printed, not the rebuttals. Given the chance, she need only cite her record to make mincemeat of her accusers.

Toward the close of 1949, I had some news of my own to volunteer to Mother. I knew how much it would hurt her. She was as fond of Faye as if she had been a daughter. But my disturbed personal life was breaking up our marriage. Mother yearned to see all her children settled into happy, useful lives. Once again, I had let her down. There seemed to be no end to her heartache. She had achieved the respect of most of the world, but personal happiness to crown her struggle always eluded her.

8

The mountaintops of the Catskills glistened white these days, and the path up the hill to Top Cottage, where I lived on alone, crackled underfoot with frost. This winter, no Roosevelt Christmas trees went on sale. We were learning slowly by trial and no shortage of errors what could be achieved and what could not at Val-Kill Farms. The fire on Mother's hearth was burning low, but she wanted to continue talking with Tommy and me, so I tossed on another log.

Mother was in one of her Griselda moods, as she liked to call them once she had recovered from those hours when the weight of guilt for her very existence bore down on her. The name was borrowed from school days, when Geoffrey Chaucer's *Canterbury Tales* was on the curriculum at Allenswood. Patient Griselda, silent and sorrowful, was one of the company of pilgrims on their way to the shrine of Thomas à Becket. "And gladly wolde he lerne, and gladly teche" was something else Mother took to heart from the Chaucer text.

The latest divorce in the family had grieved her even more than I had anticipated. "I can understand why the two of you couldn't make it work," Mother had said sadly. "I had

watched you very closely, you know." There were no re-
criminations, but she interpreted our failure as her own. This
evening, she took up the subject again after a long silence,
broken only by the crackling of the fire.

"Elliott, dear, I'm afraid I failed you *terribly* in your earlier
years."

"What do you mean, Mother?"

"I should have given so much more of my time when you
were young—you, Anna and Jimmy."

"Look, I know you're thinking about Faye and me. You
didn't have anything to do with it."

"But I *did*. If I had not kept myself so busy, instead of
building up a home for the three of you. . . . I spent so much
time away that you never knew what home could be. It was
selfishness on my part."

"Mother, it was no such thing," I protested. She brushed
the interruption aside.

"*None* of you older children experienced security. You
could never count on the advice of a father and a mother. All
you could possibly see in me was the disciplinarian, and bad-
tempered too, sometimes. Father was the one who could comfort all of you, and then he fell sick the month before your
eleventh birthday. Jimmy would be thirteen in December, but
Anna, of course, was growing up—quite the young lady at
fifteen. Father did try so *hard* to walk again. But that didn't
work, and he was away a great deal of the time after that,
wrapped up in his political career. You had already drifted
away by then."

"I had a terrific time out West. There's no reason in the
world for feeling sorry about that. Why, from the time I was
thirteen, I was practically independent, earning my way during school holidays. I've never regretted it."

"But where was the *guidance* you should have had from
Father and especially from me? Anna and Jimmy suffered just
as you did. *Nobody* was willing to devote the time to provide
you with a proper upbringing. I did begin to realize my mistakes and make an effort with Franklin and Johnny. But it

wasn't enough. One has only to look at the difficulties you
have all had in *your* married lives. You, Anna, Jimmy, Franklin; and I don't believe Johnny and his wife are completely
happy. I *have* to blame myself."

"Mother, it's not true. Sure, we've had problems. We grew
up receiving a lot of attention from all kinds of people. It was
a time of enormous change in America. We lived through Pro-
hibition, for one thing—saw people defy the law for the sake
of a drink and get away with it. Everything got so darn much
more *permissive* inside and outside of marriage."

"If I had provided a better home life, you would have had
different *standards*."

Tommy shook her head. Mrs. R. as Griselda simply could
not be argued with.

"We just didn't learn how to deal with outside people," I
said. "We were brought up to trust, not be leery and cynical
about the tricks some of them pulled on us. We were babes in
the woods, and there were plenty of wolves around. If you're
talking about *my* home life, it's true that I made a mistake early on. Betty and I were both too young to marry, and we paid
the penalty. How can you be to blame for that?"

"But then Ruth? And Anna with Curtis and now poor John
Boettiger? Jimmy and Betsy? Franklin and Ethel?"

"Remember that a lot of those difficulties stem from the
war. In my case, it meant being separated too long from Ruth.
That wasn't *your* fault. Overseas I had no time for a normal
life. I came back with my mind all over the place, and I made
more mistakes. I made them, not you. You've no cause to re-
proach yourself. No wife, no home, I had nothing I was set on
doing. I've never been happier than when you asked me to
come here and work with you."

There was no way on earth to change her attitude. She accepted as her doing the divorces of all her children, and we
certainly kept her occupied in that respect. On top of the cul-
pability she felt in Father's dying, she insisted that she was
primarily responsible for our shortcomings. Joe Lash was to
write later on of "her failure to separate her loyalty to her

children from her role as a public servant." Mother showed greater understanding. "How," she once asked herself, "does one compartmentalize one's heart?"

One tie with the past which was adjusted at this time caused her no regret. In order to complete *This Is My Story* according to schedule, she had gone into retreat on Campobello, the rock-strewn Canadian islet in the Bay of Fundy, where the fog might roll in any day of the year. Granny had owned a summer place there, and she bought a house for Father next to hers. "Campo" was where Mother took us children, the current governess and some of the servants for warm-weather vacations. It was there that she waited for Father when he made excuses to stay on in Washington to court Lucy. And it was at Campobello that he contracted polio.

"How I would like to relive the days!" he wrote to a friend in 1937, remembering the "beloved island" that spelled joy for everyone of us excepting Mother. The plain wooden house with a multitude of dormer windows was part of his estate, which was another reason for the visits she and I paid there, taking a launch—the quickest means of transport—for the choppy crossing from Lubec or Eastport on the coast of Maine.

The house had stood empty since the early years of the war. Winter storms had taken their toll of the paint. Dampness permeated the rooms where as children we had played, scratched our sunburns and mosquito bites, and tracked sand across the gray-painted floors. There was still no electricity, and Mother had to fiddle away at her typewriter by the yellow light of kerosene lamps.

The place was tolerable when other people, preferably young, stayed for a while. Then she could keep busy as she had before, setting up picnics, scrambles over the rocks, swimming parties and boat rides. When she was alone or had only Tommy and me for company, melancholy filtered into her mind like mist off the chill sea. Mother was undecided about what to do with a house where wraiths seemed to hover. She herself had no desire to remain there, yet letting it go would mean the loss of something that Father had loved. A solution offered itself one day.

"Elliott, perhaps *you* would be interested in acquiring Campo? You could use it as a summer place, and it could be available for the rest of the family too."

This struck me as a practical idea. The property became mine for $12,000. We had visions of restoring it to the shape Father had kept it in, when the painters and the handyman had been commissioned each spring to make good the winter's battering. But Mother was reluctant to return, and none of the rest of us found much opportunity to go there. Some other destiny had to be devised for the sadly neglected old house before it fell into complete disrepair.

"I think it should be sold, Elliott, if we could find a suitable buyer who would really *care* for the place," she concluded.

Armand and Victor Hammer proved to be the men we were looking for. Armand had made a fortune in oil, his brother flourished as an art dealer. Both were celebrated collectors of fine paintings—Armand paid a record-setting $3,250,000 for Rembrandt's "Juno" when it came up for sale in the fall of 1976. The brothers had the means as well as the desire to bring the house back into mint condition, which they did, exactly as it had been in Father's young manhood, which reconciled Mother to the sale.

In 1962, they offered the Campobello estate to the governments of the United States and Canada jointly as a memorial to FDR. The pity of it was that by then Mother was seventy-seven years old, her perception failing fast. She did not live to hear President Kennedy and Prime Minister Lester Pearson announce that Campo would be turned into "a symbol of Canadian-United States friendship."

Within three months of being divorced by Anna, John Boettiger found a new wife in a previously married woman who had been a neighbor of the Boettigers in Phoenix. He still corresponded with Mother, but his depression showed no signs of lifting. He was staying in the charge of a male nurse at a hotel on East 54th Street, around the corner from Madison Avenue, when his internal torment became unbearable. In the absence of the nurse, he threw himself from an upper window, leaving a note in the room for Anna.

Using that as a lead, the police telephoned. Would I go to identify the body? When I returned, there was no way of withholding an account of the death from Mother. She sat brooding, pale and withdrawn, for some minutes in her chair. Then she spoke almost to herself. "Is there nothing I might have done to help poor John? What dreadful things can happen when people *fail* each other! Destroying themselves in this terrible fashion; losing faith in living. I did try to offer him friendship, but what *good* did it do?"

Every season brought a fresh deputation of dignitaries and potentates to visit the grave in the rose garden and enjoy a talk with Mother. As she escorted them around the grounds and into the big house, most of them saw in her only what they expected to see—a gracious hostess eager to help with their problems, the symbol of a benign America that worked for peace and an end to hunger in the world.

Mohammed Riza Pahlavi, the young, hawk-eyed shah of Iran, was full of the time he met Father in Teheran. He remembered listening enthralled as FDR predicted that irrigation dams and hydroelectric power would transform a country of sand and dust into an oasis of industry serving as a buffer to Soviet expansion in the Near East. The shah was following the course outlined for him by FDR, he explained, and Mother glowed with pleasure.

Tiny, trim-bearded Haile Selassie, emperor of Ethiopia, came on a state visit, with nineteen members of his entourage. The State Department had laid out his timetable: Mother was to meet him in the rose garden; show him the library; make sure he was through by one o'clock to watch himself interviewed on a television show that had been filmed in advance; give him half an hour to rest and wash up; and serve him a belated lunch.

She took an instant liking to the diminutive "Lion of Judah," though she would have preferred to see him in belted white robe and sandals instead of double-breasted business suit. He was so overcome with awe in the library—"Study this system!" he ordered his aides—that it was a race to get him to the living room in front of the TV set. She wondered if he had ever seen one before as he sat himself down on a low stool in front of it just as the program started. When it ended, he did not stir. Mother nervously consulted her watch.

"Your Majesty, I believe you want to rest for half an hour alone. Your room is ready."

A smile appeared in his molasses-dark eyes. "Oh, no! It is not necessary to be alone. I only wanted to take off my shoes for a while, and you see my shoes are off."

Jawaharlal Nehru, first prime minister of an independent India, shunned Western dress and arrived to spend a weekend wearing tightly-fitted white trousers under a long black coat, a remarkably intellectual man, in Mother's eyes, flawed only by his later bigotry on the question of whether his country or Pakistan should take over Kashmir.

Some of her grandchildren were at Val-Kill with us. She took to her armchair by the fire, he crossed his long legs to settle himself on the rug by her feet, and the rest of us sat in an arc around him. Mother led the questioning. "What do you contemplate as India's future, Mr. Nehru?"

He was an apostle, he replied, of Mahatma Gandhi and the doctrine of nonviolence, of turning the other cheek to provocation. Eventually, the sheer force of that faith would prevail without any call for massive armaments. He was positive that democracy could be assured for his people, more than half a billion of them, once levels of education had been raised following centuries of oppression, first by the caste system imposed by the maharajas and then by the rifles of the British raj. Some form of socialism was inevitable in order to share the wealth which in the past had been concentrated in rich men's hands.

"But what about antipathy between Hindus and Moslems? Are they as irreconcilable as many believe?"

"We do have and we shall continue to have that problem. It

is an internal one which does not affect the rest of the world. It is by no means insuperable. We can solve it ourselves."

"Without outside intervention, perhaps from the Chinese?"

"We have nothing to fear in the long run from the Chinese or any other great power—the Soviet Union or even yourself." He smiled. "I am sure we shall be able to reach an understanding with all. They will respect our borders, you will see. We shall also overcome the difficulties created by hunger and a population which refuses to stop growing. In the end, the policies of nonbelligerence will gain respect and enable India to emerge as a true leader in the search for peace."

Not one of his listeners had so much as heard of his daughter Indira, who, married to another Gandhi unrelated to the Mahatma, would be a future prime minister and no more take after her father than King Lear's elder daughters patterned themselves on *him*. Nehru expounded his philosophy by the fireside, picturing India loosely allied with a demilitarized Japan guiding the uncommitted nations and new African states by setting the example of nonviolence and by holding them out of the reach of Mao's China or the USSR.

"Mrs. Roosevelt," Nehru said, "you must visit India as my guest. I should appreciate the opportunity to speak at greater length with you. Your views on the direction my country should follow would be most welcome."

She needed no more asking. The dream of seeing India had lingered from the days when it was stirred by her father. Before he married Anna Hall, he had set off to hunt tiger in the rain forests of Hyderabad in India, elephant in Ceylon and wild goat in the Himalayas. The letters of introduction he carried opened the doors of princes' palaces and the preserves favored by resplendent officers of the armies of Victoria, Empress of India, Queen of England. "This for the mere pleasure of living is the only life," said one of his letters home. Mother assembled and published them together with his own account of his expedition during our first White House year.

As a child, she spent hours on his knee, absorbing his tales

of adventure and the misery he had seen among the poverty-
stricken. "What a puzzle to me this world becomes," he exclaimed in another letter, "when we find out how many of us
are in it! And how easy for the smallest portion to sit down in
quiet luxury of mind and body to say to the other far larger
part, Lo, the poor savages! Is what *we* call right, right all the
world over and for all time?" The elder Elliott Roosevelt was
accorded too little credit in inspiring his daughter's concern
with human suffering.

"We'll see India together, you and I," he used to promise
her. After Nehru's invitation, she would get there as soon as
possible. The evening at Val-Kill influenced the remainder of
her life. She decided to travel not only to India but to as much
of the rest of the earth as could be managed, learning by looking and listening, adding her voice to the universal chorus that
pleaded for a better deal for humanity.

First another tribute to Father called for her presence: a
statue overlooking Oslo harbor to be unveiled. The State Department had it in mind to expand the trip into something
more grandiose. Of late, the undeclared war on communism
had gone badly for the United States in Asia, which Mother
had pinpointed to Truman as the key arena. Mao had ruled
China for the past half year after forcing Chiang and his de-
moralized troops off the mainland to Taiwan and some smaller
islands. Dean Acheson, Secretary of State now that Marshall
headed the Department of Defense, had defined what he
termed a "defense perimeter" for America in the Far East.
South Korea, which the Potsdam agreements had divided
along the thirty-eighth parallel from the northern portion of
the former Japanese territory of Korea, was omitted from this
perimeter. Some strategists already scented trouble there.

Mother was of an age to qualify for social security, but
Acheson wanted her in Western Europe on a goodwill mission
for America, to provide reassurance that this country stood
firm in its opposition to communists everywhere. Sweden,
Finland, Denmark, the Netherlands, Belgium, Luxembourg,
France and England were added to the itinerary.

Tommy would stay home this time. I would go instead and, at Grand'mère's request, so would my eldest daughter, Chandler, and my second son, Tony; they lived with Ruth, who had remarried. Mother boarded the flight from Idlewild Airport with the usual solitary piece of luggage, causing us to wonder whether we had overdone it—we each had packed three times more.

A literally royal reception was accorded us from the minute we arrived in Norway, where aged King Haakon had us out to his summer palace. In Sweden, another sovereign, King Gustaf, was on hand to welcome Mother. Where monarchies were no longer in style, heads of state substituted in extending us the Very Important Person treatment. Everywhere, she kept us marveling at her daily schedule—press conferences, radio broadcasts, public functions, private meetings with diplomats, speeches to women's groups and civic gatherings.

In Finland, we stole half a day and a night together at Rovanami within the Arctic Circle, where in this summer season the daylight never ended. Every Scandinavian we met impressed us with his strength of character, but the Finns, nestled up against the Soviet border, scored the highest of all. The children and I demonstrated a little fortitude of our own by taking a sauna bath in the sweltering steam of a log cabin, then plunging into an icy lake to cool off. Grand'mère was not to be tempted; morning exercises in her bedroom were enough for her.

As the days wore on, she grew increasingly troubled by what she was seeing and hearing. A letter to Acheson (noted "copy to Mr. Truman") spelled out her alarm. "Some of our industrialists and some of the members of Congress seem to have left the impression that we are not averse to going to war on the theory that we will have to go to war in the end and we might as well do it while the balance of power is on our side. I do not know that they have actually said it, but that is the impression they left, and it frightens most of the people very much indeed."

She wrote this on June 13. Less than two weeks later, sixty

thousand North Korean troops, spearheaded by Soviet-built tanks, crossed the thirty-eighth parallel to invade the South. Within forty-eight hours, Truman accepted a call by the Security Council for all the United Nations to join in enforcing an end to hostilities. He ordered General of the Army Douglas MacArthur to aid the South Koreans, while our Seventh Fleet was put on dual duty: to protect Taiwan and stay Chiang from attacking the China mainland.

The United Nations "police force," which Father had visualized as something akin to a patrolman forestalling crime on the beat, went into action like a fire brigade. When a country was already ablaze, sixteen others contributed men to serve under MacArthur's command. Nine out of ten were Americans; 55,000 of those died in battle.

State Department sponsorship of our travels made hospitality certain at every American embassy on our path. In Copenhagen as in every other capital, Mother punctiliously explained that she was *not* a member of Truman's Administration and disclaimed having any say on matters of policy. She was under heavier pressure on this supposed pleasure trip than she ever was at home.

The Netherlands supplied another royal welcome, this from Father's old favorite, Wilhelmina, who styled herself "princess" after abdicating in 1948 and having her daughter Juliana replace her as queen. Juliana joined in talking with Mother. We were given a taste of family history when we were driven to the village in western Holland which allegedly was Claes Martenszen Van Roosevelt's point of departure when he set off for New Amsterdam. Father would have been more overwhelmed than Mother appeared to be.

In the embassy at Brussels, she found herself at cross-purposes with Ambassador Robert D. Murphy, a smooth-tongued diplomat who fell out of grace with Father at Casablanca conferences and subsequently endeavored to make amends by rounding up some bottles of hard-to-find English gin to be delivered to his Commander-in-Chief for making martinis. Murphy imagined that she was nagging Washington to hurry into an accord with Moscow to ease international tension—a futile exercise in the opinion of this conservative tough-liner, who saw the Soviets only as "avowed enemies." Mother corrected him. What she prescribed to alleviate the state of fear in Europe was "some gesture"—she was not specific about its form—to spread confidence that the United States' objective was peace, not war.

From Belgium, we moved on to Luxembourg as guests of the first woman ambassador ever appointed by an American President. Little, gnomelike Perle Mesta, a queen on the Washington social scene, had been duly rewarded by Truman for her vociferous loyalty. The country in which she represented him was the tiniest on our list, 55 miles long, 34 miles wide, and smaller than Rhode Island, but our visit there had the most phenomenal aftereffect.

Our engaging hostess mentioned a trip she had made to SHAEF headquarters in Paris to meet General Eisenhower and his wife Mamie. Mother was not alone in being aware of rumors that Mamie had serious health problems to cope with. "How *is* she these days?" Mother asked, making conversation.

"Oh, she's fine, perfectly fine," Perle replied. We went on to talk of other things. There was no hint of what the consequences would be.

Next stop: Paris. Our hotel was again the embassy, and Mother resumed her scheduled pace. London provided more of the same, plus the opportunity to sit for a while on one of the four low, marble benches around the two shallow pools that flanked the statue of Father, a spot where Londoners came to eat a lunchtime sandwich in the sunlight and perhaps read his Four Freedoms declaration, carved on the back of the seats.

"Look, my dear ones," she murmured, "see the flowers by the plinth? People put them there *all* the time." I thought that Chandler and Tony were as pleased as she.

Jimmy and Franklin were waiting to welcome us back when our flight landed at Idlewild. Both of them had the bit between their teeth in their eagerness to emulate FDR. Franklin had debated running for Governor of New York this coming November, but Mother dissuaded him. "I rather think, dearest, that you need a proven record as a good liberal Democrat first." His progress in the House and in his law practice delighted her. He accepted her advice to try for another term in the Capitol before he aimed for anything higher.

Conditions were different in California. There, Earl Warren, Dewey's running mate in 1948, had held down the governorship for eight years. Jimmy had his local party's backing in his bid to oust him. What my brother asked of Mother was to intercede with Truman, whose regard for her did not extend to Jimmy. He had gone too far in his efforts to draft Ike.

Helen Gahagan Douglas was ambitious to proceed from the House of Representatives to the Senate. So was her rival in the race, Richard Milhous Nixon, twice elected from California's twelfth Congressional district, coauthor of 1948's communist-control bill, and a sparkplug of the Un-American Activities Committee.

The President was uncompromising in his apathy for Jimmy in spite of Mother. He would endorse Mrs. Douglas, but not young Roosevelt. Mother's temper brought her close to tendering her resignation from the United Nations for the third time, but she thought better of it and flew to Los Angeles to campaign for her son.

She considered Warren a gentlemanly adversary and found little fault with him, apart from his political affiliation. Nixon, on the other hand, she bitterly resented. "A very able and dangerous opportunist" was her summation. "I don't believe he really has any convictions of his own." She cared less about his labeling her a communist fellow-traveler than about his spreading lies and insinuations concerning Helen Douglas, whom Mother admired as a friend and capable Congresswoman.

Neither one of her protégés was elected. Nixon's skillful use of the McCarthy principle in branding Helen "soft on communism" shooed him into the Senate. Jimmy's loss to

Warren was interpreted by Mother largely in terms of the scheming of Ed Pauley, who declined to involve himself in raising funds for the gubernatorial campaign and dropped early hints that my brother had no hope of victory.

She took comfort from Franklin's performance. He proved that he could pull in the votes and, reelected, set about acquiring a praiseworthy record as a Congressman. There was also a crumb of consolation in the fact that Jimmy, back in his insurance business, could watch over Anna, whom he provided with a none-too-taxing job while she convalesced.

Tommy's work load had to be lightened, too. The days when she could keep up with her beloved but sometimes exasperating Mrs. R. must soon be ended. The strain of trips abroad was too much for her. Mother urged her to engage an assistant and left her the choice. With the utmost reluctance, she telephoned an employment agency. Miss Maureen Corr, tall, slim and auburn-haired, had not set eyes on her employer before Mother walked into Tommy's office one morning with some dictation for her to tackle. Tommy had contributed one more service toward bringing up Mother. Miss Corr came from Armagh in Northern Ireland; had graduated from Hunter College, which was familiar to Mother in her earliest United Nations days; had worked as an eye specialist's secretary at Columbia Presbyterian Medical Center. And she was a Catholic.

A further addition to the company at Val-Kill was in the offing. My brother Johnny and his wife invited a friend of their West Coast days to visit them. Minnewa Bell Ross, tall and shapely, wore blond hair cut short and walked lightly as a deer. The John Roosevelts introduced us to each other and did nothing to discourage the interest developing between us when we were both susceptible to the attentions that a man can pay a woman, a woman return to a man.

Minnewa and I were married that winter. Mother never went to greater lengths to have a newcomer to the family feel instantly at home and confident of her affection. After the latest Mrs. Elliott Roosevelt entered her circle to live at Top

Cottage, Mother took her to heart, anxious to excel herself this time in helping make marriage work for a child of hers.

The will she wrote the following spring named as executors Johnny, myself and Harry Hooker, her attorney, whose closeness had begun more than half a century ago when he and bustling young Franklin D. Roosevelt were partners in a Manhattan law firm. Her desire to cement the marriage of Minnewa and me carried her, I thought, to extremes. With only a few exceptions, all her household belongings—family portraits, silver, books, china and personal effects—were bequeathed with that purpose in mind.

Apart from what she wanted him to have after her death, she also chose to help Earl Miller set up house in Hollywood, Florida. After one visit to Val-Kill, he went off in possession of a mattress and box spring, a mirror, tallboy and chest of drawers, along with a scottish terrier bitch, as gifts from Mother. She had an understudy nowadays for Fala, who was getting along in years and growing cranky. Tamas, an almost identical black scottie, was his grandson. Perhaps he could sire offspring with Earl's dog to add one more generation to the line of Murray the Outlaw of Fala Hill, which was the grandfather's pedigree name. The nuptials were arranged in the yard one day when Mother was in Paris, but the groom's advances were spurned by the bride.

All through the winter and into the following spring, fear increased that a third global war was exploding in Asia. Neither the Soviet Union nor Red China was active at first in Korea, and MacArthur insisted that the Chinese would never intervene. On that assumption, he advanced northward toward the Yalu River, North Korea's frontier with Manchuria. Two hundred thousand Chinese "volunteers" promptly counterattacked across the Yalu, forcing him to evacuate his armies while the invaders penetrated seventy miles into the southern republic.

It took MacArthur three months to restore the position and clear the Chinese out of all territory below the thirty-eighth parallel. Before that had been done, the United Nations, anxious to contain and then halt the fighting, proposed a negotiated settlement of the war that was still officially minimized as a "police action." MacArthur disregarded the proposal, announcing instead a personal offer to talk terms with the opposing side in advance of his pursuit of the Chinese into Manchuria and his threat to subject China itself to air and sea attack. Twice within ten days he ignored orders from Washington to issue no further pronunciamentos without clearance from the Pentagon. On April 10, 1951, Truman summoned MacArthur home and fired him.

Mother displayed remarkable calm when the scent of hysteria tainted the air. Madam Chairman was aroused not so much by MacArthur's high-handed deeds in Korea as by the longer-term implications of Asian distrust of white Westerners. It was understandable, she thought, when Asians and Arabs alike had been dominated for so long by European colonialists and United States businessmen, but she had never experienced such personal animosity in her United Nations career.

She saw only one way of quieting the tumult in Committee Three. She must surrender the appointment in which she had found the fulfillment of her life. Chairmanship of the Commission on Human Rights should pass to someone who would not be automatically suspect because of being white, not yellow or black or brown.

Her nominee was Dr. Charles Malik, cultured, Christian and Lebanese, who had the qualifications to bridge several worlds. Washington approved the choice. She nominated Malik, and to her delight the committee elected him. There was an additional reason for her relief. As a rank-and-file committee member, she would have more open time for travel. India was waiting for her.

Malik could not have been blind to her prejudice against the Arabs. "I know you are going to stop in Israel on the way to India," he told her when he learned of her plans. "I really

don't think you should stop there without visiting some of the
Arab countries. You should see more than one country in the
Middle East."

This was reasonable, she felt. Malik made arrangements for
her journey to include stops in his country, Syria and Jordan.

The letters she wrote us in October from the Hôtel Crillon
in Paris contained few clues to her professional thinking, but
they overflowed with affection for her newest daughter-in-
law. "Minnewa dear: You have been very sweet to write so
much, and I devour every word of your letters. I am so glad
you and Elliott enjoyed your trip [to Florida] and I am so happy that at last Elliott and John see light ahead, and with plenty
of care and work, I know they'll make a real success. . . .
How I look forward to being with you all at Xmas! . . . I
wish I could bring a really good French cook home! I'm eating
too much and gaining because I never get any exercise—my
brain works a lot, however! . . . I must go to bed. My dear
love and thanks again—Mother Roosevelt."

The approach of Thanksgiving found her embroiled in Paris. Negotiations for a cease-fire in Korea had been dragging
along for the past four months; MacArthur had been welcomed home as a hero; and a campaign to impeach the President had fizzled out when a Senate inquiry found that in firing
the rambunctious commander he had the authority of the
Constitution.

Letters from Mother arrived almost every morning, some
of them dashed off in an almost indecipherable scrawl. "Darling Elliott: This is just to tell you that I think of you constantly. . . . Do write me *all* the news often. I am so interested in
everything that you consider—you and Johnny. Tell me about
Hyde Park, too, and say a word to Fala and Tamas for
me. . . . Tommy and I have slept a great deal, and I've done
some work with the advisers and tried to help the new people
where I could. . . . My love to you, Minnewa dear. Thanks
again for the flowers. All my love to you, Elliott dear, and
bless you. I think of you constantly and miss you more than I
can say. Devotedly—Mother."

The thought of being absent when turkey and trimmings were served at Val-Kill was hard for her to accept. "Where will you all be for Thanksgiving dinner and will you have it at one or in the evening?" she asked. "I'd like to call you when you are together. I'll put in a call in a.m. for a specified time and hope for the best! . . . My love to Minnewa, Johnny and Ann. A heartful to you and good luck and bless you."

Placing that telephone call had high priority on her agenda. "Minnewa dear: Thanks for your note and its information— I'll try to get a call through on Thanksgiving Day between 1 and 3 your time. . . . I hope to get home on the 20th [of December] and I count the weeks for I miss you all very much even though I'm enjoying Paris so far, not feeling over-worked. . . . Tommy sends her love and much from me— Mother R."

A few days later: "Dearest Elliott: I got your letter, which had gone all over the world, the same day I got your last one, and last night I talked to you. I just had to hear all your voices. . . . Lots of things worry me here, and I'm going to see tomorrow if I can understand this economic picture better. It looks to me as though industrialists in France and Italy were so terrible that the people not only won't fight but they'll be Communists. . . . I miss you and love you—Mother."

Now she started ticking off the days left before she could fly home. "Dear Minnewa: I've done a bit of Xmas shopping with Tommy's help here and at home, so I'm sure I can do my bit on stockings and presents on the plane. I want to give you and Elliott the Val-Kill furniture for Florida because I have little else for you, and when I know I could get that, I hoped you would want it. Let me know what I owe you for the children's presents you got for me. . . . Life is not idle for me just now. I'd like to be two people on Thursday, for I should be in Committee Three, and the General Assembly is going to meet, and I have to vote for the delegation. . . . You and Elliott will have to see that Fraser wires a little outdoor tree for each place and a wreath on each door. . . . I really want a small tree as I had last year in the livingroom. . . . Much love to you and thanks, dear. Tommy sends love to you and Elliott.''

Her holidays were festive, joyous, but from our point of view too short—no more than an interval during the General Assembly sessions. More than her usual light-weight packing was necessary for her return. When the round of meetings was finished in Paris, she was going to fly most of the way around the world before she came home again. Tommy was subdued throughout the week; Maureen, not she, would be traveling with Mother.

I drove them to Idlewild for the takeoff, set for some minutes before midnight on December 31. As they climbed into the sky, Maureen raised a glass to the health of New York, while Mother contented herself with staring down at the city, silently repeating Father's toast to the United States of America. An admiring stewardess lifted the arm between two seats, and Mother settled down to nap under a blanket before the plane put down in Paris at seven a.m.

From the Hôtel Crillon, January 1: ''Elliott darling—just a line to thank you for all that wonderful but miserable driving you did! I hope you got home safely last night. Thanks, too, so many times to you and Minnewa for a lovely Xmas and for all you have both done. . . . I would love to see you here and have you on part of the trip at least, but if you have to go to work, that will just mean we'll take some other trip together. . . .''

The great safari began on February 9 with a direct flight from Paris to Beirut, where the Mediterranean curled white on the beaches in the evening light. In the morning, she discovered that Dr. Malik or his governmental colleagues were nervous that her reputation as a pro-Zionist had preceded her. They were so uncertain of the reception awaiting her in the streets that a truckload of soldiers was assigned for escort duty. At every sightseeing stop, they jumped off the tailgate to form a cordon around her.

My free-minded mother would not stand for that, especially

when the dark-skinned crowds showed no trace of hostility. "I became thoroughly irritated by what seemed to me intolerable nonsense," she reported. "I insisted that they get rid of the soldiers at once." The troops were withdrawn, but she had a feeling nonetheless that a guard was following wherever she went.

She found a different cause for complaint when she and Maureen arrived in Damascus, to be faced by a platoon of newspaper reporters quizzing Mother in English and Arabic. "They were bitterly nationalistic and bitterly opposed to Israel, and they badgered me with questions about why I should support the Israeli cause."

From Syria, they drove to the Hashemite Kingdom of Jordan, ruled by the sickly King Talal, whose father had fallen victim to an assassin five months earlier. No royal welcome was extended in Amman, but Mother did talk briefly with two or three government officials, hearing about the plight of the several hundred thousand Palestinians forced to flee Israel when the Israeli army beat off the Arab nations' invasion. She asked to see the camps in which the refugees were quartered.

Her reactions to the spectacle of these homeless casualties of war, existing on no more than three cents' worth of food a day apiece, were extraordinary, understandable only in terms of her ardor for Israel. She acknowledged that the camps were "distressing" and "the least hopeful I had ever seen." The tents and dilapidated shacks struck her as "inadequate," which was putting it with perhaps excessive forbearance. She could not help comparing the downtrodden inhabitants with the refugees from Hitler whom she had met in Europe shortly after the war. They had impressed her because they "kept their hopes alive and tried to make their temporary quarters into 'homes' even under the most difficult conditions." Among these Palestinians, hope had died.

A woman in one tent held out her sick baby for inspection; it had been bitten by a snake the previous day. "There was nothing to prevent snakes from entering," Mother noted, "and babies lying on the floor were easy prey." Compassion did not stir in her as it had at the sight of the old woman on her knees at Zilcheim, crying, "Israel! Israel!"

That homeland was the next stop in the journey. Putting the Arab states behind her as she passed through the Mandelbaum Gate was, she said, "like breathing the air of the United States again." The contrast was dizzying. No apathy was visible among the Israelis, only "people dedicated to fulfilling a purpose." She shared in their elation over new factories that were arising and new dams that were producing crops in what until recently had been desert. The single criticism she voiced concerned the injustice of an established religion. "I was surprised to be told of a young man who had been refused the right to marry the girl with whom he was in love because she was an Orthodox Catholic." I wondered whether Mother or Maureen had unearthed that story.

"My Day" continued without interruption. There was only one change in the routine. Tommy had taken it down in shorthand, then tidied up the copy as she typed it. Maureen set it straight down on her typewriter to Mother's dictation.

A third traveler joined them for the breakneck week in Israel—the same amount of time Mother had set aside for Lebanon, Syria and Jordan combined. She had wanted David with her for the entire trip, but Malik and others advised against that. The risk for a member of David's race abroad in the Arab states was too great to be undertaken. He and Mother had a joyous reunion in Tel Aviv.

He was with her, camera clicking, at Beersheba when she encountered old Sheikh Suleiman, a rarity among Arabs in that he had not involved himself with either side in the war with Israel. In white headdress and dark burnoose, with a jeweled dagger hanging from his belt, he would have looked at home in a Cecil B. De Mille epic. Neutrality had enabled him to hold on to his wealth—and his harem. When Mother ventured a peek inside, she was astonished to see a picture of herself hanging on a wall. Astonishment increased when he asked her hand in marriage.

"What number wife would I be?" she asked with a smile.

"Number thirty-seven." It was *not* an effective way to convert her to the Arabs' cause!

Our ambassador in Karachi, Avra Warren, learned that she was not all smiles and graciousness when he proposed that she and Maureen should stay at the embassy while David was put up in a hotel. If the embassy could not accommodate all three of them, Mother retorted, they would *all* find hotel rooms. The impending fracas was resolved when Governor General Husain Malik had Mother, Maureen and David stay with him and his begum.

A crowd tens of thousands strong gathered at Karachi Airport for the flight from Tel Aviv to land. At first, Mother would not believe that they were waiting for her. Then another thought struck her. "I hadn't realized how they cared about Franklin."

She could dispense with bias when she met Pakistanis. These were people of "courage and great vitality" who surely could not fail to build a great country. Lack of trained civil servants and technicians, drastic shortages of essential equipment down even to pencils, vast defense spending for fear of invasion by India—every problem, she was certain, would ultimately be overcome.

She made speeches to the "magnificent" All Pakistan Women's Association, which had yet to convert most of its members into abandoning the tradition demanding that yashmaks be worn in public. She staged an impromptu dancing class for some youthful pupils to teach them the Virginia reel, which she had been stepping out in since White House days. And she itched to be on her way to India. She boarded the flight in a mood of soaring optimism. The faraway regime of General Agha Mohammad Yahya Khan and the loss of a million people in the fighting for Bangla Desh were unimaginable in 1952.

Prime Minister Nehru was waiting on the runway at New Delhi, together with his sister, Madame Vijaya Pandit, head of India's United Nations delegation, who carried a garland of

cloves and perfumed beads to drape around Mother's neck.
"I have come to learn," my parent exclaimed, touching
fingertips to brow in *namaskar;* one did not shake hands in
greetings here. "Eleanor Roosevelt *zindabad!*" yelled the
crowd. "Long live Eleanor Roosevelt!"

A full month had been allotted on her timetable for this climax to her journey. The first night was spent in Government
House, official home of President Rajendra Prasad, as protocol demanded, though she would not cease stressing, "I'm
here, you know, in a purely *unofficial* capacity. I don't want
anyone to make a *fuss.*" She was afraid that every kind word
she said would be taken as Washington policy.

For the remainder of her time in New Delhi, the three of
them were Nehru's guests. There were snakes in his garden,
Maureen warned Mother as she prepared for bed, and the
windows ought to be kept shut against them. "Don't you worry about that dear," was the reply. "We'll think about that in
the morning."

The more she saw of Nehru, the higher he rose in her estimation. He had, she reflected, made "an inspiring beginning"
toward establishing a unique brand of democracy and evoking
the same kind of devotion among his colleagues as prevailed
among American patriots in the 1776 revolution. She asked
how he had succeeded in getting 90,000,000 people out to vote
in the last election. He showed her a map that charted 25,732
miles of campaigning, which brought him face to face with
30,000,000 of them. She appreciated the power in the man.
That was the sort of thing Father used to do in his efforts to
enlighten America.

With her two companions, she traversed most of the sub-
continent by plane: Bombay, Trivandrum, Mysore, Ban-
galore, Agra, Jaipur, Benares, Nepal, Calcutta. "So many
crowded miles, so much want, so much ferment, so much
blending of the timeless with the new. So much human need—
and so little human communication, at least between Americans and Indians."

From New Delhi, she took a side-trip to nearby Rajghat,

where Gandhi's ashes were taken after his murder by a dissenting Hindu. She laid a wreath there and, in the hut in which the Mahatma had once lived, gave a turn or two to his spinning wheel. A woven loincloth that he had worn hung from a nail in one wall, the only other possession in the humble museum. "How little a human being really needs!" she sighed, and turned away.

David spoke afterwards about one dark day when she threatened to call off the trip and scurry home. Dr. Gurewitsch, weary of palace receptions and the hospitality of maharajas, begged off attending a ceremonial dinner for her. She had to go without him. This was enough to bring poor Griselda to the fore. In her room that night, she wrote telegrams of apology to Nehru and Dean Acheson, canceling the rest of her engagements. She spent the next day in broody silence, refusing to talk to David. But the telegrams were never sent.

Then the morning came to put on a cotton plaid dress and clean white tennis shoes and to set off for Agra and the Taj Mahal. She joined the throng that excursion trains, tour buses, cars and bullock carts brought there every day. There were barefoot men, skin color reflecting a multitude of races and castes, in turbans of pink, orange and blue, women in shawls of saffron and crimson with silver bracelets jingling on their wrists and silver rings on their toes; babies riding on a father's shoulder or on a mother's hip; schoolgirls in white pantaloons and bright tunic tops marching two by two alongside the reflecting pool.

On the steps of the principal terrace, she tied felt slippers over her white shoes—the rules prohibited rough soles inside the Taj. Her escorts made a path through the mob of commercial photographers who clamored to add her picture to the day's tally of romantic couples and honeymooners posing for good-luck pictures with the white marble wonder of the world as a backdrop.

The babble of guides added to the general bedlam. "Madam, if you will listen, please for a moment. The Taj was built by the Shah Jahan, mourning the death of his beloved wife,

Mumtaz Mahall, in childbirth in the year 1630. For twenty-two years, men labored, twenty thousand of them, to create the tomb. Four million rupees it cost then—you could say perhaps fifty million American dollars today. Even an earthquake could not destroy it. See here now, on the cenotaph of Mumtaz Mahall, this one little flower? It contains—imagine this!—thirty-five different shades of the flesh-colored stone called carnelian. . . ."

I doubt that she heard a word. She gazed at the Taj and thought of it as a kind of memorial to the other Elliott Roosevelt. "Little Nell," he had told her, "when you grow up you must go and see the Taj Mahal on a night of the full moon. There is a bench not far away, next to one of the lotus-leaf basins, where you should sit and contemplate."

This was such a night. She waited through the day, then, finding the same place where he had sat before she was born, she recaptured his feeling that this was the one unforgettable sight he had seen in India.

"I will carry in my mind the beauty of it as long as I live," she said. She had never known greater tranquil joy than this.

Book III
The Bequeathing

"THERE IS SO MUCH TO DO, SO MANY ENGROSSING
CHALLENGES, SO MANY HEARTBREAKING AND PRESS-
ING NEEDS, SO MUCH EVERY DAY THAT IS PROFOUND-
LY INTERESTING. BUT, I SUPPOSE, I MUST SLOW
DOWN."

—ELEANOR ROOSEVELT

9

Sorrow trod on the heels of happiness all through her life. She came back to Val-Kill by way of Jakarta, Manila and Los Angeles, half-way satisfied that Acheson's praise—"Mrs. Roosevelt's journey has served the public interest exceedingly well"—was not completely undeserved. What she had seen in the past two months reinforced her conviction that Americans "must show by our behavior that we believe in equality and in justice and that our religion teaches faith and love and charity to our fellow men." If that duty should be ignored, "we can lose the battle on the soil of the United States just as surely as we can lose it in any one of the other countries in the world."

She had not been home for long when grief overcame her pleasure in a job well done. Six days short of the seventh anniversary of Father's death, one more link with their life together was broken. She came downstairs one morning to find that age had taken Fala. "There is only one place for him now," she sobbed. "He must go where he always belonged."

She had a carpenter nail together a little pine box. One April

morning, when cold bit into the bones, she and I stood together in the rose garden as Fala went to his place by his master.
She had not wept at Father's burial, but the tears came this
day. I had never seen her openly give way to grief before. The
grumpy little dog had been closer to Father than any other living creature in his final days, the one truly dependable companion who stayed with him through every day and slept the
night at the foot of his bed. Fala, too, was a memento mori—
he had been there when Father died.

In lamenting the end of the scottie, Mother wept for his
master. The loss of the dog was somehow a liberation for her.
She had learned a great deal in the past few years as she put
into practice methods and principles that had been his. Many
times she had to steel herself and suppress her deepest feelings. At last, she divined something else that Father had recognized and practiced—the venting of emotion when it become overwhelming. Since 1945, she had changed almost
beyond recognition as a personality. Everyone of her family
along with the rest of the world had altered for better or
worse. But Fala had remained what he had always been to
her—Father's friend; constant and faithful.

Only a while ago, her religious faith had been questioned by
Senator Millard Tydings, ostensibly a Democrat, who made
himself a hardy political perennial by catering to the wants of
conservative Republicans in Maryland. Any cordiality he felt
for a Roosevelt vanished in 1938 when Father put him high on
the list of Congressmen whom FDR tried without success to
purge from the party.

What was Mother, Tydings demanded, an agnostic, an
atheist? Either way, he decided, she was unfit to serve in the
United Nations. She took a tolerant view of her attacker,
largely because he had more recently been a victim of the
highly specialized techniques of Senator McCarthy, who produced a doctored photograph showing Tydings chatting with
another apparent fixture on the political scene, the communist
Earl Browder.

Her reply to Tydings was mild. She believed in immortality,

she assured him, but she was dubious about the form a future life might take. Though this was not said to the Senator, she had no expectation of being united with Father after death; her deeds on earth must memorialize him. She did not think, as he had, that anyone could personally commune with God. She mourned for Fala because this, too, was farewell.

The country had started early on the search for a new President that election year. Once Truman bowed out of the contest, the choice of candidate was wide open on both sides. Truman had recalled Eisenhower to the Army after he had put in two years as head of Columbia University; his new assignment was to create a structure for the North Atlantic Treaty Organization. Ike's appeal as a father figure for Americans in an era of stress was irresistible.

Mother had reservations about his fitness for the White House. To Truman's credit, he would leave the Presidency no richer than when he entered it, a plain-living man who collected no more than his $75,000-a-year salary and approved expenses. Eisenhower was more financially ambitious. There were clear signs in the tax privileges granted to enable him to retain most of the $500,000 received for his memoirs, *Crusade in Europe.* Taxes were always much on Mother's mind, though she had personally paid in full on everything she wrote.

As President, Ike could not avoid being "tarnished," she felt, but the worship afforded him made him a certain winner, should he decide to forget his own words opposing the concept of military men running for "the most important office in the world."

In her analysis, Adlai Stevenson "would probably make one of the best Presidents we ever had," but first he should decide whether he wanted the job; she would not coax him, though she knew him well enough to recognize in him a fellow believer.

No biographer has yet paid enough attention to her total disenchantment with the foreign policies of Harry Truman. She judged the cold war to be unnecessary. A working arrangement should be struck with the Russians to end it before the world blew up. *She* was equipped, she felt, to make the opening moves by sitting down with Stalin, if only she were allowed to. Part of the gain for mankind everywhere would be the lifting of mutual suspicion, the root cause of Soviet oppression in Eastern Europe and aggression elsewhere. Adlai felt almost exactly the same way.

Her influence with us children as spring gave way to summer was decidedly limited. I could not conscientiously generate much enthusiasm for Adlai; he struck me as being too gentlemanly for political rough-and-tumble. Using Senator Henry Cabot Lodge as his mouthpiece, Ike announced, almost as though he had spun a coin to decide, that he was after all a Republican at heart, but I had served under him too long and respected him too much not to hope that he would win this race.

Jimmy's selection was Estes Kefauver, the gangling Senator from Tennessee who made crime-chasing his strong point and a coonskin cap his trademark. Franklin, who was hoping to win another two years in Congress, was partial to Averell Harriman, whose appearance as guest speaker for Father's memorial day services was engineered by my brother. Mother was quick to point out that this did not *necessarily* signify that she was endorsing Averell.

Shedding all pretense of being a Democrat, Johnny declared himself publicly as the first of Father's offspring to defect. His wife was influential in the switch. In their frequent drop-in calls on Mother, Anne made no bones of the fact that she came from a line of Grand Old Party shellbacks who had resented everything FDR stood for. For all that, Mother was pained when my brother made the seconding speech for Ike at the Republican convention. But she was glad that the delegates had proved immune to the drum-rolling oratory of General MacArthur, who had lulled some of them to sleep before he was done.

She professed herself reluctant to leave Val-Kill for the Democrats' convention in Chicago when the family was divided five ways over who Truman's successor should be. Franklin by now had taken to managing Harriman's bid for the nomination. At the last minute, Truman prevailed on her to go and plead the case for the United Nations, and I went along to admire her skill in action. She wasted no time in circulating backstage among the delegates, pinning down support for Adlai.

I saw her steal the show the moment she entered the auditorium to the cheers of her party and the brassy blare of what used to be accepted as Father's theme song for the New Deal, "Happy Days Are Here Again." On the platform, she stood in bewilderment while the standard-bearers jiggled their state's signs under her nose. Finally, the chairman's gavel hushed the din. "This demonstration was *not* for me," she began. "It was in memory of my husband. . . ."

Stevenson did not want the nomination. He had learned enough about politics in Springfield to know that Ike was unbeatable. But Mother, who rarely counted chickens when they were still in the shell, felt such confidence that she left Chicago before the ballots were counted that drafted him. She liked everything she saw in Adlai, from his tremendous respect for the office he was trying for, which meant that every speech must have a prepared text, to the gentle humor that prompted him to term Ike as "familiar as the ketchup bottle on the kitchen table."

Adlai deserved all the help she could give him, not forgetting the all-important question of where to look for campaign money. She steered him to Bernie Baruch. "I have always found that while it took a little tact and some flattery to get on with the old gentleman I got enough information with valuable experience back of it to make it worth while." Baruch coldshouldered him; Bernie liked winners best.

Her distaste for Eisenhower grew at every fresh turn on the track. He preferred not to debate with Stevenson but to score communism's "infiltration" in Washington and the dawdling pace of armistice negotiations for Korea. She was disgusted by the performance of his Vice-Presidential nominee, Richard Nixon, after his career was threatened by revelations that a group of rich Californians had set up a private slush fund for him.

She watched his weeping defense on nationwide television, flanked by his dog Checkers and what turned out to be a life-size cardboard cutout of his wife Pat. Mother detected where the idea of introducing a dog for support had originated: in FDR's sardonic words to the Teamsters Union, in which a rumor that a United States destroyer had been diverted to pick up Fala, inadvertently left behind, was turned into a jest for trouncing Dewey in 1944.

"That," she sniffed when Nixon had dried his eyes, "was an inferior imitation of Father's speech about Fala. Eisenhower should drop Nixon from the ticket immediately. He is not *worthy* to be in public life. If anything should happen to make him President, very, *very* serious times would develop for this country."

"You could be right, but I fancy Ike will make a good President."

I was given an exceedingly cool stare. "He," she snapped, "will be the tool of big business."

The new divisions in our family went deeper than into questions of politics, though politics did contribute to the tension. The John Roosevelts and the Elliott Roosevelts did not get along as neighbors. The original friendship between my brother's wife and Minnewa eroded into a sometimes unpleasant disregard for each other. Visits up and down the hill between our cottage and theirs tapered off when in their company the name of another friend of Anne's, Faye Emerson, came up too often for Minnewa's liking. She suspected a deliberate attempt to humiliate her, who had been their protégée.

The two Republican Roosevelts were jubilant over Ike's performance. At Mother's dinner table, they rubbed it in hard. "You just don't know how to pick the right horse," Mother was told. I objected to this kind of teasing as much as she did, since it always involved the risk of bringing on another Griselda mood of depression.

The riddle of what might be done to cut short the bickering

and the mutual antagonism took some soul-searching. Minnewa and I wrestled with the problem for months. I had enjoyed nearly seven years of knowing maternal love, but there was no avoiding the decision: Minnewa and I must get out of range of what she felt, right or wrong, was sniping aimed primarily at her.

Telling Mother we were leaving was probably the worst moment of my life. She had borne with some ugly quarreling between the Elliott Roosevelts and the John Roosevelts in her sitting room and at the dinner table. Sometimes no more than a mention of Faye was needed to start accusations flying in both directions. Once it had begun, the four of us would be at each other like Kilkenny cats, while Mother sat in silence, praying that a miracle would happen and the values she had tried to instill in those she loved would win out over our hostility for each other.

She was appalled to hear that I was quitting and that her effort to create a family unit of two sons and their wives living in happy harmony had failed. "Is there *no* way you could stay and make one more attempt to patch things up between yourselves?"

"I don't see any. We've tried, but it's been going on too long."

"Perhaps there's something I can do, dearest. If I talked with Anne and Minnewa together—I've been away so much, I feel it's my duty."

Her acceptance of responsibility when she was blameless was impossible to accept. "I don't think it is in any way your fault," I said. "If it's anybody's, it's mine. You've every right to be disturbed and angry and disappointed in me. I feel I'm letting you down, but I can't see any alternative."

She shook her head in bewilderment. "How *dreadful* that all these problems come up for you. I do hope things will work out happily in the end."

She agreed to the closing up of Roosevelt Enterprises. The traveling she had done and planned to do made it hard to keep up her television and radio shows. Her need for income was less pressing nowadays when fewer cries for help were heard from her children. If I stayed, she would renew the NBC contracts solely for my sake. As it was, they were allowed to expire.

There was a host of details to be attended to before fresh patterns of living could be found for each one of us. Johnny would go looking for work again and land a vice-president's job with Bobst Pharmaceutical. Anne and he counted on moving, too, with Stone Cottage put up for sale or rent. Top Cottage, which Mother had deeded to me, suffered the same fate. The prospect of the little family community breaking up terrified her.

DARLING ELLIOTT: I have been sick at heart all day for I hurt you and that is not what I ever want to do. I know what you spent on the place and what a millstone the debt has been and I know when you sold the Top Cottage it was the only thing you could do. I never said a word about it tho' I felt badly for you and for myself for I knew I would miss you sadly and I wanted above all to have your love and keep your home there. . . . I hoped you would all come back and be with me often and perhaps in the end you and Minnewa would live in my house if Johnny stayed. . . . If Johnny wanted to stay, I'd gladly hand my house over to you any time and build a cabin. . . . If you don't want to come back to Hyde Park, perhaps you'd better sell it all. Tell Johnny quickly before he puts any money into it and we'll all go on our ways. I can live much more cheaply in other countries. . . . I have never been "disturbed, angry and disappointed" in you. I've always loved you dearly, wanted you near and been proud of the fine things you have done. . . . You have weaknesses and I know them, but I never loved you less because I understand so well. I know you have tried to do the right thing and you never failed me! Living at Hyde Park itself means little to me. Keeping it for you and Johnny would have had a meaning. . . .

She would be seventy years old in two more years, and she could not face the thought of solitude. In one letter after another, her appeals continued. "You and Minnewa can always live in my house and if one of your children want to live in Hyde Park, for a young couple the playroom building could be added and with little expense. If Johnny moves now, I would not stay at Hyde Park as I cannot undertake to run the place and be there alone. . . ."

Somehow, it was clear, my brother must be induced to stay or else the last bond between the family and the place that Mother cherished in Father's name would be severed. The remaining property around Val-Kill amounted to some 250 acres, valued at roughly $400,000. With the exception of her cottage, it was made over to me, and half my interest was passed on to Johnny for a nominal ten dollars, on condition that he and Anne would live in Stone Cottage to provide company for Mother. The bulk of the land was leased out and afterwards sold for vegetable farming.

Anguish over the upset between two sons was lightened a little by her daughter's promised happiness. Anna was in good health and in love again. Partly in the cause of revealing another talent of FDR's, and partly in the quest for cash that preoccupied his children, I had been using his notes to complete a novel based on the life of John Paul Jones, Scottish-born naval hero of the Revolutionary War, that he had started in 1923. Most of the writing was done in a house Minnewa and I kept in Benedict Canyon in Beverly Hills. To help her put a new life together, Anna was engaged for research and typing, coming in every day but not always anticipating a welcome from my wife.

Anna introduced me to Jim Halsted, a middle-aged doctor from Massachusetts who worked on the Veterans Hospital staff and also taught at the University of Southern California. He had six children from his first marriage, which had recently ended in divorce. My sister and Jim, greatly taken with each other, began spending much of their time together.

They flew to New York for his introduction to Mother, who rated him "a fine person" and looked forward to one more marriage in the family. A remarkable change could be seen in my sister. Her gaiety was in flood again. "Oops, the typewriter carriage slipped above!" one letter began. "How the H are you all and when are you coming down here? . . . Lots and lots of love to you and Minnewa. I do hope you're all having a wonderful time." Closeness and affection between mother and daughter had been fully restored, which did something to ease my conscience on leaving Val-Kill.

The politician in Mother grew ever more alarmed as election day drew near. Stevenson's campaign was poverty-stricken, and the Democratic National Committee was not doing half enough for him. They seemed intent on keeping her, his greatest champion, on the sidelines, leaving her to fume at Ike's embrace for Senator William Jenner of Indiana, who had stooped to calling George Marshall "a living lie." She could only pity Eisenhower's above-the-battle refusal to condemn Joseph McCarthy for branding as a communist-serving traitor the austere general who had recommended Ike's promotion over the backs of 366 senior officers to command U.S. wartime forces in Europe.

Additional cause for concern lay closer to home. "I'm sorry Johnny is doing so much speaking," she reported to me. "They use him to offset F. junior, but it doesn't make for good feeling. Even some old Republicans have told me they thought he was going rather far as his father's son, but I haven't told him, since he'll find out, and if he feels he must, of course he must."

I preferred to sit on the sidelines myself. *John Paul Jones* was finished but never submitted to a publisher. With the winding up of Roosevelt Enterprises, Minnewa wanted us to return to California. The place for us, I thought, was Cuba. It was my ambition to establish a wholesale pharmaceutical enterprise there, simultaneously representing a group of Americans who were looking to buy radio stations in the so-called Pearl of the Antilles as a step toward introducing television.

We acquired a house in Marianao, Havana, but our timing was badly off. The two operations had been set up successfully when Fulgencio Batista, the swarthy "Little Corporal" whom Father had treated with, seized control of the government as a dictator. What Father had said about him—"He's a bastard"—gave me an idea of what to expect.

All Batista's lieutenants started cutting themselves into every foreigner's business. The approach in my case came from Havana's brand new chief of police, who walked into the office one day with a message: "*He* wants to talk to you." I kept an appointment with Batista and heard immediately what he had in mind.

"You should work with the chief as your partner," the Little Corporal grinned. "Fifty-fifty."

"We would be delighted to have you hold a half interest, Mr. President," I replied, an apprentice diplomat. "Here are the figures on what we have invested. Pay us fifty per cent of that, and we can go forward together."

"I did not mean it that way." A frown replaced the grin. "You turn over half the business. We do not pay you for it."

"But on that basis we couldn't possibly get our money out, unless you allow us to take all the profits until such time as we've recouped what's been put in."

"Oh, no! We will take fifty per cent of the profits until you have been paid off for your investment. After that, we shall want a more significant share."

I shook my head slowly. "At that rate, we'll never get our money out." Naturally, we parted with fulsome expressions of eternal goodwill. I went next to the investors in the radio-television project and recommended pulling out. One of them, a New Jersey restaurateur, elected nevertheless to stick to our original plans. Batista proceeded to pluck this *yanqui* pigeon clean.

Minnewa and I beat a retreat first for California and then for Meeker, Colorado, where she owned a ranch, renamed the Rolling R. An October 24 letter to her from "devotedly, Mother R." mentioned, "I'm glad Elliott hasn't made speeches for Eisenhower. . . . I've been bombarded with horrid letters since Johnny got bitten with the political bug."

Did we know that President Truman was about to send her to Chile for six days, heading the American delegation to President Carlos Ibanez' inaugural? "Exhausting, but it can't be much worse than the life I am already leading!"

She was out of the country on election day, when Adlai piled up over 27 million votes—more than any Democrat before him—but got swamped by Eisenhower by a plurality of more than 6 million. Against any other Republican, Stevenson would have won handily. Franklin swam against the current and was reelected. With their rosy dreams of Adlai as a President of Rooseveltian style shattered, party liberals asked themselves whether next time my brother might be ripe for the White House or, failing that, the Vice-Presidency.

Mother refrained from such speculation. Father had been forty-eight when he went in, and this son was ten years younger than that. Franklin should be patient because Adlai deserved a second chance, at least. "A funny thing happened to me on the way to the White House," he said. "I was happy to hear that I had even been placed second." In the ensuing four years, she hoped he could lead the losers and, if all went well, bring the voters to realize that he and the Presidency would make a well-nigh perfect match.

On November 12, nine days after the election, Anna and Jim were married in the little hideaway cottage they had found high on a mountain range inland from Malibu. They would keep it as a weekend place after they moved into a house provided by the Veterans Administration for Dr. Halsted on the outskirts of Santa Monica. Mother flew out to Los Angeles to join me in representing the family. She brought Tommy with her, an ailing Tommy, bothered by diabetes.

Fresh speculation had begun to build up around Mother twenty-four hours after Eisenhower's victory. She was on record as declaring that she hoped to give the remainder of her life to working for the United Nations as the most viable approach to peace. Her present five-year term on the Commission on Human Rights was far short of conclusion. But what were Ike's thoughts about retaining her after hearing of the scorn she had expressed for him in public as well as in private?

She was not left in doubt for long. John Foster Dulles, whose adolescent dream of being named Secretary of State was soon to be realized, sent her a curt note: her services would not be required by the next Administration. Henry Cabot Lodge was to succeed her.

She was well aware, she answered, that at the close of each United Nations session it was the practice of all American delegates to tender their resignations automatically, allowing the President a free hand in selecting who would represent him. "Mine will be in." Truman was furious when he heard what was happening. "You brought honor to all," he assured her. "You have been a good ambassador for America."

She tried to hide her bitter disappointment by process of sweet reason. The door to Truman's office had always been open for her, even when she was at odds with him. The State Department approved the arrangement because she could be relied on to give him first-hand information that might be sidetracked to a secretary's desk in written form. She could not expect similar access to Ike, not when Dulles stood in the way, likely to enjoy virtually unrestricted power in shaping foreign policy.

Shortly before Christmas, she gave her last speech at the United Nations. There was no sentimentality in it. She took this final opportunity to press the cause of rights for women, a subject on which the President-elect could use a modicum of enlightenment. Men still monopolized decision-making in government, she asserted, and "whatever of special value women have to offer is shunted aside." It was time they had a fair share in determining the direction their countries should take.

At lower levels in the State Department, a movement had sprung up to retain her on the Commission on Human Rights. It got nowhere. On December 30, she received a few formal lines from Eisenhower, accepting her resignation from the United Nations delegation with no word of gratitude. On December 31, sad at heart, she sent her thanks "for your extremely kind letter." The crushing of her hopes produced notunusual symptoms: she lost her voice. The midnight toast had to be left to others at her table.

She thought fondly of the pugnacious little man who was spending his final days in the White House. He had, she concluded, "remarkable understanding of the office and duties of the President." In times of crisis, he had seldom faltered. "The mistakes he made," she decided charitably, "were human mistakes in smaller things."

She would write him a farewell note before the inauguration "to tell you how grateful I am for all you have given me in the way of opportunity for service in the UN. . . . and to wish you relief from the burdens of state which I know have been overwhelming. . . ." At the inauguration, Eisenhower snubbed Truman, which was a second display of pettiness to shrink Ike's stature by my measure.

The first had shown up when we learned the reason for his brusque treatment of Mother. The fault could be traced to Perle Mesta. Telling him about our visit to Luxembourg, she had misquoted Mother's innocent question about the health of Mamie. According to the gossipy Mrs. Mesta, Mother had gone beyond asking "How *is* she these days?" to delve into Mrs. Eisenhower's supposed fondness for more than a single drink. Ike took Perle at her word. This was a slur for which Mother could not be forgiven whether or not she was his country's most able voice in the peace organization.

If she was prevented from working as a United Nations professional, she would do the next best thing. Early in January, still hoarse from mental exhaustion, she volunteered to put in as much unpaid time as the job required at the American Association for the United Nations, which was housed in the Carnegie Endowment building at the end of East 46th Street across the way from the glass-and-concrete headquarters of the establishment it was designed to support.

What this newest venture of hers lacked, she felt, was *organization.* She set about remedying that with all good speed, "unbelievably strenuous," but she eventually played a major part in the formation of 150 chapters on her missions around the country. The achievement could not be minimized when Dulles was busily hardening the lines of demarcation around the communist powers and threatening "massive retaliation" if they were overstepped, while in the Far East it seemed a toss-up who would strike the first blow, Mao Tse-tung or Chiang Kai-shek. Like most endeavors of its kind, her new affiliation suffered from a chronic dearth of income, which Mother undertook to remedy.

Raising money was her principal service at the moment for the State of Israel, too, though her ties to Zionism had been extended much farther. She had agreed to be a "world patron," an official title, of Youth Aliyah, which had come into being originally as a kind of underground railway to save Jewish children from Nazi gas chambers. And she was increasingly involved with young Brandeis University in Waltham, Massachusetts; she had addressed the first commencement of 101 students there, urging them to "have courage to live in uncertainty."

Selling bonds for Israel, stirring up followers for the United Nations association and keeping family and friends together made for hectic days as winter ended. A hastily scribbled letter arrived from Sarasota, Florida:

Tommy and I flew in from Miami last evening, and Johnny and Anne are coming for the night on their way home after two weeks' holiday. We've had lovely weather, tho' the trip to Miami last Thursday was a bit bumpy. I spoke for Israel Bonds last night, and the auditorium was packed.

Friday all day and evening was spent on AAUN with two speeches and a long business meeting. Saturday we drove over to Earl's house, and he took us to the plane. The first day I've done no work, and I felt it was rather an empty day! I felt let down and lacking in energy in Miami, but I feel it less here. Perhaps I'm getting accustomed to the war over China, etc. Tonight I speak for Israel Bonds here, peace and quiet tomor-

row, and Tuesday to Bethune-Cookman College at Daytona.
Wednesday after lunch I leave for New York. . . . If I'm to
see Johnny I'll have to go there for breakfast, and I'll have to
go and see Tiny and her kids after the AAUN meeting or before the [Sunday] service. Can you ask Jimmy and Romelle
and the kids over for lunch, since I can't get over there? Ruth
is coming East April 7, she writes, so I asked her to stay at
Hyde Park. . . .

Just before Easter, Mother squeezed in a quick trip with
Trude Lash to Israel for a meeting with Prime Minister David
Ben-Gurion, who for some reason reminded her of Father.
She returned alone, and her pride met with another battering.
The aims of the Commission on Human Rights were being
stultified by Dulles. The United States, he announced, was
abandoning the effort to frame satisfactory covenants to give
the Declaration of Rights the authority of law. The declaration would suffice as a statement of noble hopes—nothing
more.

She had not yet reached Manhattan when Tommy had to be
hurried into New York Hospital on York Avenue. What had
appeared to be a severe attack of indigestion turned out to be
something more grave when tests were made. Her diabetes
was uncontrolled, and a clot had formed in her bloodstream.
There was some question whether she would survive the night
as she lay sedated in an oxygen tent.

"All one can do is wait and pray," said Mother, "but she is
having every care, and I am so thankful she is in the hospital."

A week went by. In letters and telephone calls, she reached
out to her children for solace in what could only be anticipated as an inevitable loss. The lilies we sent for Easter, she put
on Father's grave.

April 6. "All is the same tonight with Tommy, but we feel a
very gradual deterioration, and she is not conscious. I go
there twice a day and am always where I can be reached and
will not go far away, not again even to Hyde Park. . . .

Somehow if Tommy has to be paralyzed, I think she would rather not live, don't you? On the whole, the part of her life with us has always been happy, I hope."

April 12 saw the eighth anniversary services held in the rose garden. Mother's letter to me that night carried odd echoes of the precise timetable she had painstakingly reconstructed for her understanding of the events of the same date in 1945.

> There is nothing you can say or do, but I wanted to tell you just what happened. I saw her yesterday afternoon, and she was quiet and seemed to be sleeping naturally. She has not been really conscious since the stroke a week ago. I went to Hyde Park at 4.45 this morning. Dr. Ingerman called and said she had had a hemorrhage from the abdomen in the night, but it had stopped. At 1 p.m. she called to say the crisis was over, but as soon as the people who came to lunch after laying wreaths at Father's grave had gone, Joe and Trude drove me to town and straight to the hospital. At 5, Tommy had another cerebral hemorrhage and died just as I got to the hospital. Dr. Ingerman said she had a little convulsion but seemed unconscious and died. Dr. Ingerman and I both feel she might never have fully recovered, and death is preferable to that, isn't it?
>
> I've thought these past twelve days of every possible adjustment that might have to be made, and it isn't a shock, but we are all going to miss Tommy a great deal. She was loyal and loved us all very deeply. I hope she was happy, and I think she had the kind of life she wanted.

No one compared with Tommy in Mother's heart. Nobody would act as she had as simultaneous goad and comforter for thirty years. "In many ways," Mother reflected afterwards, "she not only made my life easier, but she gave me a reason for living. In almost everything I did she was a help, but she was also a stern critic. No one can ever take the place of such a person nor does one cease missing her."

Tommy "made coming home to wherever it might be worthwhile," but Mother was sure that "she would not have wanted to live to suffer the torture of being an invalid." Those

last words contained a clue to her ultimate philosophy which
we did not detect at that time.

Her own health seemed to be unimpaired. Her cheeks were
plumper, and sometimes her feet hurt, which she ascribed to
wear and tear on the instep bones caused by endless hours of
standing at White House receptions. She paid a monthly visit
to an osteopath for treatment. The morning shower was less
likely to be taken ice-cold; she indulged herself by making it
lukewarm. If anything, she stepped up the pace of her activities, because Val-Kill meant less to her now that Tommy's
rooms stood empty.

Finding companions for her travels became more imperative. A second around-the-world trip, starting with Japan, was
in the offing. She was willing to cancel it when Dulles hemmed
and hawed over whether it was advisable in light of general
unrest in the Far East. But she could proceed as a private citizen, equipped with her usual diplomat's passport. The arrangements were complex. Columbia University was sponsor
for the Japanese segment of the journey, and Mother lined up
a $1,500 assignment from *Look* to interview Marshal Tito
when she reached Yugoslavia. Minnewa would be with her
until she left Japan, when my wife would fly to meet me in
Honolulu. David Gurewitsch would take her place as traveling companion on the European leg of the trip. Maureen
would accompany Mother all the way.

There was an essential piece of business to be tackled while
Mother was gone. Living in a hotel was miserable without
Tommy. What she was after was a Manhattan apartment to
settle down in. She left its finding in the hands of Esther Lape,
a "wise and good" friend of twenty years' standing and un-
limited resourcefulness. Whatever she came up with, Mother
would be glad to take.

She was happy at the chance to help educate the sometimes
puzzled Japanese in what Americans like herself meant when
they talked about democracy, but she felt the breeze of East-
West conflict soon after they landed in Tokyo and checked
into the Imperial Hotel. One of her first calls was at the minis-

try of labor, which had trouble applying United States occupation authorities' rules to child labor and women in industry. As she left, she was encircled by a crowd of angry women egged on by a screaming American, wife of one Fujikawa and known to be a communist.

"Go home!" they called as Mother made her way to the waiting car. "We went through one war, and we don't want any more."

"Neither do *I*," she said calmly and was driven away. Local newspapers—"somewhat unreliable"—blew up the incident with a version that had her dragged out of her seat and pummeled, but Pegler and Hearst had inured her to this kind of nonsense. It was *quite* unnecessary to ask for official protection.

Days of talks with high-ranking Japanese, women activists, students, farmers and factory hands led her to one conclusion, reported to Dean Harry Carman of Columbia University.

"They stressed they had two Occupations—one during the time when General MacArthur had given them a peace constitution which contained a clause binding them to complete disarmament and renunciation of war. The second Occupation started at the beginning of the cold war, and from then on Japan was asked to rearm and to reconsider all that she had just accepted with a good deal of difficulty. This change of policy shook the young people, who felt that if they had been deceived by the U.S. once, they could be deceived again, and the U.S. might be an imperialist nation rather than the peaceful nation they had been led to believe it was."

A question often asked was, "Is it possible to fight communism without resorting to some type of totalitarianism?"

She had a ready answer. "This is exactly the problem that Mr. McCarthy is presenting to the American people at home." She *did* wish that Mr. Eisenhower could come to grips with the intimidating Senator from Wisconsin, but there was little chance of that.

"A twinge of anxiety" affected her, she said, on the last

day of her five-weeks tour when Ambassador John Allison guided her into the Imperial Palace for an audience with Emperor Hirohito and Empress Nagako. She was awed by the thought that this solemn little man, the 124th of his line, had only recently been worshiped as a god. But the dauntless democrat in her bridled at the starchy protocol which specified even the dress she wore—sleeves long enough to cover her arms and white gloves.

Mother must be seated first on a sofa before she rose in a bow at the entry of Hirohito, who wore striped trousers and cutaway coat, and his lady in magnificent kimono and obi. As the Empress sat beside her, Mother tried to guess what quality of mind lay behind the smooth, expressionless face. Nagako was obviously a well-educated woman. What use was she making of her capacities in these radical times?

"Speak only when spoken to" was one bit of rigmarole that could be dispensed with. "When I visited Pakistan and India," Mother said briskly, "many changes were taking place, particularly in the status and activities of women. It seemed to me that women of all classes were drawing closer together and gaining in strength because of their greater knowledge of each other."

Nagako looked blank for some moments before she responded, "We need more education." Her husband broke in with a courteous attempt to turn to other subjects, but she had more to say.

"There are great changes coming about in the life of our women. We have always been trained in the past to a life of service, and I am afraid that as these new changes come about there may be a loss of real values. What is your impression, Mrs. Roosevelt?"

"In all eras of change," Mother lectured, "there is a real danger that the old values will be lost. But it seems to me much less dangerous when the intelligent and broad-minded women who have had an opportunity to become educated take the lead to bring about the necessary changes."

The Emperor appeared to have heard enough. "We serve

as an example to our people in the way we live," he concluded, "and it is our lives that have influence over them." She
took that to be the final word on how far for the time being the
emperor and empress would bend to the scourging winds of
change. With one more exchange of bows, they wished her
bon voyage.

She fell back into the practice of dictating round-robin letters, running as long as two thousand words, for Maureen to
type and mail to us, letting us know just what she was doing
and thinking about along the entire route. In Hong Kong, she
was surprised to discover that the dividing line between communism and Western-style freedom, which Dulles set great
store by, consisted of a single strand of barbed wire.

She was the governor general's guest for dinner one evening. "Maureen and I got dressed in our very best and the
governor-general's car came to take us to dinner. This time in
evening clothes and accompanied by a military aide, we drove
down to the pier and climbed aboard a little motor launch
which took us to the other side where we climbed out and I
lost my slipper on one of the steps. I fully expected to go without a slipper but I retrieved it."

The local United Nations association gave a tea party for
her. "Everybody sat on the lawn and I sat on the verandah
where I was peppered with questions for almost an hour and a
half. Most of the questions were slanted with Communist
views for there is quite a bit of pro-Communist feeling among
the Chinese in Hong Kong."

She passed up an invitation to go to Taiwan. She could not
in all politeness stop there without calling on Madame Chiang.
If they met, Mother was afraid she could not restrain herself
from telling her that the Chiangs' dream of one day ruling China again was no more substantial than their idea of democracy.

The flight from Hong Kong was delayed for engine repairs
in New Delhi as the monsoon season began. "I had my hair
done at 9.00. This was a waste of time because my permanent
has come out completely because of the heat and climatic

conditions, and the next day it was as straight as it could be and a perfect nuisance. I wish I had never tried to let it grow and yet I can't bring myself to get it cut now that it is half grown.''

In Athens, she ran into Adlai and had him in for five o'clock tea. ''In spite of his hectic travelling, he looks well. He is just back from Belgrade and why *Look* is having him write an article about Yugoslavia as well as me, I don't know. . . . I am waiting now to go out to meet David who is coming in from Paris. Maureen is about to go to sleep.'' She wished that King Paul and Queen Frederika had not omitted to ask David to lunch along with herself.

Marshal Tito and his country were equally impressive. He gave Mother two days of his time at his summer home on the island of Brioni in the Adriatic Sea, and David went too, snapping photographs. ''No one ever had a better chance for a good interview,'' our roving reporter told us, ''and I hope and pray my article will justify the reception that I have been given and still be objective enough for people to realize that, good though I think this is in trend, one can't yet be sure of the final outcome. If the Marshal lives, I think it will work out into good solutions and increasing democracy, but of the socialist variety.''

Before she got to Brioni, she had toured most of Yugoslavia, soaking in the July sunshine and soaking up the facts of life in this unique land which had broken with the Comintern to follow its own paths to socialism. That was a word which failed to send tremors through her bones. She was a firm believer in a degree of socialism for any nation where individual rights were endangered by capitalists' greed.

What struck her immediately was the pervading climate of optimism among the Yugoslavs. No one here was afraid of either the Soviets or the old enemy, Germany, which Eisenhower was now allowing to rearm. With American help, the Belgrade government was building factories and cottage industries, efficiently managed by councils of employees who aimed to show year-end profits because these were shared among the workers. Committees operated most of the farms too, and again the stress was on free enterprise. She had one complaint to lodge about the food, which was plentiful—the only place she could get orange juice was at the American embassy.

A launch of Tito's carried her from the mainland to his wonderfully wooded island, where she, Maureen and David spent two nights in a guest villa, marveling at the peace and quiet in a place where guards' Jeeps were the only cars allowed. On the first working day, she spent ten hours closeted with Tito and an interpreter. She was frankly smitten with this amazingly youthful leader of the Yugoslavs with a thrusting jaw and tanned as dark as leather.

"You cannot meet this man," she told us, "without recognizing that he has a real mind. He is a doer and a practical person. So many things that I have gathered in casual conversation throw light on what he is today. For instance, when he was in prison the warden, by way of refined torture, offered him a book, a difficult medical volume discussing reflexes, because he thought it would be beyond his comprehension, but instead the Marshal read and mastered it and did the same later with a number of books on philosophy. He has charm, he is the product of his early environment, but I think he is not only fearless but honest."

Tito piloted his own speedboat to take her to a smaller island, where they talked by the hour in a rough stone cottage while he puffed cigarettes pressed upright into a pipelike holder. He taught her that she was wrong to think of him as a communist. "He keeps telling me that it is socialism, which is only the first step toward Communism, which actually exists in this country. He calls himself a 'social democrat' and says that he became a Russian Communist because of his term in prison and the belief that the Soviet Union alone cared about the wellbeing of all the people. When he found that the Russians are as selfish and imperialistic as imperialist nations, he decided that his nation must develop in its own way."

The reporter with a scoop on her hands felt compelled to

add, "Pretty interesting as a statement, isn't it, but don't spread it around because it is part of my article."

Belgrade to Gratz—"all Russian restrictions now seem to have been lifted, so we never had to show the passes we were so carefully provided with"—Gratz to Vienna, Vienna to London, London to Paris, and she came home again early in August. She had completed her first inspection behind Churchill's "iron curtain" and liked what she had seen. Tito's blending of socialism and capitalism, in her enthusiastic opinion, could bring about better understanding between two systems which had more in common than most Americans believed. Yugoslavia, "a delightful place to visit," was a bridge between two worlds. She wished she had been able to talk with Stalin in similar fashion. But he had been dead since March.

10

Finding a new home for "dearest Eleanor" had been a service of love for Esther Lape, whose manner retained traces of the long-gone days when she had instructed students at Swarthmore and Barnard colleges. She had a habit of lecturing Mother on where her duty lay, and Mother responded to these exhortations by sharing most of her secrets with Esther, from the distant problem with Lucy Mercer down to current difficulties as they arose for us children.

The narrow, three-floor apartment at 211 East 62nd Street was ready for occupancy when Mother got back from Yugoslavia. The rent, $425 a month, was every bit as much as she wanted to pay for a place of this size. Steps from the street led down to the front door, which opened onto a little foyer with the kitchen to the rear. Up a flight of stairs were the living room and a den with two facing desks, one of them for Maureen. Lack of a dining room meant that guests must eat off folding tables. More stairs, wearisome when old legs ached, went up to the two bedrooms.

Though it was not an elaborate layout, it *was* much closer to

her office at the AAUN, and there was a small backyard in
which Tamas could run free. Mother proceeded to move in
most of her furniture and cover the walls with favorite pictures, including four amateur watercolors painted by Louis
Howe. The telephone here was unlisted; it was a source of
wonder to her how many people managed to acquire the number.

She had not long settled in when a letter arrived from Esther, touching on a subject that for the first half of 1954 kept
Mother in a state of turbulence. "After a night's reflection:
isn't there somebody not too old, vigorous, objective, devoted, in the wide circle of those that loved Franklin who would
go out to Jimmy now, confer with him and give him the sound
advice he so obviously needs?"

After almost thirteen years of marriage and three children,
Romelle was seeking a divorce. It came at a time when he was
bitten with a desire to run for Congress, "the opportunity,"
as Jimmy put it, "of doing the one thing for which I have any
fundamental training."

Romelle's accusations resulted in a crop of headlines and
breathless bulletins on radio and television that agonized
Mother. She could scarcely begin to assess the hurt she foresaw to Father's name, to liberal ideals and, most especially, to
the children born to Romelle.

Mother's sensitivity to Jimmy's domestic situation went
back to early days as a widow, when she had noticed his need
for more money "to give his wife the security she demands."
She had just extended her hand to help him again with a loan
of $100,000. In return, he gave her a note to be filed away,
putting up as security his interest in Father's estate. As she
understood it, he promised her not to enter into politics again
until his debts were paid.

Of the total loan, $75,000 had gone for the return to my
brother of a letter that was now the basis of Romelle's
charges—a photostat had been made without his knowledge
before the original came back to him. He had signed the document while he was on wartime leave from the Marine Corps,

stricken with malaria and the effects of combat duty overseas, which he could readily have avoided in consequence of the major stomach surgery he underwent eight months before Pearl Harbor day.

The letter, released by Romelle's attorneys as clear-cut proof of infidelity, named nine women—some in the public eye then, all deserving anonymity now—with whom Jimmy supposedly had attachments. Newspaper accounts accepted it as an irrefutable confession of guilt. Beyond that, private detectives had been hired on Romelle's behalf to chronicle his comings and goings and to lay hold of affidavits from alleged witnesses. Fees for these procedures amounted to $3,500.

The story broke on Friday, January 30. The same evening, Jimmy appeared at a Democratic Party rally and a fund-raising dinner for the March of Dimes, poised and making little of the lawsuit "in the grand Rooseveltian manner," as one reporter expressed it. The audience at both gatherings welcomed him with cheers.

Mother's voice trembled when I called her in New York. "What seems to me most important is to put up a good face to the world and show that Roosevelts stand together in terrible times like these. Imagine what the children must be going through," she murmured. "Do you think I ought to fly out to support him?"

"That would be about the worse thing you could do. It would only draw more attention to the case."

"Then will you act for me so that he *knows* we are all for him?"

Esther Lape inflamed Mother's fears. "I do believe," Esther declared, "that the presence now with Jimmy of a capable friend, legally and psychologically adept, would give him the support that would not only encourage him to hold onto life (the threat is obvious that he might not) but would also help him to work out wisely the case that could undoubtedly be made for him." Mother's experience in the Earl Miller suit drove her to share in part her friend's doubts about what my brother might resort to in despair.

Esther discerned "psychotic" factors at work in the case. Though Mother was of the same generation of emancipated women, she harbored some old-fashioned prejudice against the medical science of psychiatry. The investigation of anybody's mind, in her conviction, was best left to its possessor. She had no interest in the findings of Freud or any other prober of intangibles. If one could summon up the courage and self-discipline to search one's soul, it should be by no means impossible to identify one's failings and "mental quirks." Once that was done, it was simply a matter of pulling oneself up by the bootstraps.

She felt that personally she had done just this in overcoming the sense of insufficiency that lurked within her. Some of her children, bandying the language of parlor psychology, had concluded long since that hers was an inferiority complex which she willed herself to conquer. This would explain her impulsion to accept every challenge to timidity that came along, piling one on top of the other to push her fears deeper. When her concealed terror of inadequacy forced its way up in her mind, Griselda took over.

She tried to instill in each of us the bootstrap approach to mastering deficiencies of character. According to her teaching, it was quite unnecessary to turn for help to a psychiatrist or any other *outsider.* If we only fitfully followed her example, as we did, why, then it was because we were not trying hard enough, but she considered that to be her failure not ours.

She talked at length with David Gurewitsch about what could be done to protect Jimmy. The doctor did not see suicide as being an imminent danger, but my brother clearly could use an ally whom he could trust. Mother passed along Esther Lape's alarming letter to me. I went to join my brother.

The most immediate priority was to set her mind at rest about his mental state. "I must say," I reported in writing to her, "that at no time has Jimmy exhibited to me any signs of mental disarrangement that might lead him to an act of self-destruction. . . . He is not, now or ever, the type of person who will commit suicide. He has embedded in his soul the desire to compete with Father and now with Franklin and prove that he can run for political office."

The entire family urged him to withdraw from politics. Franklin held out the hope that Jimmy might try again in later years, "when he has established a sound financial, as well as a sound personal, reputation." Mother was more explicit:

> No matter what Rommie may agree to or what may happen in the next few days, I am convinced that you should not go into politics for several years. . . . I have talked with a great many people, Democrats and friends, and there is not one dissenting voice. They all feel it would be a great burden on the Party, on your running mates if you were to try to run, and that it would bring on you much censure and keep alive a great deal of feeling which, if you go to work and devote yourself to business and your children, will die down. You want to get out of publicity, not stay in, for the next few years. If you do the right thing, I don't think you need be afraid that you will never have other opportunities. Opportunities always come to people when they are honestly doing their jobs well. You will be opposed by Democrats from the top down if you go into political life at the present time, and what is more I would oppose you and feel you were doing something that the family was justified in opposing both in your interest as well as the public interest.
>
> I want to help you in every way possible to do right, but I cannot help you do what I consider is wrong. I hope you will show this letter to your lawyers. Much love, Mother.

My brother was not to be dissuaded. Winning a seat in Congress, he felt sure, would rehabilitate his name. Earning money to clear up his debts was not the main consideration. "I could be perfectly happy as a truck driver," he vowed. What was essential, he thought, was to build "a record of public service to people in the tradition of liberalism and the family name which, if it does not bury, will certainly displace the sensational charges already made."

He argued that nobody ought to condemn another merely because of disagreement with the other's approach to solving his own problems. "Certainly in our own family, we have had to believe it and practice it in order to maintain any respect or affection for each other."

Over lunch, he told me that his lawyers had warned him that to quit politics now would be taken as an admission of guilt. More than that, columnist Drew Pearson had telephoned overnight to predict that my brother could gain the seat regardless of the scandal.

I could not see it that way. "With your head bowed under the barrage of these frightful accusations, the only course open is for you to withdraw from public life."

Jimmy glared. "My head is *not* bowed, Elliott." He turned to his attorney, Sam Pecone. "Do you agree that the only thing for us to do is to fight this thing through and win?" Pecone nodded.

Jimmy held a peace conference with Romelle. Reconciliation was out of the question, but the timing of a divorce and any subsequent remarriage was important to both of them. In the meantime, they would hold their fire until a settlement could be worked out acceptable to both sides.

The family continued to apply pressure to have him take cover from the storm of publicity. It was useless. He considered the struggle to be solely his problem. "If I win it, life for Mother, Anna and for my brothers, for the ideals that we believe in, but above all, for all of our children," he wrote to Jim Halsted, "will permanently be changed for the better. I believe this with all my heart."

It turned out that he was on target and Mother and the rest not. On June 10, he was nominated by his party for the 26th District seat. A staid announcement the following day said that an out-of-court settlement had been reached with Romelle.

For Franklin, the governorship of New York was to be the next step up the ladder, but he lost the nomination. Carmine De Sapio and the sachems of Tammany chose instead to make

"Available" Harriman the candidate. Franklin glumly accepted second best: he would run for attorney general and trust that he could accumulate enough votes to make him the prime contender next time.

On November 4, Jimmy won his seat in Congress. In New York every Democrat in the races was elected—except Franklin, who lost to Jacob Javits. Newspaper columnists began writing about him not as a potential President but as a rocket that had tumbled down.

Jimmy waited until a summer Sunday in 1956 to marry again. In the rectory of the Church of the Advent in Los Angeles, Irene Owens Schultz, who had worked as his office receptionist, became the third Mrs. James Roosevelt. His letter arrived in advance for me. "I shall never forget how you stood by us when the bottom seemed to have dropped out of everything. So now that things look a little better, we want you to know we hope to make you proud and happy that you know us. . . . Say a little prayer that what I guess is our last chance to put together a good team will really stand the strains of time and that our faith and love will overcome all the obstacles we are prepared to meet." Mother asked if I would represent the family once more at the wedding.

Her seventieth birthday had come and gone, and she had reconciled herself to having it expanded into a public celebration. She agreed to let the American Association for the United Nations proceed in "really commercializing it" because that was one way to help the impoverished group reduce its debts. Toward the same end, she asked friends not to buy her presents but send a check to the cause.

The day opened with a surprise call at her front door by a choir of boys from Wiltwyck School, scrubbed clean and bearing gifts—one hundred homemade pot holders, to be precise. They broke into a serenade with what was popularly believed to be her favorite song, *Beautiful Dreamer*; it was one of the few tunes she could carry in her head. The boys made a second appearance later in the ballroom of the Waldorf-Astoria, where some thousand guests were assembled for a fund-raising AAUN dinner. This time, she was presented with an outsized birthday card signed by every Wiltwyck scholar.

Dag Hammarskjöld, the current secretary general of the United Nations, was there along with Trygve Lie and the black and eminent Dr. Ralph Bunche. Bernard Baruch came to deliver a kiss to his "dear lady," and Henry Morgenthau had a seat close by him. Andrei Vishinsky, arriving to make amends for his catcalling in the days when she was Madam Chairman, disclaimed a place of distinction on the dais. "If I were an American, I would be a Republican," he needled her.

There were some singular absentees. None of the present team of American delegates to the United Nations was in sight, which was explicable only by remembering that guilt by association had not been entirely discredited in Washington councils, and there were those, including one of her daughters-in-law, who had Mother tagged as a cryptocommunist. In Senate hearings, the United States Army had been engaged for two months in destroying Joseph McCarthy, but it would be two months more before he was finally condemned.

The message addressed to the gathering by the President was not exactly glowing: "She has carved out for herself, by her own multitudinous activities, a prominent place in our nation's life."

She found it hard to wait another two years to try to get him out of office in favor of Adlai. She scoffed at the performance so far of what Eisenhower called Modern Republicanism when GOP old-timers kept his party walking on the right of the road. "He evidently felt," she said, "he could establish his Administration in the pattern of big business, but such an approach is not necessarily either democratic or successful."

As for his Secretary of State, she detested him. Mr. Dulles was past redemption for allowing McCarthy to ride roughshod over loyal State Department employees; for his affront to Nehru in negotiating treaties with Japan without consulting in New Delhi first; for his broadcast promising Eastern Europeans that they could depend on United States backing to throw off the Soviet yoke, then doing nothing when riots broke out in East Germany.

At seventy, she liked to think that she could keep up the same pace she had set for the past forty years. She could still earn nearly $90,000 a year, but she had to push herself to make it. Getting up in the morning to face the day took longer now. Holding her weight down was a fluctuating occupation that tempted her into skipping meals some days or else nibbling only on salads. Arthritis in the neck gave her a permanent stoop in the effort to minimize pain. David became equally essential as doctor as well as friend. She swallowed a prescribed sleeping pill if the arthritis was especially bothersome at night, but this was a last resort, and she chided herself for her weakness.

An intimation of her thinking, more revealing than most readers suspected, appeared in "My Day." "Life has got to be lived—that's all there is to it. At seventy, I would say that you take life more calmly. You know that 'This, too, shall pass!'"

That column of hers had been running for so many years that writing it was a habit not much more taxing than applying the toothbrush. It served any number of purposes. It was in part a diary of domesticity: "My Scotties know when you say goodbye for any length of time and grow rather mournful." It was used to boost a play, movie or book she had enjoyed: "I have just finished reading 'The Nine Men,' a political history of the Supreme Court of the U.S. from 1790 to 1955, by Fred Rodell, professor of law at Yale University. This is a most interesting book and one I think all of us should read."

"My Day" provided her with a permanent platform for political exhortation: "I am not a Republican, but I believe that all of us Democrats and Republicans alike owe the office of the President as well as the man who occupies it respect and truth in our criticisms." And the seemingly guileless words, carefully counted to make sure there were at least eight hundred but no more than a thousand, regularly mentioned Father and gave snatches of her conclusions about life: "Justice probably can never be achieved in this world."

For two weeks in the summer of 1955, "My Day" carried a healthy scent of the outdoors. With Maureen and David, Mother arrived for a vacation at the Rolling R. No matter how much her children hurt her, she sought us out in her need for love. She had not been on a horse since she rode Dot, but she had been with us only a day or so when she decided it was time to remedy that. The column told the story by installments.

August 5. "The longer I am on Elliott's ranch here in Meeker, the more I grieve that I ever gave up riding, for this kind of riding even old ladies could do. This is to say, an old lady could if she has stayed moderately slim. Perhaps it will give me the needed incentive so that if I return here in the autumn, I will have reached a point where I feel I can get on a horse again."

August 8. "On walking into the hotel in Meeker this morning to file my column, I was overcome by the number of heads and skins covering the walls of the lobby. I am rather glad to be here in the fishing season, however, and I am sure the woods are pleasanter when the animals are not being hunted."

August 9. "After returning to the ranch, we had a late lunch and went for a ride. It was only my second attempt, so of course they were taking me at a very slow pace. I feel sure I would be completely inadequate to anything that required more than merely sitting on the horse and letting him take his own way up and down the mountains. But I enjoyed it very much and am glad to find that I am not stiff from the experience."

August 13. "I have a horse that is very sure-footed, but a bit slow. However, he follows very well, and he likes to follow one particular horse and will do exactly what that horse does—jog, trot, canter or walk, which last is, of course, what one does most of the time. I like all his gaits except his canter. I find that is rather pounding, though I know perfectly well it is partly my fault. Nevertheless, I like to fool myself into thinking he has a hard canter. I am improving, however, for this morning's ride was a three-hour journey, and it did not even tire me."

When she left Meeker, she went to visit with Jimmy in Los Angeles, departure point for her and her two stalwarts to hie off again to the Far East. She was as eager as a blue-ribbon student for more firsthand knowledge of the region and a look at the sights, with David along to make living more comfortable.

They journeyed to Japan, Hong Kong, Manila and then the fantasyland of Bali. David, younger and more starry-eyed than she, reported that "she felt the entire island population was like a monastery's, every act of daily life influenced by religion." Mother's summing up was less ecstatic: "By the time we left Bali for Jakarta and Bangkok, I felt I had seen enough dancing to last me the rest of my life."

Wherever her travels crossed the path taken by Adlai on his trip through the noncommunist world in 1953, she heard good reports about him from foreign statesmen. "He is the kind of man who listens," she was told, "who wants to learn the facts." She came home from this latest expedition even more positive that Adlai stood head and shoulders above any other candidate for the White House. Only he could restore the Presidency to what it had been in Father's years, a force for cooperation overseas and advancement at home. Justifiably, she ranked Stevenson above any of her sons in wisdom, charm and maturity. Not a day must be lost in securing him the nomination for a second time. But first this disarming and still reluctant ex-diplomat had to be coaxed into running.

"Don't you feel," he asked in her apartment one afternoon, "that there are others who would do better than I as leader of the party?"

Such modesty was not to be tolerated. "I cannot think of anyone else," she replied, "who has the ability to do the job you do in meeting the most vital needs of the day." He left not yet convinced that she was right, but already she was dashing off letters, telephoning liberal allies, rounding up recruits for Stevenson committees, and raising funds for him.

From all I could gather, there was more reticence on both sides in this relationship than in that with Gurewitsch. Mother treated Adlai like a bright child who had to be coached to win the college scholarship. Politics and little else took up the hours they spent together. There was not time for the slow baring of souls. She let no hint fall that she ever pierced his emotional defenses, raised to conceal unhappiness in his private life and the fact that as a twelve-year-old out with a gun he had accidentally killed a friend.

She paid a call at Baruch's South Carolina plantation, Hobcaw Barony, which needed a certain effort, since Father and Lucy had once shared hospitality there together. But she hoped to loosen Bernie's pursestrings for Stevenson's coming battle. A letter told Adlai how to handle him. "In devious ways Mr. Baruch will give you money when you want it in cash for specific things. If you sigh a little and say you haven't enough to meet a specific need, I think you will find it forthcoming."

Thirteen months ahead of the election, she assured herself that her favorite was prepared to fight. A word of praise was said for him at every opportunity before an audience and to friends. Eisenhower announced that he would seek another term in spite of the heart attack that kept him from his duties for nearly two months, and again Nixon would undoubtedly be his understudy.

"If that is the case," Mother snapped, "the Democrats will have to work harder than ever because I doubt if Eisenhower can stand a second term, and I doubt if the country can stand Nixon as President."

Nixon, she thought shrewdly, could be made the Achilles' heel of the Republicans. With all the malice she could muster, she took aim at him on a subsequent radio show. "I happen to remember very clearly his campaign for the Senatorship. I have no respect for the way in which he accused Helen Gahagan Douglas of being a Communist because he knew that was how he would be elected, and I have no respect for the kind of character that takes advantage and does something they know is not true. . . . I have always felt that anyone who wanted an election so much that they would use those means did not have the character that I really admire in public life."

If there was anyone more deadly than Nixon, it was Dulles. She was appalled to read his exposition of brinkmanship, written for *Life* magazine in January. "The ability to get to the verge without getting into the war is the necessary art. . . . We've had to look it square in the face—on the question of enlarging the Korean war, on the question of getting into the Indochina war, on the question of Formosa. We walked to the brink, and we looked it in the face." This most hazardous of all cold-war strategies was "utterly disgraceful," she fumed. The strange, moralizing Secretary of State "frightened most of our allies to death." The sooner he was gone, the better.

No act of his angered her more than his response when President Gamal Abdel Nasser of Egypt seized the Suez Canal from its French and British stockholders to close it to all Israeli shipping, and this when Democrats were streaming into Chicago to pick their candidate. Mother would have liked instant United States retaliation. "It is the *gravest* of errors, Elliott, for us to stand by doing nothing and allowing the Egyptians to get away with it. We should take a strong line with the United Nations to condemn this—this *terrorism*."

With Mother and Stevenson, I flew to Chicago, disenchanted with Ike but without faith in Adlai, whom I regarded as a lightweight political personality. Eisenhower looked like a certain winner again to me, so all she was achieving as Adlai's champion was condemning him to go down as a two-time loser. She had canceled all other business except the most urgent to concentrate on getting him nominated.

Campaigning for him in the early primaries had brought mixed results—negative in Minnesota, positive in the District of Columbia and California, where Jimmy had joined in, too. One of the most effective contributions she made was to go after black leaders like Ralph Bunche and Roy Wilkins of the

National Association for the Advancement of Colored People, assuring them that while he spoke guardedly about "mod-
eration," Adlai was as dedicated to expanding civil rights as
any liberal in the party.

Thanks to Jimmy, we had hotel rooms waiting for us, but it
was a while before we checked into them after landing at
O'Hare Airport. While we were en route, Harry Truman had
named *his* choice. Beating Eisenhower demanded a fighter,
which in his inflexible opinion disqualified Stevenson. The
man he was going down the line for was Governor Harriman.
"Well, that's certainly no help to *us*," Mother sighed, "but
we shall have to do the best we can." She did not relish the
thought of pitting herself against Truman; neither did Adlai.

His campaign manager, Jim Finnegan, had a car waiting for
us at the airport. Mother and Adlai shared the back seat, while
I eavesdropped from the jump seat in front of their knees.
Even now, he wavered about seeking the nomination. She
browbeat him for most of the ride into downtown Chicago.

"There are many people who could wage this campaign just
as well as myself. I don't know that I'd be the right candidate,
I don't think I should carry on as the standard-bearer——"

"You are the *only* one who can possibly do it," Mother said
flatly, "and you *will* do it."

"But I'm not sure that I want to."

"Oh, yes, you *do!*"

Downtown, she proceeded to whisk in and out of a series of
caucus meetings, where strategy for Stevenson was being for-
mulated, to establish her position forcefully and immediately.
"Adlai Stevenson is the inheritor of the beliefs of President
Roosevelt. He is the one candidate who represents the thinking of my husband."

At the Blackstone Hotel, she had to face more reporters
and cameras than she had ever faced simultaneously. How
was she going to justify opposing Truman? Her initial qualms
disappeared the moment she began to speak. She gently
deflated any reputation Harriman might have garnered as a
fighting man. She wondered aloud whether Adlai was any less

experienced for the chief executive's duties than Truman had been at Father's death. And she twitted her rival promoter about his age—five months older than she—and the outdated tradition that gave elder politicians "more influence than they should have had."

Then the session had to be broken up; she had a prearranged luncheon date with Truman in the grillroom. His wife, Bess, sent her excuses, but a handful of sharp-eared newspapermen took another table so close they could have used the same plates.

"I hope," said her luncheon partner, "you will understand that whatever action I take is because I think I am doing the right thing."

"Of course. I know you will act as you believe is right, and I know you will realize that I must do the same."

There was a grin on his creased cheeks. "What I want to do is make this convention do some real thinking about issues." Did any former champion of the political prize ring say anything different on the eve of another bout?

Each day we spent in Chicago, she tired herself out, working so long and late that she did not appear for breakfast until the unheard-of hour of nine o'clock and was not ready for her first appointment much before ten. She wore the same flowered blue dress because it was too much bother to find something else until somebody drew her attention to the monotony and she promised to do better tomorrow.

Sprightly young Jack Kennedy sought audience with her, looking for support in his bid to be the Vice-Presidential nominee. He came up to the rooms we had at the Blackstone, which were loud with the ringing of telephones and awash with friends and family. She knew something about the Kennedy clan. Everything she had heard and seen of the father, old Joe, aroused her veiled antagonism. Father had briefed her on Joe's shortcomings as wartime ambassador in London, when he advocated striking a quick peace with the Nazis at the same time as he was sewing up a dealership in Scotch whisky for himself in the United States.

The Kennedy she was best acquainted with was Jack's mother, Rose. Mother felt sorry for her, without realizing the strength of this woman or to what degree she dictated the operations of all her family.

One yardstick Mother applied to any political hopeful in 1956 was his record on McCarthyism. "I cannot be sure of the political future of anyone who does not willingly state where he stands on that issue," she said. Young Kennedy had never announced his position. The second of two spine-fusion operations, treatment for a bad back that put him onto crutches, had kept him out of the Senate when the vote was taken, 67 to 22, to censure McCarthy. Convalescence over, Kennedy ducked answering reporters' questions on how he would have voted, for or against the fellow Catholic from Wisconsin who had a sizable following in Massachusetts.

"Just where *do* you stand on McCarthyism, Senator?" Mother demanded when the introductions were over. For lack of anywhere else to sit, they faced each other from the edges of twin beds. He was as equivocal with her as he had been with the press. The vote on McCarthy had happened so long ago that it was a dead issue, he said; it had no relevance today. She could get nothing more out of him on the subject. Jimmy and Franklin had already climbed onto the bandwagon that was rolling on well-greased wheels to make Kennedy the choice for the Vice-Presidency, but that meant nothing to her.

"I do not see how I can possibly support you, Senator," she told him bluntly. "McCarthyism is a question on which *everyone* must stand up and be counted. You avoid committing yourself, while your brother Robert was actually on the McCarthy staff. I am surprised that you ask help from *me.* Good day!"

When balloting on the Vice-Presidential nomination began, Mother had left Chicago. She knew that Adlai would leave the convention free to name whomever it wanted to run with him, and she had seen to it that her views of Jack Kennedy were no secret. The Boston bandwagon was mired down in the opposition she had roused, and Estes Kefauver was given the job.

She had rounded off her sponsorship of Stevenson by putting on one of her best dresses, adorned with a big ADLAI button, and adding a flowered hat for her appearance on the platform to speak for him. She cited Father's vision of an America in which no one went ill-housed, ill-clothed or ill-fed. The world, she declared, looked once more to the United States to blaze the trail toward true democracy. Only the right leadership could accomplish the task. When she sat down to a roar of applause, she had clinched Adlai's nomination for the Presidency.

Before she got down to the business of stumping the country for him, she took two of her grandsons and young Grania Gurewitsch off for a three-week vacation to see the sights of Europe. At every stop, she mailed Adlai another note of encouragement. "I feel more certain than ever that you can win," she emphasized, as she repeated to herself, "Well, we *do* have a chance."

Starting on the September day of her return to New York, she was off and running so fast that each of us children felt compelled to give her the same warning: "You're going to have to slow down. Don't get yourself involved again in a job like this."

Even she confessed that it was "a hectic period." She flew north, south and west to praise Adlai on a day-and-night schedule so tight that she could make it work only by dozing in a plane, in the back of a car or in somebody's office chair. Now and then, she was struck by the absurdity of the electoral ritual in which she had been caught up since she was a young housewife courting votes for her husband. Motorcades, after all, were "rather silly performances." Giving the same speech over and over again left her "mighty tired of the sound of my own voice."

The lectures she had contracted to deliver had to be squeezed into the timetable somehow, and so did "My Day." One morning in Los Angeles, the calendar called for a luncheon speech, a news conference, a reception, a flight to San Diego for a TV show, then a return in time to introduce, on a television hookup with Milwaukee, Stevenson, who was speaking there. The plane back to Los Angeles landed so late that she reached the studio with only thirty minutes to spare. She dumbfounded the station's management by asking for a stenographer to take down two "My Day" columns while Adlai's local lieutenants came close to throwing fits.

But there was no letup when the state of the world was worsening day by day. Adlai spoke for Mother when he brought up the prickly question of ending further tests of the hydrogen bomb, which the United States had been conducting for four years, the Soviets for three. That would be "a moratorium on common sense," snorted Eisenhower—who came up with the same suggestion in 1958.

At the end of October, the Suez Canal crisis flared again. British and French planes bombed Egypt immediately after the Israelis invaded the Sinai Desert bordering the canal. At the same time, the Hungarians had taken Dulles at his word in his promise of American help in casting off Soviet domination. They took further encouragement from Moscow's tolerance in allowing Poland to take an independent path to socialism, and on October 23, Hungary began its suicidal battle for freedom. It would result in 200,000 Red Army soldiers storming into the country, 32,000 Hungarian dead and another 195,000 in flight as refugees.

Mother was as much outraged by what Dulles omitted to do as by the steps he actually took. "Why doesn't he take the stand he's always *talking* about and confront the Soviets to compel them to be merciful in Hungary? Why does he insist on having Israel pull out of the Sinai when *everyone* knows that it's going to bring *more* threats to Israel from the Arab countries and most *serious* repercussions in the future? That man is the worst Secretary of State in our entire history, and Eisenhower one of the weakest Presidents we have ever *had*."

But events in Budapest and in the Sinai increased the odds against Stevenson. The voters trusted Ike in times of peril. More blacks supported him than before, helping him to a plurality of close to ten million votes and victory in all but seven states. "I'm glad to be out of politics," Mother sighed when it was over, but none of us believed her.

Not all her bitterness over Stevenson's defeat had been shed when winter ended and she took up an invitation to go to Morocco. On behalf of Sultan Mohammed V, it had been extended soon after France granted his country independence in March, 1956. The diplomats from Rabat who made it had driven to Hyde Park with a huge boxful of flowers to place on the grave. Mother set greater significance by this gesture of respect a little later when she wrote to the sultan, whom she had never met, asking him to give clearance for 10,000 Moroccan Jews to leave for Israel. Though her letter went unanswered, within two weeks the emigrants were on their way.

She was curious to see what manner of man it was whose attitude toward Jews was so different from that of his fellow potentates in the Middle East. Father and I had both told her of our meeting him as a nine-year-old when his grand vizier, aged ninety, brought him to dinner on the same night as Winston Churchill during the Casablanca Conference. I took the boy up in a P-38, struggling to talk with him in French.

When David Gurewitsch outlined a vacation in North Africa planned for himself and Grania, Mother jumped at the chance to join in and visit Morocco in a party that included Minnewa and me. Sultan Mohammed was undergoing hospital surgery when we landed in Casablanca, but he rose from his chair in the audience room to welcome Mother when we presented ourselves at his palace in Rabat two days later.

The handsome young monarch with the sensitive face and smiling eyes won Mother over on sight. After refreshments and some minutes of conversation, when the rest of our party withdrew, he asked the two of us to remain. What she had seen of the land so far had given her the feeling that there was more sympathy here for the United States than elsewhere in the Arab world. As he spoke with us, running a string of beads between his long fingers, she understood why.

He reminisced about the few hours he had spent with FDR,

listening in silence as Father chatted in animated French with the grand vizier and ignoring Winston's attempts to interrupt. "Your husband gave unselfish advice," said the sultan. "I was convinced of your country's friendship. As a foreign head of state his attitude was exceptional. He spoke of our need to develop in order to improve life for our people. He foresaw some of them entering your universities to receive technical training and the employment of your experts to help us begin our work—all this, of course, when we were as yet a protectorate of France."

Would she consent to make a tour of his country to see for herself what had been done in a single year of independence? "I try to bring my people to an enlightened attitude toward all races and end discrimination against the Jews. Unfortunately, we are still very backward, lacking in education, sanitation and medical facilities, but I believe we shall succeed eventually to modernize our lives."

Mother was eager to be off on a tour of inspection. He made no effort to restrict her in any town or village from making her way into the Jewish ghettos. In appearance, the Jews were indistinguishable from the rest of the 15,000,000 population. The sultan had abolished measures to confine them, but to date few had chosen to move out. Many were waiting for the opportunity to emigrate to Israel. She sought assurance from him that their exit would not be impeded.

His reply was statesmanlike. "Because I regard them as Moroccan citizens, I shall do what I can to persuade them to stay, adding their talents to make conditions equal and better for all. But they will decide for themselves."

She was enthused by Mohammed V, who ranked as the second most influential leader among all Arabs. He had an open mind; he seemed interested in working out solutions to Arab-Israeli hostility, perhaps by linking his nation with Tunisia and Algeria to bridge differences between East and West. But not once did she express to him any concern for the plight of Arab refugees from and inside Israel. If she had, I thought she might have enlisted him in the task of setting up the forgotten homeland for Palestinians.

In a caravan of three ancient automobiles, we set out from Marrakech one morning, to bounce along dirt tracks that took us past camel herds hundreds strong and ox-powered water wheels irrigating patches of green in the drab desert. Jolted across the foothills of the Atlas Mountains, we came upon the hilltop town of Demnat, where hooded peasants drove sheep through the swirling dust. Outside the main gate in Demnat's crumbling sandstone walls, a crowd waited in the blistering afternoon sun.

"*Welcome! welcome!*" they shouted in chorus. Over the gate hung a sheet daubed with dyes into a resemblance of the Stars and Stripes, and a crudely lettered sign which said, "We always remember President Roosevelt."

She might be getting old, but she was as eager as ever to travel to the ends of the earth. "My Day" had just started appearing in the *New York Post* in 1957 when Dorothy Schiff asked Mother to lunch. "Would you like to go to China and write a series of articles for me?"

"I certainly would" was the instant reply. But the State Department turned down her application for a visa. For twelve years, she had been seeking permission to visit the Soviet Union. Was she forever, she fumed, to be frustrated by silly people who claimed that American citizens must be stayed from departing for countries where they would be beyond United States protection? A newspaper reporter like herself did not worry about taking *risks*.

Mrs. Schiff had an alternative idea. Would Mother go to Russia instead? For all the barrage of abuse the two powers let off at each other, a shaky equilibrium had been reached since each had demonstrated its capacity to pulverize the other. At a Big Four summit in Geneva, Eisenhower had gone so far as to say, "It is not always necessary that people should think alike before they can work together."

The United States and the Soviet Union still exchanged squawks across the "iron curtain," but at long last Mother won permission to fly into Moscow, her main purpose to interview Nikita Khrushchev, who after consolidating his position as premier and chairman of the Communist Party had denounced Stalin and repudiated Stalinist cruelty in a seven-hour speech a year ago.

This time, she would have to travel with more than the usual scant amount of luggage. She would be gone the best part of a month. Perhaps she would take a present for Mr. Khrushchev. She would pick up a Mark Cross attaché case on Fifth Avenue the next time she ate lunch at Old Denmark on East 57th Street, a favorite spot, which also sold the cookies she bought by the box once a month for David Gurewitsch.

Mother, he and Maureen had waited three months for their visas. His presence on a trip like this was imperative when the pains of old age nagged Mother. Arthritis in neck and shoulders made turning her head difficult. David was under constant pressure to try new treatments and medicines, but the trouble persisted. Her feet plagued her so that every chance was taken to sit down for a moment in the middle of whatever she was doing. Carrying on a conversation without the hearing aid-spectacles in place was not to be attempted.

Until now, she paid little attention to her health and disdained medical checkups. Of necessity, that had changed, but she found the change obnoxious. "Elliott, I do so *resent* this old body of mine."

David gave priority to this patient's needs. She could see him at any time without an appointment. Other patients would be directed to fellow physicians so that he might go with her to the USSR. He would be invaluable in a number of ways. He spoke fluent Russian; he would bring his camera; and he could handle the tape recorder, a device that flummoxed her.

As soon as the plane began crossing the Soviet Union, she was struck by the depths of her ignorance of this vast land of forests and lakes, glinting in the early September sunlight. "I had always thought of Russia as treeless steppes," exclaimed this astonished reader of Tolstoi and Dostoevski. A respectful

welcome awaited her at the airport, but the driver of the limousine heading into Moscow showed rather too much regard
for her advancing years. "Do you think we might get along a
little *faster*?" she asked.

A second surprise was in store after she had been ushered
into a suite in the National Hotel: sitting room, bedroom and
bath. She learned by accident that the ornate, dark furniture
had been transported from Yalta, a thousand miles away. It
was the furniture installed for Father when he stayed there in
Livadia Palace for the Big Three conference. One more token
of esteem was supplied in the petite person of Anna Lavrova,
FDR's interpreter in his Yalta talks with Stalin. David decided
that Russian hospitality was "prodigious"; Mother found it
"almost embarrassing."

No appointment had yet been fixed with Khrushchev. She
set about rectifying that on her first day. On request, she
wrote out the intended questions in letter form, submitted
them, and then waited—and waited. There was no response.

For the time being, she was too busy to be unduly concerned. There was too much to see and do for any day to be
wasted. Every morning, she would choose between two basic
outfits: long-sleeved, gray wool dress with a little cape over
the shoulders, or five-button, gray two-piece. The pearls and
the flat, striped toque which was her only hat would go with
either. She had brought two handbags, both roomy enough to
hold a full day's provisions, plus a cardigan and a double-
breasted topcoat in case the temperature dropped. She was
happy with her hair; for a change, it stayed *neat*.

The bright blue eyes took in the tourist sights: the ballet, a
circus, a state farm, where the cattle seemed scrawny, judged
by Val-Kill standards. With David and Mrs. Lavrova, she
took a rush-hour ride, straphanging in the Moscow subway,
and marveled at the grandeur of stations splendid with statu-
ary and glass chandeliers.

She waited patiently on line in Red Square to see the preserved body of Lenin in his tomb, declining the Intourist
guide's offer to slip her in ahead of the crowd. She went with

David to tour hospitals, donning surgical mask and coverall to inspect one operating room where eight or nine tables were in simultaneous use. David remembered that a young woman patient, abdomen already opened under local anesthetic, nearly rolled over onto the floor as she reached out to grasp Mother's hand the instant she heard that here was the celebrated Mrs. Franklin Roosevelt.

A pilgrimage had to be arranged to Samarkand, the walled city in Turkestan which may have been the most magnificent capital in Asia when Tamerlane, the crippled Mogul conqueror, made it his home. Her father had promised that this was to be a second place they would see together, like the Taj. In turban and caftan, the mufti pressed gifts into her hands. She was more pleased to note that his party of local officials contained two women.

The trained eyes took in a mosaic of details which she would soon try to assemble in her mind. "The Russians generally do not dress well. . . . Prices of clothes are high. . . . Most Russian travellers go where they are told when they are told to go. . . . In 1956, the Russian schools graduated about 26,000 doctors. In the United States, we graduated about 6,500. . . . None but a Communist newspaper can be bought in the Soviet Union, so the people get only the slanted Communist point of view on what is happening in the world."

In a Leningrad medical school, she felt the bits of the pattern fall into place. She fancied that the real father of the Soviet system was neither Karl Marx nor Lenin but Dr. Ivan Petrovich Pavlov, deceased uncle of her black-bearded sparring partner on Committee Three. The Soviet government had built a special laboratory for Dr. Pavlov before his death in 1936. The results of his experiments provided keys to the nature of learning.

His most celebrated subjects were the dogs housed in kennels fitted with lights and bells. A light flashed or a bell rang whenever the animals were fed, until they came to associate the sight or the sound with eating. Then the psychologist was ready for the second, conclusive stage of his study. Lights were turned on or bells pealed without feeding the dogs, who nevertheless drooled at the prospect of a meal. As David could explain, this was a conditioned response based on a need, in this case hunger. A well-fed dog would have ignored the entire procedure.

In the nursery of the Pavlov Institute, home for thirty-two orphaned or abandoned children, Mother saw the master's findings put into practice. A six-months-old baby had been conditioned to carry out simple exercises without direction from his nurse, who rewarded him with hugs and kisses. Four children, eighteen months old, who, uninstructed, performed more complicated routines were "like a drill team," my freedom-loving mother said in disapproval.

The implications frightened her. Young Russians were being raised to accept discipline by a process of life-long, Pavlovian training. With the whole economy also under control, Soviet leaders possessed the power to achieve goals well-nigh unattainable by Western countries, and not only in the USSR but in have-not nations too.

A symbol she saw everywhere was the white dove of peace with an olive branch in its beak, on wall posters, on the sides of trucks, and even in action when a living flock of the birds circled over the audience as the finale of the circus. She found it ironic that the dove "has become the symbol of an American plot to start a world war," but unfortunately that was what Russians believed. Only one week before her touchdown in Moscow, the Russians had tested an intercontinental ballistic missile.

Three weeks were almost up, and still there was no word from the Kremlin about when or whether she might meet Khrushchev. She had just returned with David, Maureen and Mrs. Lavrova to the National Hotel after a thousand-mile flight from Sochi, the health and holiday resort by the sands of the Black Sea. Only her three companions knew that at Sochi exhaustion had overcome her. Her principal comment on the place was, "I never realized how important vacations were until I heard them discussed so fervently in the Soviet Union." Three more days remained before she must leave for New York.

"I forget to tell you," Mrs. Lavrova said casually when Mother was relaxing in her suite, "but we go to Yalta tomorrow morning."

Another thousand miles to go back to where they had come from? "Well," said Mother, tight-lipped, "I'm glad you finally remembered."

She was too worn out to attend an afternoon reception where she was to have been guest of honor. Accepting David's advice, she put herself to bed, while he sat and read in the sitting room. The telephone rang; a call for Mrs. Roosevelt. She was asleep, David answered. But this was the office of Chairman Khrushchev. David apologized, but she did need the rest. Would he please hold the line for a moment?

It was a different voice this time. "Dr. Gurewitsch? You are speaking to the chairman, and I would like to speak to Mrs. Roosevelt."

"Sir, you are speaking to Mrs. Roosevelt's physician, and I am answering that Mrs. Roosevelt is not able to come to the telephone."

She awoke feeling better, and they were off again for the Black Sea the following morning, checking into a Yalta hotel that night, where a message was waiting. Chairman Khrushchev's car would be calling for them at nine-thirty a.m. tomorrow. She forced herself up hours earlier. Time must be made to visit the Livadia Palace, once the czar's summer home, now restored as a tuberculosis sanatorium. She had to see Father's accommodations at Yalta, in Winston's hostile estimation a pest hole that had ruined the health of FDR.

On the stroke of nine-thirty, they were in the car, driving down the hill to Khrushchev's comfortable villa on the outskirts of the town. At the first guarded gate, the car pulled off the road and stopped under some trees. In her topcoat, Mother fingered her watch. "Oh, dear, I do hope we are not going to be late!'' After a brief wait, the driver started off again—he had been killing time so they would arrive on the minute set for her appointment.

In a loose-fitting suit that did nothing to disguise his paunch, the stocky, bald little man was standing outside the villa, grinning a welcome. With him were his wife Nina, daughter and son-in-law. First, the visitors must be shown the flowers in his garden and a glimpse through the woods of the white walls of Yalta. Then David set up the battery-powered tape recorder, and the chairman and Mother settled down for two and a half hours, rounded off by a meal with all the family.

"I appreciate your coming here," Khrushchev began, "and I want to speak of President Franklin Roosevelt. . . . He was a great man, a capable man who understood the interests of his own country and those of the Soviet Union. We had a common cause against Hitler, and we appreciate very much that Franklin Roosevelt understood this task."

Mother proceeded to business. Disarmament was the opening subject on the agenda. The Red Army outnumbered United States armed forces. Why was that?

Because the vastness of the USSR demanded one army in the west, another in the east. Wartime America had 12 million men under arms. "In our country perished roughly the number of persons you mention as making up the army of your country—almost the same number, Mrs. Roosevelt."

Why couldn't the Soviets disband their forces, which terrified the rest of the world?

"When we increase our arms, it means we are afraid of each other. Until the troops are drawn out of Europe and military bases liquidated, the disarmament will not succeed."

Sometimes, the discussion grew sharp, but he was consistently affable, revealing nothing of the boorishness displayed three years later, when he took off a shoe to pound a desk at the United Nations General Assembly in New York. Chairman and former Madam Chairman clashed over that impalpable entity, "the will of the people," in Eastern Europe. The Americans were attempting to destroy it, he said. Communism was not to be equated with it, she retorted. Did he seriously believe that the future of the world would be communist?

He did. "As certain as it takes nine months to make a baby, as certainly communism will rule the world." It was a scientific forecast based on the works of Marx, Lenin and Engels, philosophers of revolution. His rubbery, peasant face could be very bland. "We are against any military attempt to introduce communism or socialism into any country."

Neither would cede an inch. They went around in circles except on one point. "Misunderstandings have grown between our countries," she moralized, "and there is fear on both sides. We will have to do things to create confidence. One thing is a broader exchange of people."

"I fully agree, Mrs. Roosevelt."

Walking her to the car, he asked with a smile, "Can I tell our papers that we have had a friendly conversation?"

A stickler for the truth, Mother replied, "You can say that we had a friendly conversation, but that we *differ.*"

The smile broadened. "*Now!* At least we didn't shoot at each other!" He waved good-bye.

The power of the man's personality stuck in her mind. Was there a leader in the West to match him? she asked David. But the long-sought meeting with a Soviet chief was a letdown. Too much time had been lost, she felt, for her to reestablish FDR's bridgehead of understanding with the communists, which cold war had destroyed. The new generation in the Kremlin was not easy to work with. To her way of thinking, they were as much creatures of their own preconceptions as their counterparts in Washington. Both the communist and the capitalistic universes were set on courses that made rapprochement as difficult as handling nitroglycerin.

When she landed with Maureen and David in Copenhagen, she realized that she was fearful of what she had learned. In providing material benefits and steadily improving standards of living, communism worked for the Russian people, dictatorship or not. The Soviets could use the example of what had been accomplished since the revolution in 1917 to win over the hundreds of millions in Asia, Africa and Latin America who hungered for food, better health, education and hope for the future.

American complacency was equally alarming. To imagine that bombs could resolve the contest or that the Russians would rise in revolt against their government was to bury one's head in the sand. American democracy was under challenge to make good its ideals at home and so rekindle confidence in United States leadership the world over. She would spell it all out in a book just as soon as she got back, called *On My Own*.

A year later, when she returned to the USSR with David and Edna Gurewitsch, she did not see Khrushchev. Their encounter had to wait until the Soviet chairman, touring the United States as Eisenhower's guest, came scurrying to Hyde Park with his wife and a wreath inscribed, "To the outstanding statesman of the United States of America—the great champion of progress and peace among peoples." Security agents wanted to crop the elms that lined the drive to the house as precaution against hidden snipers. Mother bridled. "I put my foot down at having my trees destroyed."

It was a frantic day at Val-Kill. Young Princess Beatrice of the Netherlands had brought a party of overnight guests, making a total of sixteen for breakfast before she left at nine a.m. In the kitchen, Charlie Curnan was cooking up a batch of borscht for the luncheon that Khrushchev and an unknown number of companions were scheduled to eat with Mother. Marg Entrup baked desserts and cookies.

Every state trooper in New York appeared to have been brought in to mount guard on the driveway, the parking lot and the dirt road leading from the highway to the cottage. Tablesful of food were ready there when the motorcade screamed up to Hyde Park long after the expected hour. In a floral silk dress and white shoes, Mother whisked the Khrushchevs around the big house and the library, then took them up to her place.

There was no time left for a meal, only for a champagne toast to friendship between the two nations. As Mother filled the glasses, the chairman's narrow eyes gleamed. "They call me a dictator. You see how little power I have? I told my wife not to drink any alcohol, and in front of me she takes champagne."

As he was hurried off back to Manhattan, he snatched a dry roll from a plate. "One for the road!" he shouted. Charlie Curnan's borscht and the rest of the spread went to feed the state troopers. "It was all rather *silly!*" Mother sighed.

David was on hand that day as he was much of the time now. All of us around her could recognize the quickening advance of old age. Getting dressed no longer took five mintues but closer to an hour. The knitting was still picked up whenever she sat down for a moment, but the needles would slip from permanently bent fingers, and she would nod off into sleep so deep that it would need more than a nudge to wake her. Something was happening that David could not yet diagnose.

I was relieved that he and his family now shared the same Manhattan brownstone with her. When the landlord raised the rent on the East 62nd Street apartment, she refused to sign a new lease and took refuge back in the Park Sheraton until David's scouting found a better home for her. Money was becoming a worry again. After the lost battle for Adlai, the number of newspapers buying "My Day" fell year by year to rock bottom, to the point where each daily column earned her approximately $30. She had no real cause for concern when book royalties and her *McCall's* pieces brought in some $60,000, but her charities kept her budgeting tight. In faltering health, she forced herself to continue on the lecture circuit, preferably at least once a week for the customary $1,000.

At seventy-five, she accepted a new job, teaching a weekly course in international law and organization at Brandeis University. This meant catching an evening flight from LaGuardia Airport, New York, for an overnight stay in Boston. In the morning, she would make her own way—"No car for me, thank you"—to Waltham, Massachusetts, for a breakfast conference in the faculty center, instruct her class, then fly back, all for $6,500 a year.

"I could not at any age," she said in self-justification, "be content to sit by the fireside and simply look on."

She liked the house that David showed her at Number 55 East 74th Street. "I want everything very simple—simple and not expensive," she told Gerhard Karplus, the architect she engaged for the remodeling after she bought it. "I don't like *gimmicks.*"

She would have two lower floors for herself and one elderly maid. The upper two would be made over into a separate apartment for the Gurewitsches to rent, with an option to buy the whole house in the end, as they did. David had an emergency call to attend to one April day when, outside her hairdresser's in Greenwich Village, she stepped off the curb behind a reversing station wagon.

Lying in Eighth Street with a ligament torn in one leg, she noticed that the driver was Puerto Rican, which might spell undeserved trouble when the police arrived. "It's all my fault," she fluttered. "I'm old enough to look both ways. There is no *need* to wait." She apologized to the strangers gathering around. "I'm sorry. I can't get up. I *shall* be able to in a little while." David arrived to tape the leg and take her home. Appointments had to be canceled, but she had nothing to complain about to the police.

They had to be involved when an announcement that she was booked to speak in St. Petersburg, Florida, produced an anonymous telephone call: Cancel the appearance, or the meeting will be bombed. "Isn't it *ironical*," she said, "that in the Communist countries I have visited there has never been so much as an unkind *word*?" Of course, she would go to St. Petersburg. People probably made such threats because she spoke up for blacks; the man who telephoned was likely to be a coward in any event.

The auditorium was filled, the introduction over, and she was about to begin when somebody took over the microphone. "Ladies and gentlemen, I have a message from the police department. Will you please vacate your seats and proceed to the nearest exit? The building must be cleared immediately. You will be readmitted just as soon as possible. I repeat—"

Mother remained on the platform for a minute or two to help maintain calm while the search for the threatened bomb got under way. She was touched by the courage of a little woman, possibly of her own age, who lingered on in the front row, protesting, "If I'm going to be blown up, I can't think of any better company to be blown up with."

"When people really mean business, they don't notify you beforehand," Mother assured herself. There was no bomb; the hall was refilled with no signs of absentees; she concluded her lecture in peace.

The onset of infirmity could not be permitted to slow her down. Every summer the entire enrollment of Wiltwyck School—from 100 to 150 waifs and foundlings, eight to fourteen years old—still came in by the busload from Esopus, New York, for a Hyde Park picnic. With help from as many grandchildren as could be rounded up, she cooked hot dogs by the hundreds, beans and corn; ordered coleslaw, cola, milk, cupcakes and a dozen gallons of ice cream. To one objection about "unnecessary expense," she responded, "When the King and Queen of England were here, we buttered the rolls. Why should we do less for these boys?"

They received a word of caution after games on the lawn were finished and lunch was to be served. "I would like you to know that I have 200 forks and 200 knives, and I want all of them back after you have eaten." Grandchildren were paid a quarter apiece to join in clearing up the debris, and then it was time for everyone to stretch out on the grass to listen as she read Rudyard Kipling's *Rikki-Tikki-Tavi* or *How the Elephant Got Its Trunk* and told tales of her travels.

Wiltwyck graduated some celebrities with memories of sunny days at Hyde Park. Floyd Patterson, once heavyweight champion of the world, was one; Claude Brown (*Manchild in the Promised Land*) another. The school had an enthusiastic patron in Harry Belafonte. He was asked over when she heard from some of her picnic guests what a hero he was of theirs. He and his wife were two of the last new friends she made. Learning that Mrs. Belafonte was to have a baby, Mother decided that the least she could do was to knit her a shawl for the crib.

Friends were needed because friendship warmed her heart, which was something her children seldom bothered with. David and Edna Gurewitsch, Joe and Trude Lash responded to her outpouring of love by loving her to a degree that should have shamed her sons and daughter. In this respect, each of us failed her. We took her generosity of spirit for granted, as we did her openhandedness when we ran short of money. We had the self-centeredness of children when we were all well into middle age.

For Johnny, a new career was opening up—a partnership in the brokerage house of Bache & Company. Republican affiliations were no handicap in his dealings with another diehard of the GOP, Jimmy Hoffa, steel-fisted boss of the Teamsters Union with enormous sums of the membership's pension fund to invest. Johnny scampered as hard as any of us to make himself rich and in the process paid no more attention to Mother's wants as a human being than we others did.

"I think he does tend to *tailor* his politics to suit his friends on Wall Street," she mused, "but of course he has every right to do so."

Franklin had concentrated on his law practice and his business interests after the dousing of his hopes for the governorship and perhaps later the White House. Until she read newspaper disclosures that the Dominican Republic was among his clients, she had no idea that he was accepting fees from the like of its tyrant president, General Rafael Trujillo Molina. Franklin was free to represent whomever he chose, but she was appalled nonetheless that a Roosevelt would consort with a dictator. "If I were asked, I should advise him to withdraw from that association publicly and *immediately*."

She was overjoyed when he did and concentrated on an altogether different business as a kingpin among dealers of imported automobiles. She received a new Fiat from him by way of celebration. He was settling down, she thought, as a stable member of society, as she wanted all five of us to be. Physically, he lived close at hand in Dutchess County, but she got no more solace from Franklin than from the rest. She wondered where his political ambition, which still flickered, would ever take him.

For some time, Anna was too far away to make up for Mother's lack of close companionship from her family, though Anna's happiness was one ray of sunshine for her consolation. Jim Halsted was appointed to a government hospital in Shiraz, Iran. With her grandchild Nina, Johnny's daughter, she spent two weeks there in the spring of 1959, grumbling when the teenage girl got home two hours late from a party, which was something my generation had been guilty of, too. "Please realize that times have changed," Anna admonished our parent, but that was not easy for a woman on the approach of her seventy-fifth birthday.

My brother Jimmy worked on conscientiously and unspectacularly in Congress, digging himself out from the leftover pile of debts. Nobody talked any longer about him as a candidate for the Presidency either, hard as he tried to cultivate men of influence in Washington. Mother had serious reservations about some of them, including Senator Lyndon Baines Johnson of Texas. The previous year, my brother arranged for him to be the star at the Memorial Day ceremony at Father's grave. There were the usual trappings of chairs set out on the lawn, prayers and tributes, with one exception. As soon as the program was over, Mother went into hiding. Lyndon and Lady Bird would have to be attended to by Jimmy. Mother had no wish to spend more time with them. If a man of Father's mold was to be elected again, it would have to be Adlai. She saw to it that they stayed in touch.

Nothing could have tempted me to give more than a moment's thought to a career in politics. Altogether too many other matters were demanding attention. One of several irons heating in the fire was the acquisition of some mountain acreage on which to build an executives' vacation retreat. I was into uranium mining with one Colorado neighbor, into drilling for oil with the son of another. Here was another Roosevelt caught up in the quest for Golconda that was almost an obsession among us five. Though the flow of letters from Mother did not cease, nobody was more negligent in writing back than I. Glib excuses evoked her misdirected sympathy: I was too busy.

Along with the rest of her jobs, new and old, she had picked a fight with Tammany and its slick boss, Carmine De Sapio, of the blue-tinted spectacles and pale silk suits. She ticked off three scores to be settled. In 1954, he more than any other backstage schemer had worked for Franklin's humiliation. In 1956, De Sapio had manipulated support for Harriman against Adlai. And she blamed the Tammany dandy for the Democrats' rout at the New York State polls in 1958. Now, with Joe Lash as a faithful lieutenant, she ranked in the top echelons of the Committee for Democratic Voters, whose primary objective in the interests of "real democracy" was the ousting of De Sapio. She looked forward to a showdown, possibly in July of 1960, when the party convened in Los Angeles.

June 30. "Elliott dearest: I got your wire today, and I will see you at the convention. Please arrange a little time when we can talk. . . . I have a sad letter from Minnewa. Is there no chance so you could perhaps find a life together possible again? There was so much loyalty and devotion between you it seems hard to believe it gone. I love you and am sad for you both."

My feelings about the approaching meeting with Mother were in confusion. I looked forward to the warmth of her love, but I dreaded seeing the fresh pain I had caused. What could be said to explain why yet another marriage was ending in disaster? Minnewa had gone through a harrowing nervous breakdown, calling for long spells in sanitariums. On medical advice, one of her family agreed that electrical shock should be part of the treatment, a traumatic experience for her which she ascribed to my doing. The antagonism engendered between us erased all hope of a reconciliation.

Mother had grown extremely fond of this daughter-in-law, hymning her praises even in "My Day" as no spouse of a child of hers had been advertised before. Minnewa "looks wonderful on horseback and rides very well." "Somehow, Minnewa manages meals for everyone—even on excursions when we all go off together." She had "a special kind of gift, both of an executive nature and in handling people."

For close to thirty years, Mother had done all she could think of to ensure the success of each of my four marriages. Four failures were the net result. I was not certain how much more goodwill I had a right to expect when she despaired of my ever becoming a balanced and useful citizen.

Politically, too, we would be at odds in Los Angeles. Like Jimmy and Franklin, I was in the camp of the Catholic John F. Kennedy, forty-three years old, who had been a favorite for nomination as Vice-President after winning a second Senate term in 1958 by a whopping 874,608 majority. Now he was off and running for President with his primary victories behind him, most notably in Protestant West Virginia. Harry Truman hinted darkly that old Joe Kennedy had bought the vote there, and Mother was inclined to believe him.

Three fellow Senators among a turnout of a dozen were on the same track—Hubert Humphrey of Minnesota, Stuart Symington of Missouri, and Johnson of Texas. Mother espied "a spark of greatness" in Humphrey's unblemished liberalism; she was noncommittal about Symington; she regarded Johnson as a distinctly slippery operator.

His voting record on civil rights, she felt, earmarked him as a bigot, not an FDR liberal; there was no indication that in the Presidency he would show a different face as he launched "the great society." The private fortune he had accumulated as a Congressman and then in the Senate disturbed her. Not only his constituents gained from the licenses he was instrumental in obtaining for Texas radio and television stations.

Federal grants helped his farming and ranching enterprises. He had a hand in his State's oil industry and in the engineering giant, Brown & Root, which enjoyed State Department help in its multinational business, including later activity in Viet Nam.

"I suppose one must conclude that everything he turns to is perfectly *legal*," Mother sniffed, "but that only goes to show that we need stricter laws."

Adlai, she thought, remained "the only mature person among the lot," but until she could hector him into a third try, she kept her partiality her own affair. Averell Harriman was one inquirer at Val-Kill who tried to coax her into declaring herself. The Democrats wanted to know where she stood to avoid the embarrassment of having the woman they looked upon as the party's grandmother step off independently at convention time.

Her attitude was as coy as a debutante's. Too well aware that three of her sons were boosting Kennedy, she chose to conceal as long as possible the melancholy truth that we rejected her counseling and that politically the Roosevelt family was split in two.

Adlai alone, in her consideration, could pick up the pieces left after the collapse of Eisenhower's last attempt to discuss terms with Khrushchev at a Paris summit the previous May. Francis Gary Powers' U-2 spy plane, shot down over Russia, and his confession about its purpose spelled the end of negotiations. Ike was looking forward to retirement on his farm in Gettysburg, Pennsylvania, leaving Nixon to face the Democrats' choice in November.

Mother closed her ears to my brothers' recitals of Stevenson's twice-proven weakness as a candidate. The friends she sought to listen to were those she knew were for Adlai. Her mail, she noted, was almost unanimously in his favor. He would have to be drafted if that was the only means of convincing him that Kennedy's youth and, more crucially, his religion made him unsuitable for the White House. Of course, if

Stevenson would accept him as running mate, she could countenance that.

Fervor for Adlai outweighed her reluctance to let the country see that the family was at loggerheads over this election. One month before she flew with David to Los Angeles, she started stumping for Stevenson, complaining like Truman that the Kennedy clan was busy rigging the convention in advance.

As would-be kingmaker, she put herself in the thick of the struggle in Los Angeles from opening day on. A Monday morning press conference on July 11 saw her at work with her bodkin, gray head bent forward to relieve the nagging pain in her shoulders, feet aching, smiling as if nothing on God's earth worried her. Would the black vote go to Kennedy? She rather doubted it. Would the South back a Catholic? She really didn't know. Was Mr. Kennedy too young for the top job? Well, she said, her sons disagreed with her on that.

On her first appearance at Convention Hall, in a new three-piece outfit and little flowered hat, the welcoming roar drowned out the amplified voice of Florida Governor Leroy Collins issuing from the podium from the moment she came through the door. The ovation swelled as she plodded along the aisle, seemingly oblivious of everything. David helped her find her chair in the designated box in the first balcony hung with a banner proclaiming "All the Way With Adlai." Easing herself down, she fidgeted with her handbag, still ignoring the commotion.

"Don't you see what's going on?" David asked in bewilderment.

He was given no answer. When it looked as though the cheering would never end, she bobbed up, raised a hand in stiff acknowledgment, then plumped down again. After the chairman's gavel had fallen and risen often enough to restore uncertain quiet, David repeated his question. "But don't you see," she answered, "that any *encouragement* of the applause would have been impolite to the speaker?"

She sandwiched in a few minutes alone with me. I sensed more than before how truly vulnerable she was, battered by the things done and left undone by me, my sister and brothers. The front she put up to the universe outside was always brave. But behind it, she was a figure of tragedy, consumed by guilt for our misdeeds.

"Are you quite certain there is nothing I can do for you and Minnewa? I do so want happiness for you both."

"I can only say that I am sorry, but there isn't a chance."

"All of us have failings, you know, but in time a husband and wife get to make *allowances* for the other's faults so long as they refuse to be *selfish* about it. Father and I learned that."

"I know you did."

"What is going to happen now?" she asked.

"It's all been settled. Another divorce. I won't contest it. I don't think we want any more court fights in the family."

"Will it be a big expense for you?"

"I guess so, but we can get into that another time."

"You must *promise* to let me know," said my unfailingly charitable mother. "Do you intend to marry again?"

"I'll let you know that, too."

My brothers and I shared the same discomfiture as we pursued our delegate chores in the arena under the commanding gaze of Mother in the box above, Jimmy a representative of California, Franklin of New York, and I of Colorado, each committed to Kennedy. The sense of disloyalty was only temporarily alleviated when we glanced up and saw the box empty as she circulated through rounds of caucus meetings, striving to apply her prestige to prop up Adlai and block the Kennedy steamroller.

If idealism could be equated with naiveté, she was too naive in imagining that she could undo what had already been secured. In spite of Franklin, she felt sure that the New York delegation might have been courted on Stevenson's behalf except for De Sapio, an elusive adversary who bested her once more.

Her reputation was her single weapon, and it was useless in the backroom dealings that were under way all around her. In alliance with the bosses, the Kennedy team was running this show, and Adlai was too persnickety to protest. The cynicism horrified her. The machine which she was powerless to stop was dictating "the people's choice."

She made the seconding speech for her candidate, indignant at the way a cordon of plain-clothes detectives treated her "as though I were made of Dresden china" when they half-carried her through the crowd to the platform while she struggled to pull her arms free. In her eyrie on the balcony, she sat out the balloting whose outcome was prearranged.

Most contenders had seen fit to fall by the wayside. Before the first count had been tallied, it was evident that Kennedy had won. She controlled herself as she left the hall, claiming afterward that the reason she dabbed her cheek with Kleenex was to rub off the lipstick traces of somebody's kiss. Within a few more hours, the party's new idol would find Johnson ready to strike a bargain and run in second place on the ticket, which only increased her distrust of them both. Mr. Johnson's ambitions soared higher than that.

By then, she was bound for home. A call to one of the old circle, Tiny, at whose home Mother had left some luggage, fetched Mrs. Martin to the airport to say good-bye. Before the flight was boarded, Kennedy was on the telephone to Mother. She was too downcast to say more than ask for Kennedy to relay what he wanted of her through Franklin.

It was tormentingly clear to her that she had just witnessed something more than the out-of-hand rejection of Adlai. His defeat was hers, too. The influence she exercised as a public figure while she pursued her private goals of self-realization counted for nothing now in the party she had served all her adult life. Her pleas had gone unheard. She had put her heart and soul into the fight for Stevenson, and she had lost.

She could dream no longer of ushering into the White House the one man she trusted completely to hold to the course set by Father and, in his image, continue striving to build a braver America and a more hopeful world. She realized at last that she was growing too old to carry the standard of FDR. She had hoped to hand over to Adlai the task of giving shape to Father's vision of betterment for humankind.

The setbacks she had suffered in the past at the hands of Truman, Churchill, Eisenhower and the rest of them had hurt, but she refused to be deterred from her chosen mission. This time, it was different. In a changing world, her generation was getting to be out of date. She felt so weary that she knew she could never summon the strength for another fight like this. But one obligation remained: to lay hold of some worthy consolation prize for Adlai, best of all the job of Secretary of State.

For a month, she avoided meeting Kennedy in spite of the overtures that were made. Concern for Stevenson's next appointment led her to consent to receive old Joe's suspect son at Val-Kill one Tuesday in August. The date was advanced to the preceding Sunday when he was booked to speak at an afternoon rally of senior citizens at the Hyde Park estate and, not unreasonably, shied away from appearing in the territory without her approval.

Forty-eight hours before the scheduled luncheon in her cottage, Johnny's thirteen-year-old daughter Sally was thrown from a horse at a summer camp in upstate New York. The concussion she suffered went unnoticed until she lost consciousness on a hiking expedition the next day, Saturday. Mother hurried to the hospital, but her granddaughter died before the night was over. Grand'mère got back to Val-Kill shortly before dawn on Sunday, to snatch an hour or so of disturbed sleep; she would not think of putting off her guest.

He came a-courting, wearing the dark business suit, white shirt and restrained tie which were to be something of a uniform in his campaigning. They talked for an hour in between bites at a meal served on two folding tables on an assortment of mismatched chinaware.

She found him less cold and calculating than at their previous unhappy get-together four years earlier. He was playing against heavy odds in taking on Nixon, who would have the advantage of entrenched authority plus Ike's endorsement as "a courageous and honest man." Every feasible Democratic and independent vote must be pulled in, and Mother's drawing power was not to be underestimated.

She had never asked favors for herself from anyone, including Father; all she could do today was underline the extent of Adlai's following without trying to pin Kennedy down into promising a specific job for Stevenson in the event of a Democratic victory.

With Senator McCarthy dead, the riddle of Kennedy's thoughts about McCarthyism could be left unsolved, but the specter of Catholicism and recollections of her dispute with Cardinal Spellman arose in her mind. With utmost delicacy, she raised what to her was the fundamental question: how did John Fitzgerald Kennedy propose to distinguish between his allegiance to his church and his duties to his country?

He was, he said, "absolutely smitten" with her when lunch was over. As usual, she was more cautious. "I will be surer of this as time goes on," she told some friends in another round-robin report, "but I think I am not mistaken in feeling that he would make a good President if elected." She expected Nixon, "tricky Dickie," to revert to form before November.

She held back from active work for Kennedy until after he addressed a Texas gathering of the Greater Houston Ministerial Association, a bold choice of audience for a speech that Mother believed owed something to their exchanges over mismatched Val-Kill china. To a smattering of applause, he laid the religious issue to rest. He vowed that his faith would not impede him as President; separation of church and state was basic to his way of thinking.

Mother was satisfied. She felt strangely weak that autumn, but she set out extolling this new suitor, underlining in every speech she made for him that separation whose importance she had impressed on the cardinal when Kennedy was a Congressman with a fresh-out-of-college manner which deceived some tourists in the Capitol into mistaking him for an elevator boy.

While seventy million people watched Kennedy's self-confident duels with a harassed opponent on television, I was caught up in trying to balance my life's account. Financially for sure, I had known better days. The uranium business was a flop, the oil wells a rather arid success. The vacation club venture could not get off the ground. In the divorce settlement, I had to take on some $425,000 in debts, not all of them my own, which meant putting up virtually everything I possessed as collateral for bank loans.

Yet at the age of fifty, long past the due date, I had just taken to heart for the first time a lesson consistently taught by Eleanor Roosevelt, practical psychologist, which could be entered on the credit side of the ledger: "We should look inward at ourselves to *recognize* our deficiencies, then do our *very* best to correct them."

I did what she had been advocating for as long as I could remember. So many of the errors I had made were due to personal shortcomings. Up to this moment, I had been eager to find excuses and blot failings from my mind instead of pledging not to repeat them. I could trace the habit to self-pity, which war service had magnified: "Live it up, man—you ain't going to be around too long!"

For fifteen years since then, I had been ignoring another of Mother's teachings: "We should think of other people's needs first, not our own." Selfishness had marked too much of what I had done. Looking out at the world instead of in at myself, I had been less than generous in spirit. From now on, I would seek to find some compassion to offer and hope to spend the rest of life a member of the human race in good standing.

12

Campaigning for Kennedy took her around half a dozen states as far apart as California and New York, New York and West Virginia. "Unfortunately," her readers were told, "I started out under a slight handicap, as I picked up a virus and was feeling far from well." The truth, far more alarming, could not be shared with them in case they pitied her, which would be intolerable.

David had traced the cause of the fatigue, so acute now that she would fall asleep on her feet and have to be helped into a chair before she toppled over. She was a victim of aplastic anemia; incurable; origin unknown. The bone marrow had lost its capacity to form blood. Transfusions could bring only temporary improvement. Sooner or later, her arterial system would begin to break down and internal hemorrhaging result.

On November 8, when Kennedy squeaked in with only 113,057 votes more than Nixon out of almost 69,000,000 cast, Mother's valiant contribution just conceivably had swung the day. Three of the states in which she labored turned up in Kennedy's column. She would have wished for only one thing more gratifying than the garland he had for her. By naming her to the United States delegation at a special General Assembly session, he gave her the opportunity to pay a farewell visit to the Commission on Human Rights, which was struggling again to write a workable covenant. She would have been better pleased if he had made not Dean Rusk but Adlai his Secretary of State instead of awarding him the inferior post of United Nations ambassador.

Franklin's reward was well deserved, she thought; for his help to Kennedy, he was appointed Assistant Secretary of Commerce in 1962, a stepping stone toward higher things if he cared to use it. After a flurry of speculation that my brother might try another climb up Capitol Hill, he decided against it; business was a safer bet for the time being.

One week before Election Day, I was married again in a quiet ceremony which we managed to keep from the newspapers and networks. In a resort hotel near Vancouver, British Columbia, Patricia Peabody Whitehead become what some of her friends liked to joke about as "the fifth wheel on the wagon." To make sure that we were not instantly awash in publicity, I guarded against security leaks by letting Mother and the family know only after we were man and wife.

I had met Patty in the course of some real-estate transactions in which she had been the agent. This mother of four was something of a rarity in that loving and being loved meant more to her than money. Otherwise, it must be said, she would have had no alternative to turning me down flat. We faced a task to challenge Hercules in unburdening ourselves of debt.

On January 20, 1961, Mother preferred not to accept the President's invitation to sit at his side in the Presidential box outside the Capitol for the Inauguration. To do so would put her in the company of old Joe, and fondness for the son did not extend to the father. Sharing a blanket with a neighbor in the stand below to fend off the icy cold, she reminisced about the March day in 1933 when Father spoke from the same spot, voice resonating as he declaimed, "This great nation will endure as it has endured, will revive and will prosper . . . the only thing we have to fear is fear itself."

"I remember how it rained," she confided, "and I was wearing a velvet hat, a *purple* hat. I rode in an open car, and my hair was purple when we reached the White House. I took one look in a mirror, but there wasn't time to do anything about it, so I put the hat back on and wore it the rest of the day." Or was that another Inaugural? In 1937, perhaps, or 1941? She could not be absolutely sure. She fumbled with the blanket and settled down to listen to the first Catholic President's crisp Harvard accent. "And so, my fellow Americans, ask not what your country can do for you—ask what you can do for your country."

She wondered vaguely what the new man in the White House intended to do about Fidel Castro. Diplomatic relations had been broken off two weeks ago, and in the final months of Eisenhower's Presidency, the Central Intelligence Agency had trained an invasion force of anti-Castro Cubans, commissioned to overthrow the communist regime in Havana. Mother's vain hope was that Kennedy would not be tempted by the Pentagon "to interfere in the internal affairs of Cuba." Father had been subjected to similar beguilements when the dictatorship in power there was of a different political color.

In March, fresh symptoms of physical decline appeared. Soreness and swelling in her legs were evidence of blood vessels clotted by phlebitis. Marooned at Val-Kill, she announced to all but those closest to her that it was nothing more than a bout of influenza.

The experience drove her to have a new will drawn by Harry Hooker, making him, Franklin and Johnny her executors. David was to be left an etching of Father, the Turner watercolors, and $10,000 in cash "for his devoted care for which he would not accept compensation during my lifetime." Joe and Trude Lash, Esther Lape, Maureen, Tiny, and Lorena Hickock were among the dozens of those she remembered, including "each person in my personal employ."

I was down to receive "what remains of Grandmother Roosevelt's pink china and two silver serving trays," Johnny for the contents of Val-Kill Cottage. All possessions not specifically allocated were to be divided among us children. Anna was bequeathed furs, jewelry and, because the Halsteds had known thin times, lifetime income from Mother's estate.

The response from my brothers and sister to the new marriage had been less than cordial, though Mother continued to flay herself emotionally because of what she interpreted as her failure to help me. An overdue letter to her was designed to set her mind at rest:

> There is nothing you can do to alleviate my situation. Don't feel sorry for me, because this is a great challenge. I think I can lick it, and if I do, it will make a great difference for the future of not only myself but all connected with or interested in me. . . . I do hope that fate will give me a chance of seeing you in the not too distant future, as I do love you with all my heart. I know I'm terrible about writing or communicating, but when one is fighting with one's back to the wall, it is hard to write and wrong to share those difficulties.

The reply came written in a hand so wavering as to be all but illegible. Seemingly, she said, the one way left for her to help her children was to die, so that we would share the inheritance. But she had been feeling better lately. Death, she regretted to say, was some distance away.

A huge box of presents arrived for Christmas, each package wrapped in bright paper whose creases told that she had saved it from gifts made to her in former years. Shirts, socks and sweaters for me, gloves and stockings for Patty, a sweater apiece for each of the four children she had brought into our marriage—all tied in ribbons and fumbled bows with old-fashioned cards attached, bearing greetings in spiderweb handwriting.

In the New Year, the two of us flew to New York to see Mother. Dinner was to be served at East 74th Street for the whole family excepting Jimmy and his wife Irene, who would be in Washington. Anna was there with her husband; back from Iran, the Halsteds were due to move to Michigan when Jim went to work in a union-operated Detroit hospital.

Mother looked ill and very old. The stoop in her shoulders was more pronounced, and the puffiness in her cheeks had not been there before. She made a sterling effort to be congenial to Patty. We were on our way down the carpeted hall to the tiny dining room when Aunt Polly floated in, encased in a woebegone chinchilla coat that covered a gold blouse and red velvet pants. Arms and hands glittered and jangled with jewelry.

"Well," she addressed Patty, "so you're the latest one, are you? What have you got to say for yourself?"

"Yes, ma'am," she blushed. "I'm the last one and the best."

She was awarded a hug for her courage. "My God, Eleanor," Polly whooped, "I think he's finally got a live one!" She invited Patty to her house on Sutton Place the following afternoon for "tea," which turned out to be rum for the hostess, Scotch for the guest. "It isn't going to be easy for you, Patty," she warned her.

Extricating ourselves from debt was a slow, slow business, but gradually a gleam or two was discernible at the end of the tunnel. As a mark of approval for my new wife, Mother donated cash for a fur coat. We settled down in Minneapolis and I legally adopted Patty's Ford, Gretchen, David and Jimmy. Mother came to see us in our latest home.

She landed at the airport holding a travel-worn, blue-canvas zipper bag: "Thank you, no. I can carry it." She survived a tumultuous reception there; a garden party that kept her standing for two and a half hours, shaking hands; rides in a series of motorcades to the scream of police sirens; a dinner party for two hundred guests at the art museum, where a display of Rooseveltiana was opening that evening as a further means of paying off the banks; and a receiving line in which three thousand ticket buyers at the exhibit felt the touch of her strong, welcoming fingers.

At every turn, she was careful to share the adulation with the woman at her side. "Yes, how *delightful* to see you! This is my daughter-in-law Patty, Elliott's wife——" A breakfast confined to chocolate Metrecal next morning, and Mother was off to the airport in another motorcade. Neither Patty nor I had found the right moment to let it be known that she was pregnant.

Livingston Delano Roosevelt was born by Caesarian section two months early. The call from Mother reached me at six in the morning. "Oh, I'm so *thrilled* for you and Patty. Now do you need anything? Remember I shall be more than glad to share the expense. If you need me, I'll come right away." Placing calls was unusual for my old-fashioned parent, set in her ways but not in her thinking, who regarded telephones with suspicion and much preferred to write. She never saw her new grandson. At five days old, Del suffered a death similar to that which was to take the life of Patrick, aged thirty-nine hours, son of Jack and Jacqueline Kennedy, a year later.

March 21, 1962. "Dearest Elliott and Patty: I must tell you again how sad I am for you both and how I wish the baby could have lived to be strong and well, but perhaps this could not be, and we have to accept often in life what is hard to understand. I know how hard it is to lose a baby and especially for Patty, and I do hope she will soon be stronger and have no more setbacks. You can bear things together, I am sure. Let me know if I can do anything for you. My love to you both."

March 22. "Elliott darling: I have just paid my income tax and find I can send you $3,000 which will I hope pay the extra medical etc. expenses you've been under. I know you must live on a budget, and unexpected expenses would upset it. My love and deep sympathy to you both."

It was out of the question for us to accept the money as a gift—only as a loan. I mailed a note to formalize that arrangement, to be stored away by Maureen along with the similar paper from my brother Jimmy, acknowledging his debt of $100,000.

Mother liked what she heard and read about young Kennedy's "new frontier," the attack he had announced as his platform on "unsolved problems of peace and war, unconquered pockets of ignorance and prejudice, unanswered questions of poverty and surplus." A request from him that they keep in contact was all she needed to pepper him with advice along much the same lines as she gave Truman.

The new Administration, she felt, was woefully short of women; she suggested that this should be remedied. His press conferences were nowhere near as effective in enthusing people as Father's fireside chats had been. Mr. President's voice sounded too shrill and cold; might she recommend speech lessons from her old teacher, assuming she was still alive?

She urged him to let the United Nations take over the problem of Viet Nam—"a tragic pit," in her words, into which Americans "were being asked to leap," but the United States build-up continued there. Would he *please* not be provoked by his two days of stormy talks with Khrushchev in Vienna into giving up the attempt to furl the banners of cold war? Withdrawals on each side would surely be the best approach to universal disarmament.

And, most important of all, it was time to cry halt to the nuclear arms race. With her seventy-seventh birthday not far off, Mother had reexamined her thinking about the use of atomic bombs. She aligned herself now with the Quakers and signed "a declaration of conscience," then warned him against being persuaded by the militarists. If Kennedy was influenced in the least by her, she was not to know, but in July, 1963, he did conclude a nuclear test ban treaty with the Soviet Union and Great Britain.

She savored the taste of one political victory, small but not insignificant, when Carmine De Sapio was swept out of power in a cleanup staged by Robert Wagner, mayor of New York. What the Tammany boss had done to Franklin and Adlai had been avenged.

She could count no longer on enjoying a day when chills or fever that might rise seven or eight degrees above normal would not force her to rest. Rather than cancel an appearance, she would have Maureen call Jimmy in California, Franklin in New York or me in Minnesota to pinch-hit, depending on what part of the country Mother was due to speak. On five or six occasions, I found myself selling bonds for Israel in Canada, Kansas City and Paterson, New Jersey. In case funds for her charities ran dry, she was writing a new book, *Tomorrow Is Now*. Some mornings, her hands were too shaky to hold a pencil, much less finish the shawl for the Belafontes' baby.

There was something else she wished to donate for a useful purpose that went unmentioned in her will. An accompanying letter took care of it—her eyes were to go to an eye bank for the blind. At the same time, she spelled out the arrangements she wanted for her funeral: a simple oak coffin, covered not with flowers but with branches of evergreen from the Val-Kill woods; her wrists to be opened for fear of being buried alive; Charlie Curnan and Les Entrup of the Hyde Park luncheonette—Marg's husband—to be her pallbearers.

Early in 1962, she made her last flight across the Atlantic to work on a television series, "Prospects of Mankind," which, to our disbelief, she had contracted to make. Back she went to the old, familiar hotels where she was greeted as if they were home—Claridge's in London and the Crillon in Paris. With her crew of three—Maureen, David and Edna Gurewitsch—she also fitted in a few days of fun, sleighing in the Swiss Alps at St. Moritz.

She reminisced: "Franklin and I came here on our honeymoon—well, it was really our second honeymoon, when his term at Columbia was over. I had *never* been so well looked after in my life. Of course, I had been here before as a schoolgirl—and that was during the Boer War! I remember getting up early in the mornings to walk with Aunt Tissie to a little café perched out above the lake. We would have our cocoa and coffee and fresh rolls with honey and watch the sun come peeping over the mountains—utter *contentment*!

"Franklin liked to climb the mountains, but I could not.

There was a lady from New York who owned a hat shop, and *she* went climbing with him. I was jealous beyond belief! We had to be home for the start of the next term at Columbia. I could not make out why I felt so *miserable* on the return crossing, and then Anna was born the following May.''

The blood transfusions needed to be supplemented by other treatment as the anemia progressed, bringing on these inexplicable fevers. David prescribed cortisone to counter the risk of concealed hemorrhages. Her condition remained a secret so well kept that one New York Congressman, Emanuel Celler, seriously proposed making a television appearance to press her candidacy for a seat in the Senate.

Nobody must know that she was failing fast. As the 1962 campaign got off the mark, she felt obliged once again to do her bit for the nemesis of Tammany, the Committee for Democratic Voters. She agreed to speak at an open-air rally for Ellis Bert, running in the 6th Assembly District.

"My head is heavy," she explained to the young man sent to escort her from East 74th Street. "You'll have to steady me when I get out of the car." To the black girl who waited with a bouquet before Mother climbed the steps to the platform set up in a Queens street, she murmured, "I had to come; I was expected." A handful of teenagers wearing lapel buttons of the newly formed Conservative Party stood in the crowd, chanting, "Communist, go back to Russia!"

If she heard them, she ignored them. In an old, light-blue print dress, she spoke for fifteen minutes, drumming up votes for the reform ticket. The chanting resumed as she made her way through the audience afterward, shaking every hand within reach. She slumped into the seat of the returning car. "I don't feel very well," she complained for the first time.

David was away at sea aboard the peace ship *Hope,* on a voyage to Peru to which he had committed himself earlier. Mother would not hear of him canceling the trip, though he was the only doctor in whom she placed any faith. Jim Halsted and Anna were pressing for other consultants to be brought in on the case. Mother threatened to dispense with medical attention altogether before she would deliver herself into the hands of an outsider.

On the eve of David's return, the physician he had recommended in his absence gave her a transfusion of fresh blood. Her temperature shot up and stayed perilously high. As soon as David saw her, he ordered an ambulance to hurry her to Presbyterian Hospital.

Jimmy telephoned me in Minneapolis. "Mummy's in the hospital. It looks like the beginning of the end." Anna flew in from Detroit, bringing her husband with her, to install themselves in a back bedroom on the third floor of Mother's brownstone. I came with Patty to stay in the Summit Hotel on Lexington Avenue. Johnny and Anne had a Manhattan apartment of their own. Franklin and Sue were close by in Dutchess County. Jimmy and Irene had already arrived from Washington. The watching and waiting were about to begin.

There were times when Mother recognized nobody, yet incredibly to all of us, "My Day" continued into August, albeit spasmodically. Anger was the spur and the feeling that overwhelmed her, a consuming rage first with her inability to force herself back to health and then because she was not to be allowed to die. All this fussing with testing blood and temperature and bone marrow was so *useless*. There was little anyone but David could do to comfort her.

Conflict broke out between him on the one hand, Anna and her husband on the other. My sister was fearful that compassion might tempt Dr. Gurewitsch into acceding to Mother's wish and inject an overdose to end her torment. At Anna's insistence, specialists were summoned, and David was thrust into the background, to spend more time in his apartment upstairs, less downstairs with Mother.

No sooner was she able to leave her bed than she demanded to be taken home—she was expected at Campobello for the dedication of a bridge spanning the waters of the Bay of Fundy from the Maine shore, a memorial to Father. David and Edna would fly up there with her, Trude would drive her back. During much of the time on the journeys to and fro, she was only dimly aware of what was happening. Again she implored David to hasten her exit.

On September 26, she was readmitted to the hospital, refusing all visitors beyond the family and the four dearest friends for fear that anyone else would see her reduced so low. Even Adlai was turned away. "I love you dearly," said the note he sent, "and so does the whole world."

She needed oxygen now to help her breathe and saline solution fed constantly into her bloodstream. So many injections had been given that the nurses had to search for areas of unscarred skin. If no one else would grant her desire, she would have to see to it herself. She spat out the pills she was handed, or held them under her tongue. It was nonsensical to go on any longer. She remained in the hospital for three weeks.

She was carried home on a stretcher seven days after her seventy-eighth birthday, four days after U-2 reconnaissance revealed that Soviet missiles were being installed in Cuba, ninety miles from the Florida coast. As she lay dying in her second-floor bedroom, it seemed that the peace for which she had striven in memory of Father was to die with her.

She did not care to hear about it. When Joe Lash offered to read the newspapers to her, she whispered, "It'll never come together. Nobody makes sense." He puzzled over her meaning. Then her mind cleared for a moment. "All I want"—and his dedication to her led him to expect some crystalline pronouncement about the state of the world—"is to be turned over."

Anna took complete charge, replaying the role she had created for herself in Father's terminal years. She ran the household; paid the bills from Mother's account; brought in her daughter Sistie and son Buzz and his wife to help with the errands. After seventeen years away, my sister was back in power behind the scenes at a center of universal attention.

I walked twenty blocks uptown and twenty blocks back twice a day to sit with Mother. She lay in a three-quarter bed with a tall headboard in a room that seemed bizarre in its brightness when daylight streamed in through the bay win-

dow, hung ceiling to floor with red velvet curtains. The gleaming chrome of hospital equipment, the jars and tubes and
charts were new. In front of the window stood the Queen
Anne desk at which she had so often sat up late, writing her
round dozen letters a day. At the foot of the bed was Granny's old hope chest, stocked with blankets, and by Mother's
side a simple dressing table, its top covered with the photographs she had traveled with and the silver-backed comb,
ready if she ever again could do her hair and tie it with a bedtime ribbon. Across the room, on the fireplace mantel, a gold
pendulum clock ticked time away.

Holding her still hand, I spent hours studying that room,
listening to the clock. Only rarely she stirred into consciousness, to open misted eyes and press my fingers before she
faded back into sleep. Once, at the thrust of yet another hy-
podermic, I watched her wake and mutter, "Let me die."

I preferred to walk, not ride, between the house and the hotel. There was plenty to think about and much to regret.
Throughout her life, she had received scant solace from her
family. We had been blind to her immense capacity for love,
compassion and understanding, developed with such effort
over the past seventeen years. Perhaps our neglect deepened
her insight into human failing and her understanding for all
mankind as a result. She and I had spent too long apart of late,
and too much had been left unsaid. She had been told too seldom of my love and my need for hers. I wondered now if she
remembered.

She had been home a week when analysis of the latest hospital tests was completed. The illness ravaging her was tuberculosis, spreading unimpeded through her body. It had lain
dormant and unrecognized in her for nearly half a century,
since she caught what she imagined to be influenza in the
wake of the epidemic that swept the world after the First
World War, accounting for 548,000 Americans in a total of
20,000,000 dead. Her illness coincided with the era when she
learned about Lucy and Father.

Disdain for checkups and her belief that willpower was a

cure-all had left the lung damage undetected by X-rays until now. There was no clue in the medical records, dating to childhood, which she provided for David. But the cortisone he had treated her with induced a side effect. The medication had rekindled the tuberculosis—the disease which once had attacked him, the disease which had drawn them together in the first place as fellow passengers on a fog-bound flight in Ireland.

Talking to the newspapers was another responsibility Anna took on. Mother's condition usually was "very much the same," as my sister told it, without letting the world know that the life of the woman it had honored was coming to its close. My sister blamed David for prescribing cortisone. I saw no reason for faulting him when, on the basis of her medical history, the foremost experts in his profession would scarcely have hesitated to specify the same treatment.

In Washington, the conferences had gone on day and night for more than a week: how to end the Cuban crisis before it exploded into a nuclear and possibly exterminating war? Kennedy sensed on the Russians' part a desire for compromise; they had overreached themselves. The United States would quarantine the island by sea and air to prevent further Soviet armaments from reaching Castro. If Khrushchev promised to order on-site missiles dismantled and removed, Kennedy would pledge there would be no repetition of invasion like the Bay of Pigs debacle. On October 28, agreement was struck between them.

Peace had been saved, but in our family the waiting and watching went on, the period uncertain, the outcome not. Workaday jobs to be done prevented all of us but Anna from staying on every day. With Congress in session, Jimmy had to commute between New York and the capital. Franklin resorted to a similar routine. Jim Halsted shuttled to and from Detroit. Johnny's Wall Street job made him the best placed.

I was with Patty on a business trip to Miami Beach when Franklin traced us at the home of a friend there. The telephone muffled his voice. "I'm sorry, old man, but Mummy's gone." There would have to be an autopsy, which revoked one more wish of hers—the bequest to the eye bank could not be fulfilled.

We took the first available flight to New York on that seventh day of November. As the jet droned northward, I began to attempt—it would be months before it was half-way complete—to figure how history would assess her, a rare and independent spirit who emerged from the shadow cast by her husband's image to attain her own renown. There were so many imponderables that it was hard to judge.

If Truman had heeded her in the beginning when she echoed Father's hopes, the world might have been spared the cost of cold war in cash, casualties and human misery. But Truman had gone along with Churchill and the Pentagon's ancient regime. If she had been given the opportunity to open discussions with Stalin in 1945, how much smoother would relations between East and West have been?

Instead, she had been allowed to leave her imprint at the United Nations. In spelling out equal and inalienable rights for mankind as the foundations of freedom, peace and justice, a lantern had been lit. No matter if the flame flickered, it marked the road to betterment if the citizens of all countries, old or new, would assert their will, by ballots or bullets as the case may be, to set out on the journey.

More than anything else, she made of herself a measure of what could be accomplished if you abided by your principles and held on to your faith. She transmuted the dross of a guilt-ridden life into gold. Idealism as she practiced it had proved its worth in human affairs. But now the last of the undaunted idealists was dead, and there was no telling whether her like would be seen again.

On the day after her death, Johnny asked Anna and his brothers to meet in his apartment at noon before we heard the terms of the will. Harry Hooker had predeceased his client; an attorney from the same law firm donned a pair of Ben Franklin spectacles to read aloud the six typed pages.

There were no surprises. So far as the cash estate was involved, it was to be held in trust, as expected, with income paid quarterly to Anna. Mother had looked for money only for handing out to others. What remained amounted to roughly $150,000 in all, little more than a single year's earnings when her activities were at their peak.

In the files lay Jimmy's note for $100,000 and mine for $3,000. Both of us would honor them with all the speed we could muster.

Anna and Johnny supervised arrangements for the funeral. The service would be held at St. James's, Hyde Park, at three o'clock, burial in the rose garden next to Father. Lunch was to be served in Johnny's Stone Cottage at noon. More than a thousand invitations went out by telegram, the most distinguished guests were telephoned. Tickets were printed for the luncheon and admission to the church. My brother had a talent for organization. "Red tickets for the VIPs," he announced briskly, "green for the semi-VIPs, blue for the non-VIPs."

Patty and I put up in a motel, the Halsteds and the Lashes stayed in Val-Kill Cottage, where the oak coffin rested in state, not under evergreen boughs but covered with a magnificent floral blanket. At its head was placed a portrait of Father, gleaming in lamplight in the shadowed parlor. A bouquet of violets and gardenias arrived from Aunt Polly.

The evening before the funeral, we gathered in Mother's sitting room. Tomorrow, we should be wearing identification badges complete with photographs to clear our way through the throng, the police cordons, the carefully screened photographers and reporters assembling in a multitude that swarmed along the highway and up the drive to the big house.

At nine-thirty, my sister rose to her feet. Her words could have been Mother's. "We'll have a hard day tomorrow. It's time for bed."

Somehow, 250 people had to be shoehorned into Stone Cottage for lunch. My sister-in-law Anne paced the rooms, praying for the rain to hold off, while servants arranged fresh flowers and gave the furniture a final dusting. The limousines came swaying over the bumps in the dirt road. A black Continental brought John and Jacqueline Kennedy with his brother Robert and wife Ethel. On their heels came Dwight Eisenhower, alone. Harry and Bess Truman were there, along with Lyndon and Lady Bird Johnson. Aunt Polly, in unadorned black, cast her eighty-one-year-old eyes on Governor Nelson Rockefeller. Adlai Stevenson, gray with grief, scarcely touched the cold turkey, ham or molded salad.

Three or four dozen limousines, each numbered like their occupants by instruction of Johnny, drove in procession to the church. Protocol presented a problem. Jimmy was for having Presidents take the lead in chronological order. I disagreed. "Mother died, not Kennedy or Ike or Truman. The first cars should be for the family." That was how it was settled, with Jimmy, Anna, myself and wives and husband riding fourth in line through the ranks of onlookers who packed the roadsides in the rain.

Mother was laid to rest in the rose garden in accord with Father's wish, set down a quarter of a century ago: "I hope that my dear wife will be buried there also and that the monument contain no device or inscription except the following on the south side——" The stonecutter had done his work. ANNA ELEANOR ROOSEVELT 1884-1962. David Gurewitsch, camera in hand, heard Truman's comment: "I told her she was the First Lady of the World."

When the last guest had left, we returned for a while to Johnny's cottage to talk over plans for two memorial services. Anna and John would concern themselves with the first, in New York's Cathedral of St. John the Divine; Jimmy and Franklin with the second, in Washington Cathedral.

Adlai Stevenson, who mounted the pulpit in scarlet robes to address a congregation of ten thousand in the Cathedral of St. John the Divine, said of Mother, "She would rather light a candle than curse the darkness." Which was as true as something Aunt Polly sniffed at the funeral: "What *nonsense!* Eleanor would have hated all this fuss."

* * *

Ten years passed. On another day of drenching rain, I went back to Hyde Park. With my brothers and sister, I was invited to witness the fulfilment of seven lines in Mother's will: "During my lifetime I have given away from time to time part of my manuscripts and other works of mine, files, documents, correspondence, papers and memoranda of every kind. All the rest of such property which may belong to me at the time of my death I give and bequeath to the Franklin D. Roosevelt Library. . . ."

The Eleanor Roosevelt wing of matching gray fieldstone was about to be declared open. A soddened marquee sheltered the guests as they sat on little chairs unfolded on the grass. Governor Rockefeller, coming in by helicopter, was late, and time dragged. Some familiar faces were in the crowd, Joe Lash in a black beard and Marion Dickerman among them.

When courtesies had been exchanged and little speeches delivered, the rain turned to drizzle, and the children of Franklin and Eleanor Roosevelt posed together outside for the photographers.

Here we were on parade together again: Johnny, fifty-six years old, the epitome of a successful stockbroker in his gray business suit with oblong square of pocket handkerchief; Franklin, soon to be fifty-eight, assuming a head-of-the-family air; Jimmy, sixty-four, flashing his version of Father's smile; Anna, white-haired and hollow cheeked at sixty-six, guardian of the more revealing documents stored inside these walls and carrying on some of Mother's work in philanthropy. I would be sixty-two in September, and I felt a stranger. More mountains remained to be climbed, but with Patty to accompany me, I didn't doubt they could be conquered.

We five not-so-young Roosevelts had continued to walk our separate ways, heedless of Mother's yearning to unite us as a family worthy of our name. There was no trace of kinship. We had broken with each other as we had with her. We had lived in a reflection of our parents' glory. I knew that we should never meet as a family again.

There was only one thought that softened that realization. Where we failed her memory, her grandchildren honored it. The next generation of Roosevelts was growing up accepting the tenets of her faith, realizing the validity of what both Father and Mother believed: *I am my brother's keeper.* It applied to a family, a nation and the world.

Index